An Introduction to the Grammar of English

Revised edition

An Introduction
to the Grammar of English

Revised edition

Elly van Gelderen
Arizona State University

John Benjamins Publishing Company

Amsterdam / Philadelphia

The paper used in this publication meets the minimum requirements of American National Standard for Information Sciences – Permanence of Paper for Printed Library Materials, ANSI Z39.48-1984.

Library of Congress Cataloging-in-Publication Data

Gelderen, Elly van.
  An introduction to the grammar of English / Elly van Gelderen. -- Rev. ed.
    p. cm.
Rev. ed: 2010.
Includes bibliographical references and index.
1. English language--Grammar. 2. English language--Grammar, Historical. 3. English
        language--Social aspects. 4. English language--Syntax. I. Title.
PE1106.G38   2010
428.2--dc22   2009043299
ISBN 978 90 272 3270 0 (HB; alk. paper) / 978 90 272 1168 2 (PB; alk. paper)
ISBN 978 90 272 8862 2 (EB)

John Benjamins Publishing Co. · P.O. Box 36224 · 1020 ME Amsterdam · The Netherlands
John Benjamins North America · P.O. Box 27519 · Philadelphia PA 19118-0519 · USA

Table of contents

Foreword

To the student:

You don't have to read long books or novels in this course – no *Das Kapital, Phenomenology of Spirit, Middlemarch*, or *War and Peace*. There isn't too much memorization either. It should be enough if you become familiar with the keywords at the end of each chapter. Use the glossary, if it is helpful, but don't overemphasize the importance of terminology.

The focus is on arguments, exercises, and tree drawing. You need to practice from the first week on, however, and you may also have to read a chapter more than once. Pay attention to the tables and figures; they often summarize parts of the text. The course is not particularly difficult but, once you get lost, go for help!

The book is divided in four parts (Chapters 1 to 3, Chapters 4 to 6, Chapters 7 and 8, and Chapters 9 to 11), with review sections after each. Chapter 1 is the introduction; skip the 'about the original edition' and 'preface to the second edition', if you want.

About the original edition

The philosophy behind the book hasn't changed in the second edition so I have adapted the preface to the first edition here and have then added things special to the second edition.

This grammar is in the tradition of the Quirk family of grammars, such as the work of Huddleston, Burton-Roberts, Aarts & Wekker, Quirk, Greenbaum, Leech, and Svartvik whose work in turn is based on a long tradition of grammarians such as Jespersen, Kruisinga, Poutsma, and Zandvoort.[1] However, it also uses the insights from generative grammar.

While following the traditional distinction between function (subject, object, etc.) and realization (NP, VP, etc), the book focuses on structure and makes the function derivative, as in more generative work. The book's focus on structure can be seen in the treatment of the VP as consisting of the verb and its complements. Abstract discussions, such as what a constituent is, are largely avoided (in fact, the term constituent is since it

---

1. These are all well-known references, so I have refrained from listing them in the references.

is a stumbling block in my experience), and the structure of the NP and AP is brought in line with that of the VP: NPs and APs have complements as well as modifiers.

A clear distinction is made between lexical and functional (here called grammatical) categories. Lexical categories project to phrases and these phrases have functions at sentence level (subject, predicate, and object). In this book, the functional categories determiner, auxiliary, and (phrasal) coordinator do not project to phrases and have no function at sentence level. They function exclusively inside a phrase or connect phrases. Hence, determiner, auxiliary, and coordinator express realization as well as function. Complementizers and those coordinators that introduce clauses do head the CP in this second edition. The reason that I have changed the S' from the first edition into a CP is two-fold. (a) The S' is confusing since it is not an intermediate projection and (b) the CP is more in line with current syntactical frameworks. The CP can function as subject, object, and adverbial. In a generative syntax book, I would of course have all functional categories project to phrases such as DP, QP, and TP, but for an introductory grammar book, I think having the lexical categories (and the C) project is a better choice. The distinction between lexical and functional category is of course not always clearcut, e.g. adverbs, pronouns, and some prepositions are in between. I do bring this up.

On occasion, I do not give a definitive solution to a problem because there isn't one. This lack of explanation can be caused either because an analysis remains controversial, as in the case of ditransitive verbs and coordinates, or because of the continual changes taking place in English (or any other language for that matter). Instead of giving one solution, I discuss some options. I have found that students become frustrated if, for instance, they can reasonably argue that a verb is prepositional in contexts where 'the book says' it is an intransitive verb. The emphasis in this book is on the argumentation, and not on presenting 'the' solution. The chapter where I have been quite conservative in my analysis is Chapter 6. The reason is that to provide the argumentation for a non-flat structure involves theta-theory, quantifier-float, and the introduction of the TP and other functional categories. This leads too far.

The book starts with a chapter on intuitive linguistic knowledge and provides an explanation for it based on Universal Grammar. At the end of each chapter, there is a discussion of prescriptive rules. In my experience, students want to know what the prescriptive rule is. Strangely enough, they don't want the instructor to tell them that, linguistically speaking, there is nothing wrong with splitting an infinitive or using *like* as a complementizer. They want to (and should) know the rule. I have not integrated the topics in the chapters since I want to keep descriptive and prescriptive rules separate although that is sometimes hard. The topics are added to give a flavor for the kinds of prescriptive rules around and, obviously, cannot cover all traditional usage questions.

The chapters in this book cover 'standard' material: categories, phrases, functions, and embedded sentences. There are a few sections that I have labeled optional, since, depending on the course, they may be too much or too complex. The last chapter could either be skipped or expanded upon. It should be possible to cover all chapters in one semester. The students I have in mind (because of my own experience) are English, Humanities, Philosophy, and Education majors as well as others taking an upper level grammar course in an English department at a university. I am assuming students using this book know basic 'grammar', for instance, the past tense of *go*, and the comparative of *good*. Students who do not have that knowledge should be encouraged to consult a work such as O'Dwyer (2000).

Even though I know there is a danger in giving *one* answer where more than one is sometimes possible, I have provided answers to the exercises. It is done to avoid having to go over all exercises in class. I hope this makes it possible to concentrate on those exercises that are interesting or challenging.

I would like to thank my students in earlier grammar courses whose frustration with some of the inconsistencies in other books has inspired the current work. I am sure this is not the first work so begun. Many thanks also to Johanna Wood for much helpful discussion that made me rethink fundamental questions and for suggesting the special topics, to Harry Bracken for great comments and encouragement, to Viktorija Todorovska for major editorial comments to the first edition, to Tom Stroik for supportive suggestions, to Barbara Fennell for detailed comments and insightful clarifications, and to Anke de Looper of John Benjamins for her insights on the first edition. For help and suggestions with the (originally planned) e-text as well as the paper version, I am very grateful to Lutfi Hussein, Jeff Parker, Laura Parsons, and to Susan Miller.

Preface to the second edition

It was time for an updated version of *A Grammar of English*. Some of the example sentences read as if they were 10 years old and they are. Thus, Bill Clinton hasn't been the US president for a long time and Benazir Bhutto and Yasser Arafat are no longer alive. It is also so much more accepted to use corpus sentences, and these examples may speak more to the users. To keep the text clean of references, I give very basic references, e.g. "CBS 60 Minutes", and not always the exact date. It is now so easy to find those references that I think they aren't needed. Many contemporary example sentences come from Mark Davies' *Corpus of Contemporary American English* and the *British National Corpus*; the older ones from the *Oxford English Dictionary* or from well-known plays.

I have updated the cartoons, added texts to be analyzed, rearranged and added to the Special Topics, and provided more figures and tables. There is also a website that lists relevant links, repeats practice texts from this book for analysis, and contains some resources: http://www.public.asu.edu/~gelderen/grammar.htm. I have deleted the 'Further Reading' section since it was useless: too much detail on the one hand and then very general references to introductory textbooks on the other hand. I think the students who would use this section are smart enough to figure out other references for themselves.

Due to a computer error that changed N' and V' etc into N and V (after the second page proofs had been corrected), the first edition of this book had to be physically destroyed and what ended up the first edition in 2002 was actually a reprint. There were a few typos that survived this process. I hope that these are corrected and that not too many new ones have been created.

I am very happy that the first edition has been useful in a number of different settings and places, e.g. in Puerto Rico, Norway, Turkey, Spain, Macedonia, The Netherlands, the US, and Canada. I have used it myself with a lot of satisfaction, and would like to thank many of my students in ENG 314 at Arizona State University. The areas that I personally did not like in the first edition are the flat auxiliary verb structures in Chapter 6 and the S' (and S) in Chapter 7. As mentioned, I have only changed the S' to CP, but haven't introduced a DP, TP, or an expanded TP because this isn't appropriate for the audience. I have eliminated traces and use what looks like a 'copy' or sometimes the strike-through font. In Chapter 6, I have also introduced timelines for tense and aspect since students often ask about the names of tenses.

I would like to thank some of the same people as I did for the first edition, in particular Johanna Wood, Harry Bracken, and Laura Parsons. For comments in book reviews and beyond, I would like to thank Anja Wanner, Carsten Breul, Christoph Schubert, and Nina Rojina. I am especially grateful to Mariana Bachtchevanova, Eleni Buzarovska, Lynn Sims, James Berry, Amy Shinabarger, James Dennis, Wim van der Wurff, and Richard Young for detailed comments after teaching with the book, and also to Terje Lohndal. Thanks to Alyssa Bachman for providing a student perspective and helping me add to sections that were less clear. Continued thanks to Kees Vaes and Martine van Marsbergen.

Elly van Gelderen
Apache Junction, Arizona
November 2009

Abbreviations

Adj	Adjective		N′	N-bar, intermediate category
AdjP	Adjective Phrase		neg	negative
Adv	Adverb		NP	Noun Phrase
Adv-ial	Adverbial		ObjPr	Object Predicate
AdvP	Adverb Phrase		OED	Oxford English Dictionary
AUX	Auxiliary		P	Preposition
BNC	British National Corpus		pass	passive auxiliary
BrE	British English		pf	perfect auxiliary
C	Complementizer or		PO	Prepositional Object
	Coordinator		PP	Prepositional Phrase
CP	Complementizer Phrase		Pre-D	Pre-determiner
	(or Coordinator Phrase)		Pred	Predicate
COCA	Corpus of Contemporary		prog	progressive auxiliary
	American		Pron	pronoun
D	Determiner		RC	Relative Clause
(D)Adv	Degree Adverb		S	Sentence (or Speech on time line)
DO	Direct Object		SC	Small Clause
E	Event time		SU	Subject
e.g.	'for example'		SuPr	Subject Predicate
i.e.	'namely'		V	Verb
inf	infinitive marker to		V′	V-bar, intermediate category
IO	Indirect Object		VGP	Verb group
N	Noun		VP	Verb Phrase

? Questionable sentence.
* Ungrammatical sentence.
^ May occur more than one.

List of figures

List of tables

Chapter 1

Introduction

1. Examples of linguistic knowledge
2. How do we know so much?
3. Examples of social or non-linguistic knowledge
4. Conclusion

All of us know a lot about language. Most of the time, however, we are not conscious of this knowledge. When we actually study language, we attempt to find out what we know and how we acquire this linguistic knowledge. In this chapter, a number of instances will be given of what speakers of English intuitively or subconsciously know about the grammar of English, both about its sounds and its structure. The remainder of the book focuses on syntax, i.e. the categories, phrases, and the functions of phrases to account for our intuitive knowledge. The chapter also discusses social, i.e. non-linguistic, rules. These are often called prescriptive rules and some of these prescriptive rules are dealt with as 'special topics' at the end of each chapter.

1. Examples of linguistic knowledge

Speakers of a language know a lot about their languages. For instance, we know about the sounds (phonology), the structure of words (morphology), and the structure of sentences (syntax).

1.1 Sounds and words

If you are a native speaker of English, you know when to use the article *a* and when to use *an*. All of us know how to do this correctly though we might not be able to formulate the rule, which says that the article *a* occurs before a word that starts with a consonant, as in (1), and *an* occurs before a word that starts with a vowel, as in (2):

(1)   a nice person, a treasure
(2)   an object, an artist

If a child is given a nonsense word, such as those in (3), the child knows what form of the article to use:

(3)   ovrite, cham

The rule for *a(n)* does not need to be taught explicitly in schools. It is only mentioned in connection with words that start with *h* or *u*. Teachers need to explain that what looks like a vowel in writing in (4) is not a vowel in speech and that the *a/an* rule is based on spoken English. So, the form we choose depends on how the word is pronounced. In (4) and (5), the *u* and *h* are not pronounced as vowels and hence the article *a* is used. In (6) and (7), the initial *u* and *h* are pronounced as vowels and therefore *an* is used:

(4)   a union, a university
(5)   a house, a hospital
(6)   an uncle
(7)   an hour

The same rule predicts the pronunciation of *the* in (8). Pronounce the words in (8) and see if you can state the rule for the use of *the*:

(8)   The man, the table, the object, the hospital...

Examples (1) to (8) show the workings of a phonological (or sound) rule. The assumption is that we possess knowledge of consonants and vowels without having been taught the distinction. In fact, knowledge such as this enables us to learn the sound system of the language.

Apart from the structure of the sound system, i.e. the phonology, a grammar will have to say something about the structure of words, i.e. the morphology. Speakers are quite creative building words such as *kleptocracy, cyberspace, antidisestablishmentarianisms*, and even if you have never seen them before, knowing English means that you will know what these words mean based on their parts. Words such as *floccinaucinihilipilification*, meaning 'the categorizing of something as worthless or trivial', may be a little more difficult. This book will not be concerned with sounds or with the structure of words; it addresses how sentences are structured, usually called syntax. In the next subsection, some examples are given of the syntactic knowledge native speakers possess.

1.2   Syntactic structure

Each speaker of English has knowledge about the structure of a sentence. This is obvious from cases of ambiguity where sentences have more than one meaning. This often makes them funny. For instance, the headline in (9) is ambiguous in that 'cello case' can mean either a 'court case related to a cello or someone called Cello' or 'a case to protect a cello':

(9)   Drunk Gets Ten Months In Cello Case.

In (9), the word 'case' is ambiguous. We call this lexical ambiguity since the ambiguity depends on one word's multiple meanings. The headlines in (10) to (12) are funny exactly because *drops, left, waffles, strikes* and *idle* are ambiguous:

(10)   Eye drops off shelf.
(11)   British left waffles on Falkland Islands.
(12)   Teacher strikes idle kids.

Word ambiguities such as (10) to (12) are often produced on purpose for a certain effect, and are also called 'puns'. Some well-known instances from Lewis Carroll appear in Table 1.1.

Table 1.1. Alice's Ambiguities

"Mine is a long and sad tale!" said the Mouse, turning to Alice and sighing. "It is a long tail, certainly," said Alice, looking with wonder at the Mouse's tail, "but why do you call it sad?"
"How is bread made?" "I know that!" Alice cried eagerly. "You take some flour -" "Where do you pick the flower?" the White Queen asked. "In a garden, or in the hedges?" "Well, it isn't picked at all," Alice explained; "it's ground-" "How many acres of ground?" said the White Queen.

There are also sentences where the structure is ambiguous, e.g. (13) and (14). In (13), the monkey and elephant can both be carried in or just the monkey is. In (14), planes can be the object of flying or the subject of the sentence:

(13)   Speaker A: I just saw someone carrying a monkey and an elephant go into the circus.
        Speaker B: Wow, that someone must be pretty strong.

(14)   Flying planes can be dangerous.

Cartoons thrive on ambiguity and the combination of the unambiguous visual representation with the ambiguous verbal one often provides the comic quality, as in Figure 1.1.

Figure 1.1. Structural Ambiguity (Hi & Lois © KING FEATURES SYNDICATE)

The aim of this book is to understand the structure of English sentences; ambiguity helps understand that structure, and we'll come back to it in Chapter 3.

Knowing about the structure of a sentence, i.e. what parts go with other parts, is relevant in many cases. In a *yes/no* question, the verb (in bold) is moved to the front of the sentence, as from (15) to (16):

(15) The man **is** tall. *declaration*
(16) **Is** the man tall? *Question*

This rule is quite complex, however. Starting from (17), we can't simply front any verb, as (18) and (19) show. In (18), the first verb of the sentence is fronted and this results in an ungrammatical sentence (indicated by the *); in (19), the second verb is fronted and this is grammatical:

(17)   The man who **is** in the garden **is** tall.
(18)   *Is the man who in the garden is tall?
(19)   **Is** the man who is in the garden tall?

These sentences show that speakers take the structure of a sentence into account when formulating questions (see also Chapter 3). We intuitively know that *the man who is in the garden* is a single unit and that the second verb is the one we need to move in order to make the question. This is not all, however. We also need to know that not all verbs move to form questions, as (20) shows:

(20)   *Arrived the bus on time?

Only certain verbs, namely auxiliaries (see Chapter 6) and the verb *to be*, as in (16) and (19), are fronted.

Apart from *yes/no* questions, where the expected answer is *yes* or *no*, there are *wh* questions, where more information is expected for an answer. In these sentences, the *wh*-word is fronted as well as the auxiliary *did*. In (21), *who* is the object (see Chapter 4) of the verb *meet* and we can check that by putting the object 'back', as in (22), which is possible only with special intonation:

(21)   Who did Jane meet?
(22)   Jane met WHO?

This rule too is complex. Why would (23a) be grammatical but (23b) ungrammatical?

(23)   a.   Who did you believe that Jane met?
       b.   *Who did you believe the story that Jane met?

Without ever having been taught this, native and most non-native speakers know that about the difference between (23a) and (23b). With some trouble, we can figure out what (23b) means. There is a story that Jane met someone and you believe this story. The speaker in (23b) is asking who that someone is. Sentence (23b) is ungrammatical because *who* moves 'too far'. It is possible, but not necessary here, to make precise what 'too far' means. The examples merely serve to show that speakers are aware of structure without explicit instruction and that *who* moves to the initial position.

Thus, speakers of English know that (a) sentences are ambiguous, e.g. (13) and (14), (b) sentences have a structure, e.g. (17), (c) movement occurs in questions, e.g. in (16) and (21), and (d) verbs are divided into (at least) two kinds: verbs that move in questions, as in (19), and verbs that don't move, as in (20). Chapter 3 will give more information on the first two points, Chapter 11 on the third point, and Chapter 6 on the difference between auxiliaries and main verbs. The other chapters deal with additional kinds of grammatical knowledge. Chapter 2 is about what we know regarding categories; Chapter 4 is about functions such as subject and object; Chapter 5 about adverbials and objects; Chapter 9 about the structure of a phrase; and Chapters 7, 8, and 10 about the structure of more complex sentences.

2.   How do we know so much?

In Section 1, we discussed examples of what we know about language without being explicitly taught. How do we come by this knowledge? One theory that accounts for this is suggested by Noam Chomsky. He argues that we are all born with a language faculty that when "stimulated by appropriate and continuing experience, ... creates a grammar that creates sentences with formal and semantic properties" (1975: 36). Thus, our innate language faculty (or Universal Grammar) enables us to create a set of rules, or grammar, by being exposed to (rather chaotic) language around us. The set of rules that we acquire enables us to produce sentences we have never heard before. These sentences can also be infinitely long (if we have the time and energy). Language acquisition, in this framework, is not imitation but an interaction between Universal Grammar and exposure to a particular language.

This need for exposure to a particular language explains why, even though we all start out with the same Language Faculty or Universal Grammar, we acquire slightly different grammars. For instance, if you are exposed to a certain variety of Missouri or Canadian English, you might use (24); if exposed to a particular variety of British English, you might use (25); or, if exposed to a kind of American English, (26) and (27):

(24)   I want for to go.
(25)   You know as she left. (meaning 'You know that she left')
(26)   She don't learn you nothing.
(27)   Was you ever bit by a bee?

Thus, "[l]earning is primarily a matter of filling in detail within a structure that is innate" (Chomsky 1975: 39). "A physical organ, say the heart, may vary from one person to the next in size or strength, but its basic structure and its function within human physiology are common to the species. Analogously, two individuals in the same speech community may acquire grammars that differ somewhat in scale and subtlety. . . . These variations in structure are limited . . ." (p. 38).

Hence, even though Universal Grammar provides us with categories such as nouns and verbs that enable us to build our own grammars, the language we hear around us will determine the particular grammar we build up. A person growing up in the 14th century heard multiple negation, as in (28), and would have had a grammar that allowed multiple negation. The same holds for a person from the 15th century who has heard (29). The Modern English equivalents, given in the single quotation marks, show that many varieties of English now use 'any' instead of another negative:

(28)   *Men neded not in no cuntre A fairer body for to seke.*
        'People did not need to seek a fairer person in any country.'
        (Chaucer, *The Romaunt of the Rose*, 560–1)

(29)   *for if he had he ne nedid not to haue sent no spyes.*
        'because if he had, he would not have needed to send any spies.'
        (*The Paston Letters*, letter 45 from 1452)

Linguists typically say that one variety of a language is just as 'good' as any other. People may judge one variety as 'bad' and another as 'good', but for most people studying language, (24) through (27) are just interesting, not 'incorrect'. This holds for language change as well: the change from (28) and (29) to Modern English is not seen as either 'progress' or 'decay', but as a fact to be explained. Languages are always changing and the fascinating part is to see the regularities in the changes.

Society has rules about language, which I call social or 'non-linguistic', and which we need to take into account to be able to function. These are occasionally at odds with the (non-prescriptive) grammars speakers have in their heads. This is addressed in the next section.

3.   Examples of social or non-linguistic knowledge

We know when not to make jokes, for instance, when filling out tax forms or speaking with airport security people. We also know not to use words and expressions such as *all you guys, awesome,* and *I didn't get help from nobody* in formal situations such as applying for a job or in a formal presentation. Using *dude* in the situation of Figure 1.2 may not be smart either. We learn when and how to be polite and impolite; formal and informal. The rules for this differ from culture to culture and, when we learn a new language, we also need to learn the politeness rules and rules for greetings, requests, etc.

Figure 1.2. How to use 'dude'! (Used with the permission of Mike Twohy and the Cartoonist Group. All rights reserved)

When you are in informal situations (e.g. watching TV with a friend), everyone expects 'prescriptively proscribed' expressions, such as (30). In formal situations (testifying in court), you might use (31) instead:

(30)   I didn't mean nothin' by it.
(31)   I didn't intend to imply anything with that remark.

The differences between (30) and (31) involve many levels: (a) vocabulary choice, e.g. *mean* rather than *intend*, (b) phonology, e.g. *nothin'* for *nothing*, (c) syntax, namely the two negatives in (30) that make one negative, and (d) style, e.g. (30) is much less explicit. People use the distinction between formal and informal for 'effect' as well, as in (32):

(32)   You should be better prepared the next time you come to class. Ain't no way I'm gonna take this.

Style and grammar are often equated but they are not the same. Passive constructions, for instance, occur in all languages, and are certainly grammatical. They are often advised against for reasons of style because the author may be seen as avoiding taking responsibility for his or her views. In many kinds of writing, e.g. scientific, passives are very frequent. This book is not about the fight between descriptivism ('what people really say') and prescriptivism ('what some people think other people ought to say'). As with all writing or speech, this book makes a number of choices, e.g. use of contractions,[1] use of 'I' and 'we' as well as a frequent use of passives, and avoidance of very long sentences. This, however, is irrelevant to the main point which is to provide the vocabulary and analytical skills to examine descriptive as well as prescriptive rules. The field that examines the status of prescriptive rules, regional forms as in (24) to (27), and formal and informal language, as in (30) to (32), is called sociolinguistics.

Some prescriptive rules are analysed in the special topics sessions at the end of every chapter. The topics covered are split infinitives (*to boldly go where . . .*), adverbs and adjectives, multiple negation, as in (30), case marking and subject-verb agreement, the use of passives, the use of *of* rather than *have* (*I should of done that*), the preposition *like* used as a complementizer (*like I said ...*), dangling modifiers, singular and plural pronouns, relative pronouns, and the 'correct' use of commas. There are many more such rules.

4.   Conclusion

This first chapter has given instances of rules we know without having been taught these rules explicitly. It also offers an explanation about why we know this much: Universal Grammar 'helps' us. Other chapters in the book provide the categories and structures that we must be using to account for this intuitive knowledge. The chapter also provides instances of social or non-linguistic rules. These are often called prescriptive rules and some of these are dealt with as 'special topics' at the end of each of the chapters. This chapter's special topic discusses one of the more infamous prescriptive rules, namely the split infinitive.

The key terms in this chapter are **syntax; lexical and structural ambiguity; puns; linguistic as opposed to social or non-linguistic knowledge; descriptive as opposed to prescriptive rules; formal as opposed to informal language; innate faculty; and Universal Grammar.**

---

1.   A copy-editor for the first edition changed the contracted forms to full ones, however, and I haven't put the contractions back where they had been changed.

Exercises

A.   Using the words **lexical and structural ambiguity**, explain the ambiguity in (33) to (37):

   (33)   light house keeper   *structural*
   (34)   old dogs and cats   *structural*
   (35)   She gave her dog biscuits.   *structural*
   (36)   Speaker A: Is your fridge running?   *lexical*
           Speaker B: Yes.
           Speaker A: Better go catch it!
   (37)   Fish are smart. They always swim in schools.   *lexical*

B.   Do you think the following sentences are **prescriptively correct or not.** Why/why not?

   (38)   It looks good.   *YES*
   (39)   Me and my friend went out.   *NO*
   (40)   Hopefully, hunger will be eliminated.
   (41)   There's cookies for everyone.   *NO*

Class discussion

C.   Can you think of something you would say in an informal situation but not in a formal one?

   Suggestion: If you have access to the internet, check the British National Corpus (BNC at http://www.natcorp.ox.ac.uk/) or the Corpus of Contemporary American English (COCA at http://www.americancorpus.org/) to see if this use is found. If you wonder what a corpus is, it is a carefully selected set of texts that represents the language of a particular time or variety (British in the case of the BNC and American in the case of the COCA).

D.   Has your English ever been corrected? Can you remember when?

E.   List some stylistic rules. In the text, I mentioned the avoidance of the passive. You might check http://www.libraryspot.com/grammarstyle.htm with links to a collection of grammar and style books.

F.   Discuss why prescriptively 'correct' constructions are often used in formal situations.

G.   You may have heard of best-selling 'language mavens' such as William Safire or Edwin Newman. Safire was a political commentator who also wrote a weekly column in the Sunday *New York Times*. Titles of his books include *Good Advice, I Stand Corrected: More on Language*, and *Language Maven Strikes Again*. Newman, a former NBC correspondent, writes books entitled *A Civil Tongue* and *Strictly Speaking*. These lead reviewers to say "Read Newman! Save English before it is fatally slain." (backcover)

–   Why are there language authorities?
–   Why do people listen to them?

H.   Have you seen titles such as 'An History of the English Language'? Is this correct according to our rule in Section 1.1? Google it and see if 'a history' or 'an history' is more frequent.
           NO

Keys to the exercises

A.   (33) shows structural ambiguity: [[light house] keeper] or [light][house keeper].

(34) shows structural ambiguity: [old dogs] and [cats] or [old [dogs and cats]]

(35) again shows structural ambiguity: She gave [her] [dog biscuits] or She gave [her dog] [biscuits].

(36) shows lexical ambiguity: *running* can be physical running or running as an engine does.

(37) shows lexical ambiguity: *schools* has two meanings.

B.   (38) is ok since *good* is an adjective giving more information about the pronoun *it* (see Chapter 2 and special topic).

(39) is not prescriptively correct since the subject should get nominative case (see Chapter 4 and special topic) and because many people are taught not to start with themselves first.

(40) is not since *hopefully* is not supposed to be used as a sentence adverb, i.e. an adverb that says something about the attitude of the speaker (see Chapter 5 and special topic of Chapter 2).

(41) is not since the verb is singular (*is*) and the subject is plural (*cookies*). This violates subject-verb agreement (see Chapters 3 and 4).

Special topic: Split infinitive

In a later chapter, we will discuss infinitives in great detail. For now, I just want to discuss the prescriptive rule against splitting infinitives that almost everyone knows and show that split infinitives have occurred in English at least for 700 years. Infinitives are verbs preceded by a *to* that is not a preposition but an infinitive marker. Some examples are given in (42) to (44), where the infinitive and its marker are in bold:

(42)   **To err** is human.

(43)   It is nice **to wander** aimlessly.

(44)   **To be** or not **to be** is **to be** decided.

The prescriptive rule is not to split this infinitive from its marker, as stated in (45):

(45)   Do not separate an infinitival verb from its accompanying *to*, as in Star Trek's 'to *boldly* go *where no man has gone before*'.[2]

---

2.   This is the version from the early episodes of *Star Trek* which was much criticized for the split infinitive. Later episodes changed *no man* to *no one* and that's how the 2009 film version has it.

Swan writes that "[s]plit infinitive structures are quite common in English, especially in an informal style. A lot of people consider them 'bad style', and avoid them if possible, placing the adverb before the *to*, or in end-position in the sentence" (1980: 327). Fowler writes as follows:

> The English-speaking world may be divided into (1) those who neither know nor care what a split infinitive is; (2) those who do not know but care very much; (3) those who know & condemn; (4) those who know & approve; & (5) those who know & distinguish. (1926 [1950]: 558)

Fowler himself disapproves of the use of the split infinitive. Quirk & Greenbaum are less critical.

> The inseparability of *to* from the infinitive is . . . asserted in the widely held opinion that it is bad style to 'split the infinitive'. Thus rather than:
>> ?He was wrong to *suddenly* leave the country
> many people (especially in BrE) prefer:
>> He was wrong to leave the country suddenly
> It must be acknowledged, however, that in some cases the 'split infinitive' is the only tolerable ordering, since avoiding the 'split infinitive' results in clumsiness or ambiguity. (1973: 312)

Split infinitives have occurred from the Middle English period, i.e. from 1200, on, as (46) to (52) show.

(46)   I want somebody who will be on there not to legislate from the bench but **to** faithfully **interpret** the constitution. (George Bush, quoted in *The Economist*, 6 July 1991)

(47)   Remember **to** always **footnote** the source.

(48)   [This] will make it possible for everyone **to** gently **push up** the fees. (*New York Times*, 21 July 1991)

(49)   . . .to get the Iraqis **to** peacefully **surrender**... (*New York Times*, 7 July 1991)

(50)   fo[r] **to** londes **seche**
       'To see countries.' (Layamon *Brut* Otho 6915, early 13th century)

(51)   Y say to ʒou, **to** nat **swere** on al manere
       'I say to you to not curse in all ways.' (Wyclif, *Matthew* 5, 34, late 14th century)

(52)   Poul seiþ, þu þat prechist **to** not **steyl**, stelist,
       'Paul says that you who preaches to not steal steals.' (*Apology for the Lollards* 57, late 14th century)

Would you change these? If so, how? In this book, I have not avoided them on purpose and know of at least one instance where I have split an infinitive.

Chapter 2

Categories

1. Lexical categories *PARTS OF SPEECH*
2. Grammatical categories
3. Pronouns
4. What new words and loanwords tell us!
5. Conclusion

In this chapter, I provide descriptions of the categories or parts of speech. Categories can be divided into two main classes: lexical and functional. The lexical categories include Noun, Verb, Adjective, Adverb, and Preposition and are called lexical because they carry lexical meaning. They are also called content words since they have synonyms and antonyms. As we'll see in the next chapter, syntactically, lexical categories are the heads of phrases.

There are also functional or grammatical categories: Determiner, Auxiliary, Coordinator, and Complementizer. These categories are called grammatical or functional categories since they do not contribute much to the meaning of a sentence but determine the syntax of it. They do not function as heads of phrases but merely as parts or as connectors. I'll refer to them as grammatical categories. Prepositions and adverbs are a little of both as will be explained in Sections 1.2 and 1.3 respectively, as are pronouns, e.g. *it, she,* and *there,* to be discussed in Section 3.

When languages borrow new words, these will mainly be nouns, verbs, and adjectives, i.e. lexical categories. Therefore, the difference between lexical and grammatical is often put in terms of open as opposed to closed categories, the lexical categories being open (new words can be added) and the grammatical ones being closed (new words are not easily added). Section 4 will examine this in a limited way.

1.   Lexical categories

The five lexical categories are Noun, Verb, Adjective, Adverb, and Preposition. They carry meaning, and often words with a similar (synonym) or opposite meaning (antonym) can be found. Frequently, the noun is said to be a person, place, or thing and the verb is said to be an event or act. These are semantic definitions. In this chapter, it is shown that semantic definitions are not completely adequate and that we need to define categories syntactically (according to what they combine with) and morphologically (according to how the words are formed). For example, syntactically speaking, *chair* is a noun because it combines with the article (or determiner) *the*; morphologically speaking, *chair* is a noun because it takes a plural ending as in *chairs*.

1.1   Nouns (N) and Verbs (V)

A noun generally indicates a person, place or thing (i.e. this is its meaning). For instance, *chair, table*, and *book* are nouns since they refer to things. However, if the distinction between a noun as person, place, or thing and a verb as an event or action were the only distinction, certain nouns such as *action* and *destruction* would be verbs, since they imply action. These elements are nevertheless nouns.

In (1) and (2), *actions* and *destruction* are preceded by the article *the*, *actions* can be made singular by taking the plural *-s* off, and *destruction* can be pluralized with an *-s*. This makes them nouns:

(1)   The **actions** by the government came too late.
(2)   The hurricane caused the **destruction** of the villages.

As will be shown in Chapter 4, their functions in the sentence are also typical for nouns rather than verbs: in (1), *actions* is part of the subject, and in (2), *destruction* is part of the object.

Apart from plural *-s*, other morphological characteristics of nouns are shown in (3) and (4). Possessive *'s* (or genitive case) appears only on nouns or noun phrases, e.g. the noun *Jenny* in (3), and affixes such as *-er* and *-ism*, e.g. *writer* and *postmodernism* in (4), are also typical for nouns:

(3)   **Jenny's** neighbor always knows the answer.
(4)   That **writer** has modernized **postmodernism**.

Syntactic reasons for calling nouns nouns are that nouns are often preceded by *the*, as *actions* and *government* are in (1), as *destruction* and *villages* are in (2), and as *answer* is in (3). Nouns can also be preceded by *that*, as in (4), and, if they are followed by another noun, there has to be a preposition, such as *by* in (1) and *of* in (2), connecting them.

The nouns *action* and *destruction* have verbal counterparts, namely *act* and *destroy*, and (1) and (2) can be paraphrased as (5) and (6) respectively:

(5)   The government **acted** too late.
(6)   The hurricane **destroyed** the villages.

Just as nouns cannot always be defined as people or things, verbs are not always acts, even though *acted* and *destroyed* are. The verb *be* in (7), represented by the third person present form *is*, does not express an action. Hence, we need to add state to the semantic definition of verb, as well as emotion to account for sentences such as (8):

(7)   The book **is** red and blue.
(8)   The book **seemed** nice (to me).

Some of the morphological characteristics of verbs are that they can express tense, e.g. past tense ending *-ed* in (5), (6), and (8); that the verb ends in *-s* when it has a third person singular subject (see Chapter 4) and is present tense; and that it may have an affix typical for verbs, namely *-ize*, e.g. in *modernized* in (4) (note that it is *-ise* in British English). Syntactically, they can be followed by a noun, as in (6), as well as by a preposition and they can be preceded by an auxiliary, as in (4). Some of the major differences between nouns and verbs are summarized in Table 2.1 below.

Table 2.1. Some differences between N(oun) and V(erb)

		Noun (N)		Verb (V)
Morphology	a.	plural *-s* with a few exceptions, e.g. *children, deer, mice*	h.	past tense *-ed* with a few exceptions, e.g. *went, left*
	b.	possessive *'s*	i.	third person singular agreement *-s*
	c.	some end in *-ity, -ness -ation, -er, -ion, -ment*	j.	some end in *-ize,-ate*
Syntax	d.	may follow *the/a* and *this/that/ these/those*	k.	may follow an auxiliary e.g. *have* and *will*
	e.	may be modified by adjective	l.	may be modified by adverb
	f.	may be followed by preposition and noun	m.	may be followed by noun or preposition and noun
Semantics	g.	person, place, thing	n.	act, event, state, emotion

In English, nouns can easily be used as verbs and verbs as nouns. Therefore, it is necessary to look at the context in which a word occurs, as in (9), for example, where Shakespeare uses *vnckle*, i.e. 'uncle', as a verb as well as a noun:

(9)   York: Grace me no Grace, nor **Vnckle** me,
      I am no Traytors **Vnckle**; and that word Grace
      In an vngracious mouth, is but prophane.
      (Shakespeare, *Richard II*, II, 3, 96, as in the First Folio edition)

Thus, using the criteria discussed above, the first instance of 'uncle' would be a verb since the noun following it does not need to be connected to the verb by means of a preposition, and the second 'uncle' is a noun since 'traitor' has the possessive *'s*. Note that I have left Shakespeare's spelling, punctuation, and grammar as they appear in the First Folio Edition.

Other examples where a word can be both a noun and a verb are *table, to table; chair, to chair; floor, to floor; book, to book; fax, to fax; telephone, to telephone*; and *walk, to walk*. Some of these started out as nouns and some as verbs. For instance, *fax* is the shortened form of the noun *facsimile* which became used as a verb as well. Currently, when people say *fax*, they often mean *pdf* (portable document format), another noun that is now used as a verb. A sentence where *police* is used as noun, verb, and adjective respectively is (10a); (10b) is nicely alliterating where *pickle* is used as a verb, adjective, and noun; and (10c) has *fast* as adjective, adverb, and noun:

(10) a. **Police police police** outings regularly in the meadows of Malacandra.
b. Did Peter Piper **pickle pickled pickles?**
(Alyssa Bachman's example)
c. The **fast** girl recovered **fast** after her **fast.**
(Amy Shinabarger's example)

As we'll see, other words can be ambiguous in this way.

As a summary to Section 1.1, use Table 2.1. Not all of these properties are always present of course. Morphological differences involve the shape of an element while syntactic ones involve how the element fits in a sentence. The semantic differences involve meaning, but remember to be careful here since nouns, for instance, can have plural *-s* in (1) and (2) above.

Differences (e) and (l) will be explained in the next section. They are evident in (11), which shows the adjective *expensive* that modifies (i.e. says something about) the noun *book* and the adverb *quickly* that modifies the verb *sold out*:

(11) That **expensive** book sold out **quickly.**

1.2 Adjectives (Adj) and Adverbs (Adv)

Adverbs and Adjectives are semantically very similar in that both modify another element, i.e. they describe a quality of another word: *quick/ly, nice/ly*, etc. As just mentioned, the main syntactic distinction is as expressed in (12):

(12) **The Adjective-Adverb Rule**
An adjective modifies a noun;
an adverb modifies a verb and (a degree adverb) modifies an adjective or adverb.

Since an adjective modifies a noun, the quality it describes will be one appropriate to a noun, e.g. nationality/ethnicity (*American, Navajo, Dutch, Iranian*), size (*big, large, thin*), age (*young, old*), color (*red, yellow, blue*), material/personal description (*wooden, human*), or character trait (*happy, fortunate, lovely, pleasant, obnoxious*). Adverbs often modify actions and will then provide information typical of those, e.g. manner (*wisely, fast, quickly, slowly*), or duration (*frequently, often*), or speaker attitude (*fortunately, actually*), or place (*there, abroad*), or time (*then, now, yesterday*). *As well* and *also*, and negatives such as *not* and *never,* are also adverbs in that they usually modify the verb.

When adverbs modify adjectives or other adverbs, they are called degree adverbs (*very, so, too*). These degree adverbs have very little meaning (except some that can add flavor to the degree, such as *exceedingly* and *amazingly*) and it is hard to find synonyms or antonyms. It therefore makes more sense to consider this subgroup of adverbs grammatical categories. They also do not head a phrase of their own, and when it looks as if they do, there really is another adjective or adverb left out. The *very* in (13) modifies *important*, which is left out:

> (13)   How important is your job to you? **Very.**
>   (from CBS 60 Minutes 1995).

Some instances of the use of the adjective *nice* are given in (14) and (15). Traditionally, the use in (14) is called predicative and that in (15) attributive:

> (14)   The book is **nice.**
> (15)   A **nice** book is on the table.

The adverbs *very* and *quickly* appear in (16) and (17):

> (16)   This Hopi bowl is **very** precious.
> (17)   He drove **very quickly.**

In (14) and (15), *nice* modifies the noun *book*. In (16), the degree adverb *very* modifies the adjective *precious*; and in (17), it modifies the adverb *quickly*, which in its turn modifies the verb *drove*. (We will come back to some of the issues related to the precise nature of the modification in Chapters 3, 4, and 9). In the 'special topic' section at the end of this chapter, it will be shown that speakers often violate rule (12), but that these so-called violations are rule-governed as well.

Sentence (16) shows something else, namely that the noun *Hopi* can also be used to modify another noun. When words are put together like this, they are called compound words. Other examples are given in (18) and (19):

> (18)   So the principal says to the [**chemistry** teacher], "You'll have to teach physics this
>   year." (from Science Activities 1990)
> (19)   Relaxing in the living room of his unpretentious red [**stone** house], …
>   (from Forbes 1990)

Some of these compounds may end up being seen or written as one word; others are two words e.g. *girlfriend, bookmark, mail-carrier, fire engine, dog food,* and *stone age*. When we see a noun modifying another noun, as in (18) and (19), we will discuss if they are compounds or not. The space and hyphen between the two words indicate degrees of closeness.

Often, an adverb is formed from an adjective by adding *-ly*, as in (17). However, be careful with this morphological distinction: not all adverbs end in *-ly*, e.g. *fast,* and *hard* can be adjectives as well as adverbs and some adjectives end in *-ly*, e.g. *friendly, lovely, lively,* and *wobbly*. If you are uncertain as to whether a word is an adjective or an adverb, either look in a dictionary to see what it says, or use it in a sentence to see what it modifies. For instance, in (20), *fast* is an adjective because it modifies the noun *car,* but in (21), it is an adverb since it modifies the verb *drove*:

(20)   That **fast** car must be a police car.

(21)   That car drove **fast** until it saw the photo radar.

In a number of cases, words such as *hard* and *fast* can be adjectives or adverbs, depending on the interpretation. In (22), *hard* can either modify the noun *person,* i.e. the person looks tough or nasty, in which case it is an adjective, or it can modify *look* (meaning that the person was looking all over the place for something, i.e. the effort was great) in which case *hard* is an adverb:

(22)   That person looked **hard.**

As a reader of this sentence, what is your preference? Checking a contemporary American corpus, i.e. a set of representative texts, I found that most speakers use *hard* as an adverb after the verb *look*. Do you agree?

Some of the 'discrepancies' between form and function are caused by language change. For instance, the degree adverb *very* started out its life being borrowed as an adjective from the French *verrai* (in the 13th century) with the meaning 'true', as in (23):

(23)   *Under the colour of a **veray** peax, whiche is neuertheles but a cloked and furred peax.* 'Under the color of a true peace, which is nevertheless nothing but a cloaked and furred peace.' (Cromwell's 16th century Letters)

Here, what looks like a *-y* ending is a rendering of the Old French *verrai*. What's worse for confusing Modern English speakers is that, in Old English, adverbs did not need to end in *-lich* or *-ly*. That's why 'old' adverbs sometimes keep that shape, e.g. *first* in (24) is a 'correct' adverb, but *second* is not. The reason that *secondly* is prescribed rather than *second* is that it was borrowed late from French, at a time when English adverbs typically received *-ly* endings.

(24)   … **first** I had to watch the accounts and **secondly** I'm looking at all this stuff for when I start my business. (from a conversation in the BNC Corpus)

A last point to make about adjectives and adverbs is that most (if they are gradable) can be used to compare or contrast two or more things. We call such forms the comparative (e.g. *better than*) or superlative (e.g. *the best*). One way to make these forms is to add *-er/-est*, as in *nicer/nicest*. Not all adjectives/adverbs allow this ending, however;

qualifiers?

some need to be preceded by *more/most*, as in *more intelligent, most intelligent*. Sometimes, people are creative with comparatives and superlatives, especially in advertising, as in (25) and (26), or in earlier forms as in (27):

(25) mechanic: "the **expensivest** oil is …"
(26) advertisement: "the **bestest** best ever phone".
(27) To take the **basest** and **most poorest** shape … (Shakespeare, *King Lear* II, 3, 7)

There are also irregular comparative and superlative forms, such as *good, better, best; bad, worse, worst*. These have to be learned as exceptions to the rules, and can be played with, as in the pun 'When I am bad, I am better'.

To summarize this section, I'll provide a table listing differences between adjectives and adverbs. Not all of these differences have been discussed yet, e.g. the endings -*ous*, -*ary*, -*al*, and -*ic* are typical for adjectives and -*wise*, and -*ways* for adverbs, but they speak for themselves.

Table 2.2. Differences between adjectives and adverb

		Adjectives (Adj)		Adverbs (Adv)
Morphology	a.	end in -*ous*, -*ary*, -*al*, -*ic*; mostly have no -*ly*; and can be participles	d.	end in -*ly* in many cases, -*wise*, -*ways*, etc. or have no ending (*fast, now*)
Syntax	b.	modify N	e.	modify V, Adj, or Adv
Semantics	c.	describe qualities typical of nouns, e.g: nationality, color, size	f.	describe qualities of verbs, e.g: place, manner, time, duration, etc. and of adjectives/adverbs: degree

1.3 Prepositions (P)

Prepositions typically express place or time (*at, in, on, before*), direction (*to, from, into, down*), causation (*for*), or relation (*of, about, with, like, as, near*). They are invariable in form and have to occur before a noun, as (28) shows, where the prepositions are in bold and the nouns they go with are underlined:

(28) **With** their <u>books</u> **about** <u>linguistics</u>, they went **to** <u>school</u>. *? awkward*

On occasion, what look like prepositions are used on their own, as in (29):

(29) He went **in**; they ran **out**; and he jumped **down**.

In such cases, these words are considered adverbs, not prepositions. The difference between prepositions and adverbs is that prepositions come before the nouns they relate to and that adverbs are on their own.

Some other examples of one word prepositions are *during, around, after, against, despite, except, without, towards, until, till,* and *inside*. Sequences such as *instead of, outside of, away from, due to,* and *as for* are also considered to be prepositions, even though they consist of more than one word. Infrequently, prepositions are transformed into verbs, as in (30):

(30)　They **upped** the price.

Some prepositions have very little lexical meaning and are mainly used for grammatical purposes. For instance, *of* in (31) expresses a relationship between two nouns rather than a locational or directional meaning:

(31)　The door **of** that car.

Prepositions are therefore a category with lexical and grammatical characteristics. Here, however, I will treat them as lexical, for the sake of simplicity. A partial list is given in Table 2.3.

Table 2.3. Some prepositions in English

about, above, across, after, against, along, amidst, among, around, at, before, behind, below, beneath, beside(s), between, beyond, by, concerning, despite, down, during, except, for, from, in, into, inside, like, near, of, off, on, onto, opposite, outside, over, past, since, through, to, toward(s), under, underneath, until, up, upon, with, within, without

2.　Grammatical categories

The main grammatical categories are Determiner, Auxiliary, Coordinator, and Complementizer. As also mentioned above, it is hard to define grammatical categories in terms of meaning because they have very little. Their function is to make the lexical categories fit together.

2.1　Determiner (D)

The determiner category includes the articles *a(n)* and *the*, as well as demonstratives, possessive pronouns, possessive nouns, some quantifiers, some interrogatives, and some numerals. So, determiner (or D) is an umbrella term for all of these. Determiners occur with a noun to specify which noun is meant or whose it is. If you are a native speaker, you know how to use the indefinite article *a* and the definite article *the*. For non-native speakers, figuring out their use is very difficult.

The indefinite article is often used when the noun that follows it is new in the text/conversation, such as the first mention of *Florida manatee* in (32) is. The second and third mentions of it are preceded by the definite article *the*:

(32)　The fate of **a Florida manatee** that has wandered into northern New Jersey waters remained unclear Saturday night. **The wayward male** – known as Ilya – has been stuck near a Linden oil refinery, and officials say plunging temperatures and a lack of food were endangering its life. And while **the gentle sea cow** appears to be in good health, it had been huddling near an outfall pipe at an oil refinery – the only place it could find warm water. (from Huffington Post)

There are four demonstratives in English: *this, that, these,* and *those,* with the first two for singular nouns and the last two for plural ones. See (33a). Possessive pronouns include *my, your, his, her, its, our,* and *their,* as in (33b). Nouns can be possessives as well, but in that case they have an -*'s* (or *'*) ending, as in (33c):

(33)   a.   **That** javelina loved **these** trails.
       b.   **Their** kangaroo ate **my** food.
       c.   **Gucci's** food was eaten by Coco.[3]

In (33b), *their* and *my* specify whose kangaroo and whose food it was, and the possessive noun *Gucci's* in (33c) specifies whose food was eaten.

Determiners, as in (32) and (33), precede nouns just like adjectives, but whereas a determiner points out which entity is meant (it specifies), an adjective describes the quality (it modifies). When both a determiner and an adjective precede a noun, the determiner always precedes the adjective, as in (34a), and not the other way round, as in (34b) (indicated by the asterisk):

(34)   a.   **Their** irritating dog ate my delicious food.
       b.   *Irritating **their** dog ate delicious my food.

Interrogatives such as *whose* in *whose books, what* in *what problems,* and *which* in *which computer* are determiners. Quantifiers such as *any, many, much,* and *all* are usually considered determiners, e.g. in *much work, many people,* and *all research.* Some are used before other determiners, namely, *all, both,* and *half,* as in (35). These quantifiers are called pre-determiners, and abbreviated Pre-D. Finally, quantifiers may be adjectival, as in *the many problems* and in (36):

(35)   **All** the books; **half** that man's money; **both** those problems.
(36)   The challenges are **many/few.**

Numerals are sometimes determiners, as in *two books,* and sometimes more like adjectives, as in *my two books.* Table 2.4 shows the determiners in the order in which they may appear. I have added the category adjective to the table since some of the words that are clear determiners can also be adjectives. The categories are not always a 100% clear-cut, and (37) tries to shed some light on the difference.

---

3.   Believe it or not, *Gucci* and *Coco* are names of real dogs!

finite sentences

Table 2.4. Determiners

	Pre-D	D	Adj
quantifier	all, both	some, many, all, few(er)	many, few
	half	any, much, no, every, less, etc.	
article		the, a	
demonstrative		that, this, those, these	
possessive		my, etc., NP's	
interrogative		whose, what, which, etc.	
numeral		one, two, etc.	one, two, etc.

(37) **The Determiner-Adjective Rule**
A Determiner points to the noun it goes with and who it belongs to;
An Adjective gives background information about the noun.

2.2 Auxiliary (AUX)

This category will be dealt with in detail in Chapter 6. For now, it suffices to say that, as its name implies, the auxiliary verb functions to help another verb, but does not itself contribute greatly to the meaning of the sentence.

Verbs such as *have, be,* and *do* can be lexical verbs or auxiliaries. In (38a), *have* is a lexical verb because it has a meaning 'to possess' and occurs without any other lexical verb. In (38b), on the other hand, *have* does not mean 'possess' or 'hold', but contributes to the grammatical meaning of the sentence, namely past tense with present relevance. It therefore is an auxiliary to the lexical verb *worked*. The same is true for *be* in (39). In (39a), it is the only verb and therefore lexical; in (39b), it contributes to the grammatical meaning emphasizing the continuous nature of the event. Lexical and auxiliary uses of *do* are given in (40a) and (40b) respectively:

(38) a. I **have** a book in my hand.
      b. I **have** worked here for 15 years.

(39) a. That man **is** a hard worker.
      b. That reindeer may **be** working too hard.

(40) a. She **did** her homework.
      b. She **did**n't sleep at all.

Because auxiliaries help other verbs (except when they are main verbs as in (38)), they cannot occur on their own. Thus, (41) is ungrammatical:

(41) *I must a book.

2.3 Coordinator (C) and Complementizer (C)

In this section, we discuss two categories that join other words or phrases. Coordinators are relatively simple and join similar categories or phrases. Complementizers introduce subordinate clauses and look remarkably similar to prepositions and adverbs. We abbreviate both as C.

Coordinators such as *and* and *or* join two elements of the same kind, e.g. the nouns in (42):

(42)   Rigobertha **and** Pablo went to Madrid **or** Barcelona.

They are also sometimes called coordinating conjunctions, as in Figure 2.1, but in this book, we'll use coordinator. There are also two-part coordinators such as *both … and*, *either … or*, and *neither … nor*.

FOXTROT

Figure 2.1. Connecting sentences (Reprinted with the permission of Universal Press Syndicate. All rights reserved)

Complementizers such as *that, because, whether, if*, and *since* join two clauses where one clause is subordinate to the other (see Chapter 7 for more), as in (43). The subordinate clause is indicated by means of brackets:

(43)   Rigobertha and Pablo left [**because** Isabella was about to arrive].

They are also called subordinating conjunctions or subordinators. We will use complementizer. Like prepositions, coordinators and complementizers are invariable in English (i.e. never have an ending), but complementizers introduce a new clause whereas prepositions are connected to a noun. Some examples of complementizers and some of their other functions (if they have them) are provided in Table 2.5.

Table 2.5. A few complementizers

C	Example of C use	Other use	Example of other use
after	**After** she left, it rained.	preposition	**after** him
as	Fair **as** the moon is, it…	degree adverb	**as** nice
because	(43)	–	
before	**Before** it snowed, it rained.	preposition	**before** me
for	I expect **for** you to do that.	preposition	**for** Santa
if	**If** she wins, that will be great.	–	
so	He was tired, **so** he went to sleep.	adverb	**so** tired
that	I know **that** the earth is round.	D	**that** book
when	I wonder **when** it will happen.	adverb	He left **when**?
while	She played soccer, **while** he slept.	noun	A short **while**

There is a group of words, namely *yet, however, nevertheless, therefore*, and *so*, as in (44), that connects one sentence to another:

(44) "you are anxious for a compliment, **so** I will tell you that you have improved her".
(Jane Austen, *Emma*, Vol 1, Chap 8)

Some grammarians see these as complementizers; others see them as adverbs. With the punctuation as in (44), the complementizer scenario is more obvious since *so* connects the two sentences. However, *so* sometimes appears at the beginning of a sentence, in which case it could be an adverb expressing the reason why something was done. I leave it up to you to decide what to do with these. You may remember from Section 1.2 that *so* can also be a degree adverb, as in *so nice*.

We can now formulate another rule, namely the one in (45):

(45) **The Preposition-Complementizer-Adverb Rule**
A Preposition introduces a noun (e.g. **about** *the book*);
a Complementizer introduces a sentence (e.g. **because** *he left*); and
an Adverb is on its own (e.g. *She went* **out**; and **Unfortunately**, *she left*).

These categories are often ambiguous in Modern English because prepositions and adverbs can change to complementizers.

3. Pronouns

In this section, I discuss the different pronouns in English. Pronouns are a hybrid category since they do not carry much lexical meaning but they can function on their own, unlike articles and complementizers, which need something to follow them. This makes them hard to classify as lexical or grammatical categories.

Personal pronouns, such as *I, me, she, he* and *it*, and reflexive pronouns, such as *myself, yourself*, and *herself*, are seen as grammatical categories by many (myself included). The reason is that they don't mean very much: they are used to refer to phrases already mentioned. However, in this book, I label personal and reflexive pronouns the same way as nouns, since they function like full Noun Phrases as Subjects and Objects (more on this in Chapter 4). Thus, a determiner such as *the* cannot stand on its own, but *she*, as in (46) from Shakespeare, can:

(46) 'Twere good **she** were spoken with,
For **she** may strew dangerous coniectures
in ill breeding minds. (*Hamlet*, IV, 5, 14)

Personal pronouns can be divided according to number into singular and plural and according to person into first, second, and third person. For example, *I* and *me* are first person singular, and *we* and *us* are first person plural. The second person pronoun *you* is used both as singular and as plural. Third person singular pronouns *he/him, she/her,* and *it* are further divided according to gender; the third person plural pronouns are *they* and *them.*

Pronouns look like the determiners we saw in the previous section. Almost all determiners, except the articles, can stand on their own, e.g. demonstratives, such as *that* in *that is a problem.* Thus, they are very much like pronouns, but they can in principle have a noun following. Therefore, I will label something a D if it can have a noun following it but a pronoun if it can't.

Apart from personal and reflexive pronouns, there are some possessive pronouns that occur on their own, and are therefore not determiners. Examples are *mine, yours, his, hers, ours,* and *theirs,* as in (47a). These pronouns appear when the noun they specify has been left unspecified. Thus, (47a) could be rewritten as (47b), with *mine* replaced by *my e-mail*:

(47) a.   That e-mail is not **mine**, but it is **yours**.
      b.   That e-mail is not **my** e-mail, but it is **your** e-mail.

The result is awkward, however, and I will suggest that *mine* and *yours* are really independent pronouns, not determiners with the noun left out.

The other determiners, namely interrogatives, quantifiers, and numerals can occur independently too, as in (48). It will be up to you as the reader to decide whether these are independent pronouns or are really determiners preceding nouns that have been left out:

(48)   **What** would be solved if **all** chose **two**?

Indefinite pronouns, such as *anyone, anybody, everyone, someone, something,* and *nothing,* occur frequently and are in many ways similar to personal pronouns. There are many other indefinites that are similar to adverbs, e.g. *anywhere, nowhere, sometime,* and *somewhere,* or to degree adverbs, e.g. *somewhat.* They are pro-forms and can stand in for an adverb. When I label them in the answers to the exercises, I will indicate that they are pronouns as well adverbs.

In this section, we discussed several types of pronouns. Some occur independently (*I, you,* and *mine*) and others occur with a noun and are Ds (*my* and *whose*). There are other pronouns we will encounter, mainly relative ones and adverbs such as *then* and *there.*

4.   What new words and loanwords tell us!

Some of the new words of the late 20th and early 21th century are *geocache, sudoku, podcast* (from the *Oxford English Dictionary* online), *spyware, mouse potato, agritourism* (from the *Merriam Webster* online), and *facebook, google, kindle, twitter, sustainability, pwned*, and *texting*, to name but a few, and they are all lexical categories! Some of the new words or expressions are loanwords (e.g. *sudoku* is from Japanese, *pwn* possible from Welsh), some are extensions of other meanings (*bookmark a site* from *bookmark a book*), some are clipped (*weblog* becomes *blog*), others come from special (*pwned* from internet gaming) but all are lexical, rather than grammatical categories.

Lewis Carroll's *Jabberwocky* includes a number of 'nonsense' words. As an exercise, at the end of the chapter, you'll be asked what category each of these is. For now, it is enough to point out that they are all lexical:

> 'Twas brillig, and the slithy toves
> Did gyre and gimble in the wabe:
> All mimsy were the borogoves
> And the mome raths outgrabe.
>
> "Beware the Jabberwock, my son!
> The jaws that bite, the claws that catch!
> Beware the Jubjub bird and shun
> The frumious Bandersnatch!"
>
> He took his vorpal sword in hand:
> Longtime the manxome foe he sought -
> So rested he by the Tumtum tree
> And stood a while in thought. (…)

There are other phenomena that the lexical/grammatical distinction sheds light on. For instance, children learn lexical categories before grammatical ones, and people with aphasia can have difficulties with either lexical or grammatical categories (see Exercise E below). So there is empirical (from the outside world) evidence for the distinction made in this chapter.

5. Conclusion

The lexical categories discussed in this chapter are defined in semantic, morphological, and syntactic terms, i.e. according to meaning, word form, and position in the sentence. The main factor determining the category (in English) is the position in relation to other words. You could also try to find a synonym and that might help you decide on the category.

Grammatical categories can mainly be defined (as their name implies) in terms of their grammatical function and it is often hard to find a synonym. Pronouns have characteristics of both. A summary table is provided as Table 2.6, but review Tables 2.1 to 2.4 and Rules (12), (37), and (45) as well.

Table 2.6. The categories in English

Lexical	N	cloud, sun, love, kitchen, house
	V	know, see, paint, swim
	Adj	good, nice, friendly
	Adv	actually, now, there, sometimes, where
	P	to, from, on, in front of
Grammatical	D	the, that, my, one, whose
	AUX	may, have, be
	C	and, that, because
Pronouns	Pron	I, yourself, who, mine, someone

The key terms in this chapter are **lexical category (Noun, Verb, Adjective, Adverb, Preposition** and **Pronoun)** and **grammatical category (Determiner, Auxiliary, Coordinator** and **Complementizer)**, or **open** as opposed to **closed**.

Exercises

A.   Identify each word in the short text below.

We found this place accidentally and have been returning almost weekly. We just love it. It is so simple and yet so wonderful and the staff is great. They are always smiling and just so nice. There is almost always a line. A must!
(review of the *Fry Bread House* in Phoenix, slightly adapted)

B.   Compose some sentences   (a)   where an adjective modifies a noun,

(b)   where an adverb modifies an adjective, and

(c)   where an adverb modifies another adverb and the two together modify a verb.

C.   Find the prepositions, coordinators, and complementizers in the text below.
MUnicycling is the act of riding a one-wheel bike off road. It is also known as Rough Terrain or All Terrain Unicycling and, in the past decade, has become the hottest trend around in the unicycling community. Off road terrain is, of course, uneven and mountains have gradients, rocks and other obstacles to get in the way of the intrepid unicyclist. Whilst jumping over rocks provides the fun element, cycling uphill on a unicycle demands incredible strength and lung capacity. Additional balancing skills, including the ability to back-pedal, are also needed to safely negotiate a downhill section on a unicycle. As a result, above average fitness levels are required. (from http://mountain-biking.suite101.com/article.cfm/mountain_biking_on_a_unicycle)

D.   To what categories do the nonsense words belong in Lewis Carroll's "Jabberwocky", given in Section 4 above? Which arguments did you use to decide on these?

E.   Choose five words that are grammatical categories and look them up in a dictionary. How do dictionaries deal with them?

F.   Broca's aphasia results in a loss of grammatical categories, such as determiners and auxiliaries, but not in a loss of lexical categories, such as nouns and verbs. It is sometimes called agrammatism. Wernicke's aphasia results in a loss of meaning, but not in a loss of grammatical categories. Which sentence exemplifies which aphasia?

I.   I could if I can help these like this you know … to make it.

II.   Well … front … soldiers … campaign … soldiers … to shoot … well … head … wound … and hospital … and so …   (from O'Grady et al. 1987: 280; 278)

G.   The excerpt below is from D.H. Lawrence's *Snake*. Find the **adjectives and adverbs** in the two excerpts below and see how they are used. What do they modify? Are there compounds?

Snake   *compound*
A snake came to my (water-trough)

A D F.   On a hot, hot day, and I in pyjamas for the heat,
To drink there.

In the deep, strange-scented shade of the great dark carob-tree
I came down the steps with my pitcher
And must wait, must stand and wait, for there he was at the trough before me.

…

And voices in me said, If you were a man
You would take a stick and break him now, and finish him off.

But must I confess how I liked him,
How glad I was he had come like a guest in quiet, to drink at my water-trough
And depart peaceful, pacified, and thankless,
Into the burning bowels of this earth?

…

H.   Most people, if asked to provide or repeat the first line of Dylan Thomas' poem, partially given below, will say 'Do not go gently . . .' with *gently* as an adverb modifying the verb. Why is *gentle* grammatical as well?

Do Not Go Gentle into That Good Night,

Do not go gentle into that good night,
Old age should burn and rave at close of day;
Rage, rage against the dying of the light.

Though wise men at their end know dark is right,
Because their words had forked no lightning they
Do not go gentle into that good night

Good men, the last wave by, crying how bright
Their frail deeds might have danced in a green bay,
Rage, rage against the dying of the light.

Wild men who caught and sang the sun in flight,
And learn, too late, they grieved it on its way,
Do not go gentle into that good night.

Look at the cartoon in Figure 2.2. Explain why *gently* is used rather than *gentle*.

Figure 2.2. *Gently into that …* (© 2008 Jan Eliot. Reprinted with the permission of Universal Press Syndicate. All rights reserved.)

I. First, circle the verbs (and auxiliary verbs) in Wallace Stevens''Anecdote of the Jar' and then identify the categories of the other words, i.e. N, Adj, Adv, P, Det, C, and Pronoun. Are there any words that you are unsure about? Make an educated guess as to their category.

> I placed a jar in Tennessee,
> And round it was, upon a hill.
> It made the slovenly wilderness
> Surround that hill.
>
> The wilderness rose up to it,
> And sprawled around, no longer wild.
> The jar was round upon the ground
> And tall and of a port in air.
>
> It took dominion everywhere.
> The jar was grey and bare.
> It did not give of bird or bush,
> Like nothing else in Tennessee.

J. Identify all the words in the following sentence taken from Shakespeare. Are there any that look unusual?

(49)   Ile serve thee true and faithfully till then. (*Love's Labor's Lost*, V, 2, 840)

K. Look at the first 10 instances of *fast* in the BNC or COCA and see how many are adjectives and how many are adverbs.

Class discussion

L. In class, it has been argued that lexical categories can be borrowed from one language into another (e.g. *karaoke, taco, sauerkraut*) or 'invented' (*e-mail, chat-room, web navigator*). Can you think of a preposition or a pronoun that has been borrowed or made up? What does your answer mean for the status (lexical/grammatical) of these categories?

M. Morris Bishop wrote the following in *The New Yorker* (27 September 1947, p. 30). How do you like the prepositions in the last line?

> I lately lost a preposition
> It hid, I thought, beneath my chair
> And angrily I cried, 'perdition!
> Up from out of in under there."
> Correctness is my vade mecum,
> And straggling phrases I abhor,

And yet I wondered, "What should he come
Up from out of in for?"

N.   Identify all the adjectives in (50), the completed (19), and discuss some aspects, e.g. the
category of *capital*:

(50)   Relaxing in the living room of his unpretentious red stone house in an
upper-middle-class section of his capital city, Tegucigalpa, Callejas spoke
about his plans.

Keys to the exercises

A.   The difference between verb (V) and auxiliary (AUX) will only become completely clear in
Chapter 6. Note that I classify pronominal adverbs as Adv/Pro(-form). See the last part of
Section 3 on this. Are there other questions that came up?
      We (Pron) found (V) this (D) place (N) accidentally (Adv) and (C) have (AUX) been
(AUX) returning (V) almost (Adv) weekly (Adv). We (Pron) just (Adv) love (V) it (Pron). It
(Pron) is (V) so (Adv) simple (Adj) and (C) yet (Adv) so (Adv) wonderful (Adj) and (C) the
(D) staff (N) is (V) great (Adj). They (Pron) are (AUX) always (Adv) smiling (V) and (C) just
(Adv) so (Adv) nice (Adj). There (Adv/Pro) is (V) almost (Adv) always (Adv) a (D) line (N).
A (D) must (AUX used as N)!

B.   a.   The **cute** kitten slept soundly; That was not **pleasant**;
            He is this very **abrasive** politician.
      b.   He is this **very** abrasive linguist; That computer was **extraordinarily** irritating; The
            extremely unpleasant judge was impeached.
      c.   I can see [**very** well] from here; He went [**extremely** quickly];
            He said that she drove [**too** fast].

C.   The prepositions are: *of, off* (unless you consider *off road* as a compound), *as, in, (around* is
an adverb), *in, Off, (of course* is one adverb), *(to* in *to get* is an infinitive marker), *in, of, over,
on, including, on, As,* and *above*. The coordinators are one *or* and four instances of *and*.
There is one complementizer, namely *whilst*.

D.   'Twas brillig (Adj), and the slithy (Adj) toves (N)
      Did gyre (V) and gimble (V) in the wabe (N):
      All mimsy (Adj) were the borogoves (N)
      And the mome (Adj) raths (N) outgrabe (V).
            "Beware the Jabberwock (N), my son!
            The jaws that bite, the claws that catch!
            Beware the Jubjub (N) bird and shun
            The frumious (Adj) Bandersnatch!"

He took his vorpal (Adj) sword in hand:

Longtime the manxome (Adj) foe he sought -

So rested he by the Tumtum (N) tree

And stood a while in thought. (…)

E.   Five grammatical categories: all (D), my (D), have (AUX), though (ADV and C), since (C and P). If you look some up in a dictionary that is historically based (e.g. the Oxford English Dictionary), you will run into trouble because there is so much information. For instance, *the* is listed as 'demonstrative', 'pronoun, and 'article'. A less historical dictionary might just give 'article'.

F.   I is Wernicke; II is Broca.

G.   The adjectives, adverbs, and compounds are listed below. Most of these are tricky and probably hard to do until you have reached Chapters 5 and 10. So don't worry!

Adjectives: *hot, deep, great, dark, glad, peaceful, pacified, thankless, burning.*

Adverbs: *there (twice), now, how.* Compounds: *water-trough (twice), strange-scented, carob-tree.*

A short analysis: Lawrence's *Snake* is about reflection and lack of action. It describes a still, beautiful scene, which is emphasized by the use of adjectives such as *hot* (l. 2) and *deep, strange-scented, great*, and *dark* (l. 4). There is also a conflict between the peace of the moment (and nature) and the voices (of education, etc.). The conflict is emphasized by the use of the adjectives *peaceful, pacified, thankless* as opposed to *burning*. It is the snake that is seen as peaceful, hence, *depart peaceful* and not *depart peacefully*.

H.   Grammatically speaking, having an adverb such as *gently* modify *go* is correct but Dylan Thomas chose *gentle*. Suddenly, another interpretation becomes available, one where the person addressed in the poem should not 'become gentle'. Now, because of its form, *gentle* modifies the implied 'you'. The effect is very different. The Stone Soup cartoon plays on the distinction nicely. The kids are not **going** gently, i.e. in a gentle manner; they are off with BBQ tools and much energy.

I.   I (Pron) placed (V) a (D) jar (N) in (P) Tennessee (N)

And (C) round (Adj) it (Pron) was (V), upon (P) a (D) hill (N)

It (Pron) made (V) the (D) slovenly (Adj) wilderness (N)

Surround (V) that (D) hill (N).

　　The (D) wilderness (N) rose (V) up (Adv) to (P) it (Pron)

　　And (C) sprawled (V) around (Adv), no (Adv) longer (Adv) wild (Adj)

　　The (D) jar (N) was (V) round (Adj) upon (P) the (D) ground (N)

　　And (C) tall (Adj) and (C) of (P) a (D) port (N) in (P) air (N).

It (Pron) took (V) dominion (N) everywhere (Pron/Adv).

The (D) jar (N) was (V) grey (Adj) and (C) bare (Adj).

It (Pron) did (AUX) not (Adv) give (V) of (P) bird (N) or (C) bush (N).

Like (P) nothing (Pron) else (Adj) in (P) Tennessee (N).

Possible difficult words: *no longer, wild, nothing,* and *else.* The Oxford English Dictionary labels *else* an adverb. I think it is an adjective since it is a synonym of 'other' and the order of adjectives and indefinites is often inverted, as in *someone strange.*

J.   (49)   Ile (Pron and AUX) serve (V) thee (Pron) true (Adv) and (C) faithfully (Adv) till (P) then (Adv).

K.   I checked the BNC and the first 10 instances of *fast* that I found are listed here:

Adv: … the cold spreading too **fast**, of my not being able to live with it.

I have never had to run so **fast** in a job in my life

Following **fast** on its heels is Ko Samui

He turned quickly, and left the station as **fast** as he could.

They go **fast** enough as it is.

Adj: … take a **fast** step forwards

… progression from **fast** to slow to **fast** again

The prototype **fast** reactor at Dounreay

… a **fast** new locomotive.

… a **fast** enough speed of about 60 miles an hour.

Special topic: Adverb and adjective

The rule stated in (12) above is often ignored by native speakers. In its simple form, it reads: an adjective modifies a noun; an adverb modifies a verb, adjective, or adverb. The reason that the rule is not always followed is that English is changing. For instance, *real* is being used as a degree adverb and is becoming more like other degree adverbs such as *too, so,* and *very* that lack the -*ly* ending. In (14) to (17) above, examples of the 'correct' use of adjectives and adverbs are given. Some additional prescriptively correct uses are listed here in (51) to (55), where the adjective modifies a noun:

(51)   She waited **impassive** while they made it in **safe.**
(52)   I list them **separate.**
(53)   He tested **positive.**
(54)   In an article on nails: Color them **unusual!**
(55)   Headline: 911 system stretched **thin.**

Explain what the adjectives in (51) to (55) modify. What happens if you add a -*ly* and make the adjective into an adverb? The meaning changes since now the adverb modifies the verb.

Examples of 'incorrect use' are listed in (56), (57), and (49) above, all from an earlier variety of English. One of the reasons for this is mentioned in Section 1.2, namely that in Old English adverbs have no endings:

(56)   Tis **Noble** Spoken. (*Anthony and Cleopatra*, II, 2, 99)

(57)   Thou didst it **excellent.** (*Taming of the Shrew*, I, 1, 89)

There may be other reasons. Explain why (58) to (61) are prescriptively incorrect:

(58)   In formal speech:
         You did that **real good.**

(59)   'because if she doesn't do **good** in school, then …' (Judge in Texas, quoted in a newspaper)

(60)   It looks **beautifully.**

(61)   Does the clutch feel any **differently**? (The Tappet Brothers on 'Car Talk')

These sentences illustrate three problems speakers encounter. First, as mentioned, *really* is losing its ending when it is degree adverb, as in (58). As Swan (1980: 12) writes: "In informal conversational English (especially American English), *real* is often used instead of *really* before adjectives and adverbs". Note that nobody uses *real* in (62). Why might that be the case?

(62)   **Really**, you shouldn't have done that.

Secondly, the adverb counterpart to the adjective *good* is not *good*, as in (58) and (59), or *goodly*, but *well*, as in (63), the rewritten version of (59). *Well* is also used as adjective, as in (64). It is no wonder speakers become confused! In (64), *good* can replace *well*. Please explain why:

(64)   You did that **really well.**

(65)   I am **well**, thank you.

Thirdly, speakers tend to overreact when they see an adjective next to a verb and hypercorrect themselves. Hypercorrection occurs when speakers are so unsure that they think about the prescriptive rule too much and confuse themselves. They think that if an adjective is next to a verb, it has to modify the verb and be an adverb, as in (60) and (61). The poem by Dylan Thomas cited above shows, however, that this is not always necessary.

As a last point, a comment on *hopefully* is necessary. Swan (1980: 296–7) mentions that there are two uses: one is 'full of hope', as in (65), and the other use, as in (66), "shows the speaker's attitude", and means 'it is hoped'. According to Swan, "[s]ome people consider the second use 'incorrect'. Both functions will be dealt with in Chapter 5:

(65)   They waited **hopefully** for a positive response.

(66)   **Hopefully**, that concert is worth going to.

It is not clear why *hopefully* should have attracted all this attention. There are several other adverbs like it, e.g. those in (67) to (70):

(67)   **Naturally**, I'd like you to stay with us for a few days.

(68)   **Amazingly**, he arrived on time.

(69)   **Fortunately**, the bus wasn't late.

(70)   **Funnily enough**, I'd been thinking about that.

In (67) to (70), the adverbs all express the speaker's attitude and this is a legitimate use of an adverb; they do not all have to modify the verb, although many used to in earlier varieties of English. More on this in Chapter 5.

Chapter 3

Phrases

1. The noun phrase (NP)
2. The adjective phrase, adverb phrase, verb phrase, and prepositional phrase
3. Phrases in the sentence
4. Coordination of phrases and apposition
5. Finding phrases and building trees
6. Conclusion

Sentences can be divided into groups of words that belong together. For instance, in *the nice unicorn ate a delicious meal*, *the*, *nice*, and *unicorn* form one such group and *a*, *delicious*, and *meal* form another. (We all know this intuitively). The group of words is called a phrase. If the most important part of the phrase, i.e. the head, is an adjective, the phrase is an Adjective Phrase; if the most important part of the phrase is a noun, the phrase is a Noun Phrase, and so on. Indicating the phrases renders the structure of the sentence clearer and less ambiguous, as we'll see.

One can indicate phrases by putting brackets around them and we will occasionally do so. However, brackets are (visually) confusing and, as an alternative, 'trees' are used with branches connecting parts of phrases. The grammatical categories Determiner and Coordinator do not form phrases of their own but function inside a Noun Phrase (NP), Verb Phrase (VP), Adjective Phrase (AdjP), Adverb Phrase (AdvP), or Prepositional Phrase (PP). The grammatical category Auxiliary functions inside a Verb Group (see Chapter 6) and the Complementizer connects one sentence to the other and is head of a CP, as we'll see in Chapter 7.

In Sections 1 and 2, the structure of phrases is examined. The head of a phrase is important, but often this is intuitively understood. The trickiest part of this chapter concerns the intermediate categories N′ (N-bar) and V′ (V-bar). In Section 3, the structure for a full sentence and its phrases is discussed. Phrases are very often coordinated by means of *and* or *or* and a structure for this is given in Section 4. In Section 5, more precise rules are given on how to identify phrases and on how to construct trees.

1.   The noun phrase (NP)

An NP such as *the nice unicorn* is built around a noun, namely, *unicorn*. This noun (or N) is called the head of the NP. We can find the head in a simple way by thinking how we'd shorten the phrase and still keep the essential part, as in a telegram. For instance, we might shorten (1) to (2):

(1)   [The nice unicorns from that planet] are visiting us regularly.
(2)   Unicorns visit regularly.

More will be said on heads below.

In addition to the head, NPs can contain determiners (e.g. *the*) and adjectives (*nice*) as well as other elements (e.g. *from that planet*). A tree structure for a simple NP is given in (3). The lines, called 'branches', indicate how the phrase is divided up, and branches come together in 'nodes':

(3)

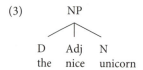

A different structure for (3) looks like (4):

(4)

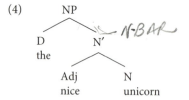

A structure such as (4) expresses the relationships more accurately than (3). In (3), it is unclear whether *the* is more closely connected to the adjective or the noun, but from (4), it is clear that *the* specifies *nice unicorn*. A structure as in (3) with more than two branches is a flat structure since the hierarchies are not clear. Using this book, you will learn to draw structures such as (4) and to avoid trees such as (3).

There are a number of things to note. First, the top node of (4), i.e. where the branches come together, is an NP because the head of the phrase is an N. Shortening the NP would tell us that. Secondly, the node in between the NP and N is called N' (pronounced N-bar). It is an intermediate node and some people call it NOM and students in my grammar classes have called the N' the small NP or the placeholder. Third, note that *nice* in (4) is itself the head of an Adjective Phrase (see 1.3 as well) and we could indicate that as in (5):

(5)

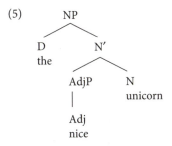

One way to go about constructing this tree is (a) to find the head *unicorn*, (b) to label the entire phrase as NP, and (c) to draw branches from the NP down to D on the left and, if there is more than one word left, to N′ on the right. The N′ functions as place-holder until you can put the N down. More step by step suggestions on how to draw trees can be found in the last section. *see 45*

On occasion, it may be hard to find the head of an NP, or to identify the entire NP. For instance, the initial group of words in (6), adapted from one of Dr. Seuss' books, is centered around a noun. Which noun do you think is the head and how extended is the NP?

(6)   [The pleasant wocket in my pocket that I adore] loves cranberry chutney.

The right answer is that *wocket* is the head because if you had to shorten the sentence, you might say *the wocket loves chutney*. Thus, *pleasant* and *in my pocket* and *that I adore* add additional information. Another way to shorten the sentence is to use a pronoun, as in (7). This is called pronominalization. If the group of words in *the pleasant wocket in my pocket that I adore* can be replaced by one pronoun, it has to be a phrase:

(7)   It loves cranberry chutney.

You can also find the entire phrase by examining which parts say something about the head, i.e. modify it. For instance, in (6), both *pleasant* and *in my pocket* have no other function in the sentence than to modify the head *wocket*.

An important function of the head is to determine the agreement with the verb. This will be more obvious in the next chapter though. I have repeated (1) as (8) with brackets indicating that the head of the subject NP is *unicorns*. The singular and plural number underneath the nouns and verb show that the head of the NP, *unicorns*, agrees with the auxiliary verb *are* in (plural) number, not the closer noun *planet*:

(8)   [The nice [unicorns] from that planet] are visiting us regularly.

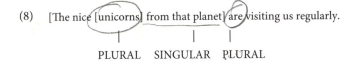

             PLURAL   SINGULAR   PLURAL

We could represent (6) as (9), where I have left the *that I adore* out for simplicity:

(9)

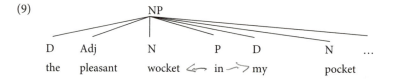

This structure indicates that the NP is composed of six words, but it does not say whether *in* is more connected to *my pocket* or to *wocket*. This is again a flat structure since we don't see what goes with what. It is even worse than (3). Therefore, as mentioned, we will avoid this kind of tree.

More hierarchical structures for this sentence are given in (10ab). To draw those trees, you could start by grouping what goes together, e.g. the PP *in my pocket*, and by circling the head. Since the head is an N, you have to put down the NP and then go to the D on the left (and put *the* underneath D) and the N′ on the right. You need an N′ because you have more than just the head *wocket*. Then, if you put *pleasant* on the left, you need another N′ on the right and you get (10a). If you first want to put the PP on the right, you need an N′ on the left to be a placeholder for the adjective and the noun and the results is (10b). We'll do a lot of practice with this:

(10)   a.

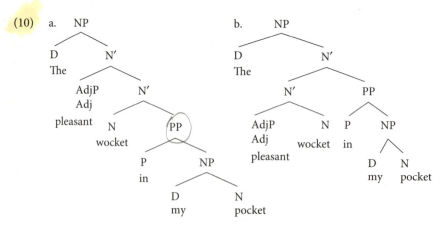

In (10a), *in my pocket* goes together with *wocket*. In a structure, this close connection is expressed by having the line, i.e. 'branch', that goes upwards connect to the same point, i.e. 'node'. This means they are 'sisters' in the structure. In (10b), *pleasant* and *wocket* are put closer together, i.e. are sisters. Both structures are possible. The meaning difference between (10a) and (10b) is minimal, but this is not always the case as sentences such as (20) and (22) below show. Note again that *pleasant* is itself the head of a phrase and that I indicate that by means of and Adj head inside an AdjP. The ultimate tree is not as important as understanding why you represent a tree in a particular way, as I have just tried to do for (10).

In (10), I am representing *my pocket* as an NP because it has a D and an N head. If the NP had been a pronoun or a name, the structure would have been as in (11). Pronouns and names such as *Jennifer, Edward, Malacandra* cannot have other elements modify/specify them and therefore we will see them as full phrases, as in (11ab):

(11) a. NP   b. NP
          | |
          she   Edward

Under very special circumstances, proper names can be modified, as when there are many persons called *Edward* and you want to make sure it is *the nice Edward*. This is not common with names, and it is very uncommon with pronouns.

Some heads are trickier to identify than others. For instance, in *one of those pages*, the head is *one*, and in *a piece of paper*, *piece* is the head. Frequently, a Relative Clause, such as *who wore that ugly hat* in (12) is part of an NP, as shown by brackets, modifying the head *person*:

(12)   [The person [who wore that ugly hat]] is the queen.

A structure for (12) will be given in Chapter 10. For now, just understand that it is part of the NP.

Structures such as (10) are called trees. As mentioned, the lines connecting parts of the trees are called branches, and the points where the branches come together are called nodes. The nodes are usually labelled, e.g. N, N′, or NP. Remember that N′ is an intermediate node between the top NP and the N. Such intermediate nodes allow one to indicate which elements are grouped together and thus make trees less flat. They are placeholders for a group of words that go together.

2. The adjective phrase, adverb phrase, verb phrase, and prepositional phrase

2.1 The adjective phrase (AdjP) and adverb phrase (AdvP)

AdjPs are built around adjectives, which indicate properties of nouns; AdvPs are built around adverbs which indicate qualities of verbs, adverbs, and adjectives. Since adjectives and adverbs have this qualifying function, they themselves are (optionally) accompanied by a degree marker such as *very, too, extremely, really*. The latter are adverbs of a special kind: they always modify another adverb or adjective and never modify a verb. They are comparable to the determiner in the NP, and more like grammatical than lexical categories. They do not expand into an AdvP of their own since degree markers such as *extremely very* do not occur.

An example of an AdjP is given in (13a) and of an AdvP in (13b). The (D)Adv indicates a degree adverb but, from now on, just Adv will be used:

(13) a. AdjP
         (D)Adv   Adj
           so   nice

      b. AdvP
         (D)Adv   Adv
          very   quickly

In (13a), the head of the AdjP is the adjective *nice*, and this head is modified by a degree adverb *so*; in (13b), the adverb *quickly* expands into a phrase and is modified by the degree adverb *very* that does not form a phrase of its own. That's why I choose not to make *very* the head of an AdvP.

An AdjP can be pronominalized, as in (14), but pronominalizing an AdvP, as in (15), sounds slightly awkward:

(14)   I was happy and **so** was she.
(15)   He behaved nicely, and she behaved **so/thus**.

2.2   The verb phrase (VP)

A VP is built around a verb and the latter can be in the present or past tense (they are past in (16abc)). Some VPs include other obligatory material, i.e. words or phrases that cannot easily be left out, such as the NP in (16a), the PP in (16b), and the AdjP in (16c). These obligatory parts are called complements and will be discussed in the next chapters:

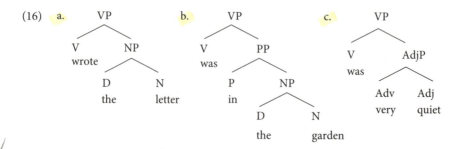

(16) a. VP   b.   VP   c.   VP
         V   NP   V   PP   V   AdjP
       wrote   was   was
         D   N   P   NP   Adv   Adj
        the   letter   in   very quiet
                               D   N
                              the garden

The VP can also include optional material that explains when, where, why, and how the action or state that the verb describes took place. These optional elements function as adverbials and will be discussed in Chapter 5.

As in the case of the NP, a VP can be pronominalized. An example is given in (17), where the (bolded) VP *washed the dishes* is replaced by *do so*. Some linguists call these pro-VPs or pro-forms, since they do not stand for nouns. It is up to you whether you call them pronoun or pro-form:

(17)   Gijsbert **washed the dishes** and Mariken **did so** as well.

2.3   The prepositional phrase (PP)

A PP is built around a preposition. As mentioned in the previous chapter, prepositions indicate relations in space and time. PPs include a P and an NP, as in (18):

(18)
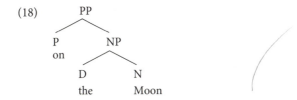

PPs can be replaced (pronominalized) by the adverbs *then, when, how, there*, etc.

In this section, it is necessary to jump ahead to Chapters 4, 5, 9 and 10 where functions are discussed. Up to now, we have looked at the names of categories and phrases, e.g. N and NP. Depending on where phrases are situated in the tree, they play a particular function, such as subject and object. Functions will not be put in the tree structure because it should be clear from the tree what they are.

With respect to PPs, it is not always easy to determine what role they play and their function in a sentence is manifold. For instance, in the ambiguous (19), an often used sentence in linguistic circles, does the PP function inside the NP, or are the NP and PP independent of one another?

(19)   She saw the man with glasses.   *PREP AMBIGUITY*

The answer to both questions can be 'yes' because the sentence is ambiguous. In the one case, the PP *with glasses* modifies the *man* and functions inside the NP *the man with glasses*; in the other case, the PP is independent of the NP since it modifies the VP and specifies how the seeing was done. The structure for the former reading is as in (20a) and for the latter reading as in (20b):

(20)   a.   b.
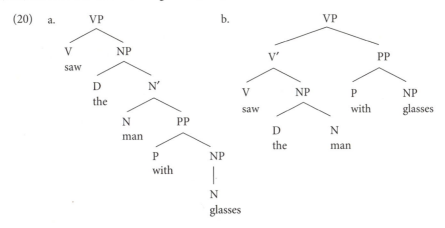

Thus, a particular tree structure disambiguates the sentence. In (17a), the PP *with glasses* is right next to the N *man* (i.e. PP is sister to N) and therefore modifies *man*; in

(17b), the same PP is right next to the V′ *saw the man* (i.e. PP is sister to V′) and hence says something on how the seeing of the man is done. For now, don't worry about (17b) too much. You may have noticed the use of V′ (pronounced V-bar) in (17b). A V′ (like the N′ in an NP) is an intermediate category in the VP. In (17b), we need to group the V and NP together so we need a label for that and we use a 'small VP' or placeholder until we can put down a branch for the V.

Groucho Marx uses structural ambiguity a lot, as in (21) below. Consider how the PP *in my pajamas* in (21) is ambiguous, in at least two ways:

(21)   I once shot an elephant in my pajamas. How he got in my pajamas I'll never know.

When you read the first line you think that the speaker was wearing pajamas, but the second line makes that impossible and you have to rethink the sentence. Now, there are two interpretations left: (a) the elephant was wearing the pajamas of the speaker while being shot and (b) the elephant was shot inside the pajamas. I have represented the two interpretations in (22). In (22a), the elephant is wearing the pajamas and, in (22b), the elephant is shot in the pajamas:

(22)   a.   b.

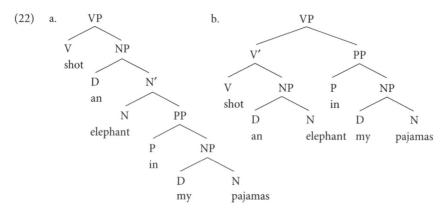

As explained in Chapter 1, structural ambiguity is different from lexical ambiguity. With lexical ambiguity, a word has two meanings, e.g. *case* in (9) in Chapter 1. Another instance is (23), a well-known joke also attributed to Groucho Marx, where the preposition *outside* is lexically ambiguous. *Outside* and *inside* look like each other's opposites in expressing a location, but in fact *outside* has an additional meaning, namely 'in addition to; except for':

(23)   Outside of a dog, a book is a man's best friend; inside it's too hard to read.

3.   Phrases in the sentence

Having provided a tree structure for all of the phrases whose heads are lexical catego-ries, I will now show how to combine these into a sentence. The basic structure for a sentence, i.e. S, is shown in (24):

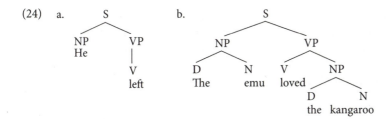

Thus, the initial element in the sentence is generally an NP (and, as we'll see in the next chapter, the function of this NP is subject). The NP is a daughter of the sentence S (i.e. immediately below S and connected by a tree branch). The rest of the sentence is the VP which can be more complex (as seen in (22b) above), as can the NP (as seen in (10)).

The relationships that are relevant in a tree are sister and daughter/mother. In (24ab), the NP and VP are sisters to each other and daughters of S. Sisters have a close relationship. Thus, in (20a), the relationship between the V *saw* and the NP *the man with glasses* is a direct one since they are sisters, but the relationship between *glasses* and the V *saw* is an indirect one.

As we'll see in the next chapter, each phrase has a function to play in the sentence. These functions can be read off the tree. For instance, in (24ab), the NP is the subject and the VP is the predicate; in (16a), the verb *wrote* is the head of the VP and its sister, the NP *the letter*, is the object.

4.   Coordination of phrases and apposition

Phrases and categories can be coordinated, as long as they are the same kind. For instance, two NPs are coordinated in (24), two prepositions in (26), and two VPs in (27):

(25)   We see scorpions all the time in [the house] and [the garden].
(26)   The dog went [under] and [over] the fence.
(27)   I [read books] and [listened to music].

When the elements that are coordinated are not the same, e.g. an NP and a PP in (28), the sentence becomes ungrammatical:

(28)   *I read [a book] and [to Janet].

Coordination can be used to recognize phrases and categories. If you know one phrase or category, then the other phrase or category will be the same.

The structure for coordinate constructions is controversial. A number of linguists argue that the relationship between the coordinated phrases in, for instance, (29) is completely equal and hence that a structure as in (30a) is appropriate. Others claim that the first phrase is somewhat more important and use (30b). Note that I have not labelled the node above *and* in (30b) since its name is controversial:

(29)   Books and magazines sell easily.

(30)   a.

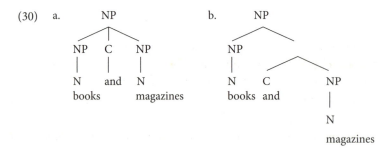

Arguments can be found for either structure. For ease of representation, I'll use (30a), but feel free to use (30b). We can usually switch around the NPs in (29) and this seems to be an argument in favor of (30a) since both NPs have the same status. However, when we move part of the *books and magazines*, for instance, because the second NP is a very long one, as in (31), *and* remains with the second NP and this speaks in favor of (30b) since *and magazines discussing political issues* is a unit (indicated by brackets in (31)), but *books and* is not:

(31)   I read books yesterday [and magazines discussing political issues].

In Chapter 7, we'll look at coordinating sentences. The basic question about which structure to pick is relevant there too. Two-part coordinators were mentioned in the previous chapter, e.g. *both Mary and John*; I will not provide a structure for these.

Apposition differs from coordination. It occurs when two NPs are used side by side but with the same reference, as in (32) to (34). In (32), the added information is not crucial for the meaning of the sentence since many of us know who Napoleon was, and I could have chosen another way to describe him. If we saw or heard (33) and (34), however, without a context, we wouldn't know who was meant by 'we' or 'my friend':

(32)   **Napoleon Bonaparte, the past Emperor of France**, went to war against most of Europe.

(33)   **We the people of the United States**, …, do ordain and establish this Constitution for the United States of America. (from the *Preamble to the US Constitution*)

(34)   **My friend Bill** sent a letter.

In appositives, the second NP can replace the first, or could be rephrased by a relative clause, as in (35). The structure could be as in (36), close to that of a relative clause:

(35)   We, who are the people of the United States, ….

(36)

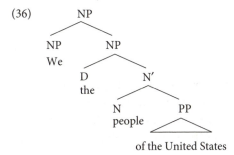

5.   Finding phrases and building trees

5.1   Finding the phrase

A phrase is a group of words forming a unit and united around a head, e.g. a noun or a verb. Since phrases are syntactic units, a number of rules apply to them. Some of these have been discussed above, namely pronominalization and coordination. Three additional ones can be used, namely deletion, replacement by a *wh*-element, and movement. These five rules are listed in Table 3.1. If I have a hunch that, for instance, *to the store* in (37) is a phrase, how do I prove that? Let's apply the rules and see:

(37)   She ran to the store.

I can pronominalize *to the store* as *there*, coordinate it, delete it, replace it, and move it, as shown in the Table.

Table 3.1. Finding a phrase

	Rules	Examples
a.	A phrase can be pronominalized:	*She ran [there].*
b.	It can be coordinated with a phrase of the same kind:	*She ran [to the bookstore] and [to the library];*
c.	It can be deleted:	*She ran [...].*
d.	It can be replaced by a *wh*-element:	*[Where] did she run?*
e.	It can be moved:	*[To the store] she ran.*

The five criteria in Table 3.1 confirm that *to the store* in (37) is a phrase. We know that it is a PP because a Preposition, namely *to*, is the head.

All phrases can be pronominalized and coordinated. However, not all phrases can be deleted. The initial NP is very important, and in English, sentences are ungrammatical without it. Thus, changing (37) into (38) produces an ungrammatical sentence:

(38)   *Ran to the store.

In Chapters 4 and 5, we will discuss what kinds of phrases can be deleted and what kinds cannot.

5.2   Building trees

We can build trees from top to bottom or from bottom to top. Experiment with this a little to see what you personally like best. Let's do the phrase *the boy with the red hat* using both ways. Either way, we first need to decide what the head is. We'll argue the head is *boy* (e.g. because we pronominalize the phrase with *he* not *it*). This means the phrase is an NP.

Starting from the top, let's put down the NP first. If there is a determiner, the first branch to the left will always be a D, so D is the daughter of NP:

(39)

Now, we have to be careful **not** to make the next branch go to N because then there won't be space for both the N *boy* and the PP *with the red hat*. Instead, we'll put down an N′ which can be expanded. Remember that N′ is a placeholder for more than one branch:

(40)
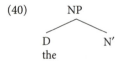

Now, the branches coming down from N′ need to be put in, as in (41):

(41)
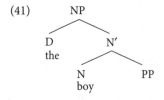

After this, finishing the tree is easy. We'll draw branches from PP to P and NP, and then have to start all over again with the NP. After the NP is finished, we make sure that we have put all the words under the categories. The result will be as in (42):

(42)

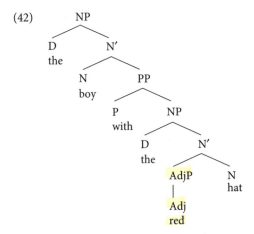

Sometimes you will see the tree in (42) drawn as in (43). This makes it easier to see the actual sentence. You have to wait until the end to put the words in. Either tree is fine, though I usually use (42):

(43)

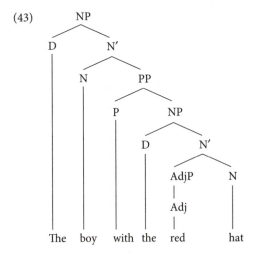

When a phrase is not a branching phrase, e.g. the AdjP *red* in (42) and (43), we still indicate that it can have a head (and other elements) by having it go to the Adj. To save space, I sometimes leave out the branches, as in (44):

(44)   AdjP
        Adj
        red

It is also possible to draw a tree starting from the bottom. In this case, it is handiest to put the category of each word on top of it, as in (45a). Then, we need to find what goes with what. In this case, *red* and *hat* combine, so we'll draw branches to connect them, as in (45b):

(45) a.   D   N   P   D   Adj   N
            the   boy   with   the   red   hat

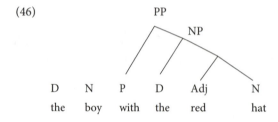

  b.

            D   N   P   D   Adj   N
            the   boy   with   the   red   hat

Then, D has to be combined with it and then P, with the result of (46):

(46)

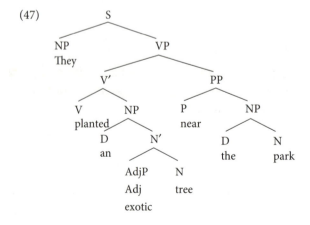

            D   N   P   D   Adj   N
            the   boy   with   the   red   hat

Now, the PP has to be connected to *boy* since it modifies it, and then D has to be connected. The result will be the same as that in (42) and (43). We'll need to make sure all nodes have labels, e.g. we need to put in the N′. The disadvantage of this tree is that the branches are not of equal length and that this becomes confusing in seeing what goes together.

A few more trees to look at are given in (47) and (48). In (47), the PP *near the park* shows where the tree was planted because it is the sister to the V′ *planted an exotic tree*. In (48), the PP *without leaves* is sister to the N *trees*, so it is the *tree* that is without leaves.

(47)

(48)

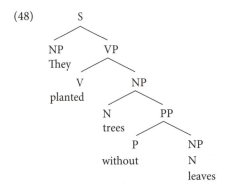

Notice that I am indicating that *leaves* is the head of the NP but that it could be modified by an adjective; the pronoun *they* cannot.

Finally, one can use a computer to draw trees either by purchasing a tree-drawing font or by just using the line-drawing feature that's part of most word processing programs. In the latter case, use tabs to space out the nodes and then draw the branches after the nodes are in. Experiment a little with this.

6. Conclusion

In this chapter, phrases and their tree structure are introduced. A lexical category such as a noun typically has other elements around it that go with it (i.e. modify it). This group of words and the head form a phrase. All lexical categories (N, V, Adj, Adv, and P) head phrases and each of these phrases is discussed.

Phrases are combined into sentences (or S), as in (24) above. A sentence includes an NP and a VP. In the next chapter, we discuss the functions of the NP and VP in the sentence. A structure for phrases that are coordinated and appositives is also given in (30).

The key terms in this chapter are **phrases (NP, VP, AdjP, AdvP and PP); S; flat as opposed to non-flat/hierarchical structures; ambiguity; pronominalization; coordination and apposition.** The most important thing is to learn to draw trees.

Exercises

A.   Draw the tree structures for (49) and (50):

    (49)   They saw the lights.
    (50)   The rabbit planted carrots.

B.   What do trees express?

C.   First identify the phrases in (51) to (53) by putting brackets around them. Then try to draw trees for (51) and (53) but not for (52) (we get to that sentence in the next chapter):

    (51)   Dumbledore submits his tax-return on time every year.
    (52)   Kim's painting made Voldemort extremely unhappy.
    (53)   Hagrid remained a lover of dragons during his life.

D.   Draw brackets around all the NPs in the first paragraph of the text below. Note that names, pronouns, and nouns on their own also need to be marked as noun phrases.

    Man rescued after 4 months at sea
    A U.S. Navy frigate rescued a man off the coast of Costa Rica last week. The man says his crippled sailboat was adrift at sea for almost four months. The 24-foot sailboat appeared battered and broken, and the navy spokesperson said his crew was stunned when Van Pham appeared and waved at the frigate.
      Van Pham told crew members of the Navy frigate that he had set out for a brief trip between Long Beach and Catalina Island when high winds broke his mast. His radio, he said, failed to work and he found himself adrift. Van Pham survived because he ate the fish that he caught in the water around him, as well as a few seagulls. He drank rainwater collected in a bucket and he appeared to be in generally good health.

E.   Draw brackets around all the PPs in the second paragraph of the text in D.

F.   Sentence (54) has a fairly complex initial NP. Try to draw the tree first for this NP and then fit it into an S:

    (54)   The man with the monstrously ugly umbrella left the house.

G.   Sentence (55) is ambiguous. Explain which of the two trees expresses that the Martian has the telescope?

    (55)   She spotted the Martian with a telescope.

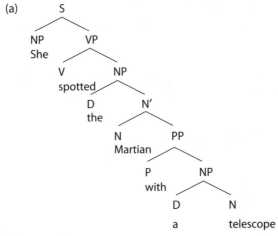

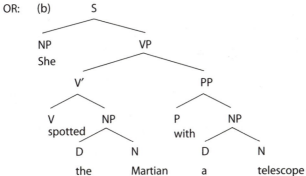

H.   Draw a tree for (56). Is (56) ambiguous? If so, explain how:

(56)   They like a house with a porch with rocking chairs.

I.   Put brackets around all the phrases in (57) and (58). How would you draw these sentences as trees?

(57)   Tom and Jerry make very good ice cream.
(58)   They washed dishes and cleaned the sink.

J.   Give some reasons justifying your choice of some of the phrases in (51).

Class discussion

K.   In Chapter 1, Section 1.2, two instances of structural ambiguity are given. The headlines in (59) to (61) are likewise structurally ambiguous. Can you explain their ambiguity using brackets indicating the structure?

(59)   Complaints about NBA referees growing ugly.

(60)   Enraged cow injures farmer with ax.

(61)   Two sisters reunited after 18 years at check-out counter.

L.   Discuss the structure of *one of these, a piece of chalk*, and *all those arguments*.

M.   Draw brackets around the phrases for the intended meaning of 'throw it away in a waste basket' and around those for the meaning PJ heard in Figure 3.1.

Figure 3.1. From inside or into? (FAMILY CIRCUS © 2008 BIL KEANE, INC. KING FEATURES SYNDICATE)

Keys to the exercises

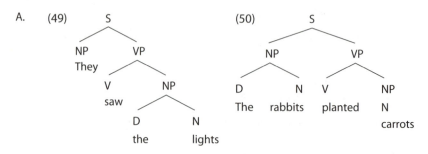

A.   (49)

B.   Trees indicate what goes with what, e.g. which phrases modify which head.

C.   In (51), [Dumbledore] is an NP and [submits his tax-return on time every year] is a VP; [his tax-return] is an NP; [on time] is a PP and [every year] is an NP. All put together, it looks as follows: [[Dumbledore] [submits [his tax-return] [on time] [every year]]]. In

(52), [Kim's painting] is an NP and [made Voldemort extremely unhappy] is a VP; [Kim]
is another NP; [Voldemort] an NP; and [extremely unhappy] an AdjP. With brackets, it
looks like: [[Kim's painting] [made [Voldemort] [extremely unhappy]]]. In the next
chapter, we will see a structure with an added bracket. In (53), [Hagrid] is an NP;
[remained a lover of dragons during his life] is a VP; [a lover of dragons] an NP; [of
dragons] a PP; [dragons] an NP; and [during his life] a PP. With brackets: [[Hagrid]
[remained [a lover [of [dragons]]] [during his life]]]

(51)

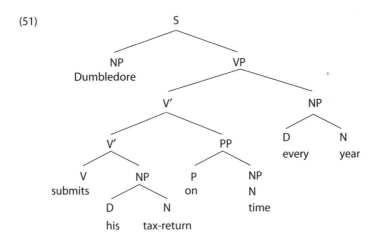

(53)

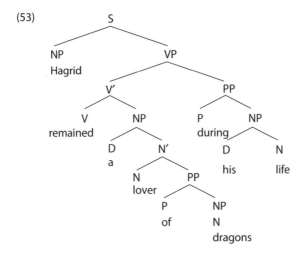

D.   The NPs: [Man] rescued after [4 months] at [sea]

[A U.S. Navy frigate] rescued [a man] off [the coast of [Costa Rica]] [last week]. [The man]
says [his crippled sailboat] was adrift at [sea] for almost [four months]. [The 24-foot
sailboat] appeared battered and broken, and [the navy spokesperson] said [his crew] was
stunned when [Van Pham] appeared and waved at [the frigate].

E.   The PPs: Van Pham told crew members [of the Navy frigate] that he had set out [for a brief trip [between Long Beach and Catalina Island]] when high winds broke his mast. His radio, he said, failed to work and he found himself adrift. Van Pham survived because he ate the fish that he caught [in the water [around him]], as well as a few seagulls. He drank rainwater collected [in a bucket] and he appeared to be [in generally good health].

F.   (54)

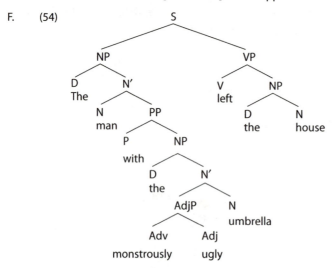

G.   In (a), the Martian has a telescope; in (b), the 'she' uses the telescope to spot the Martian. We can figure this out from looking at who the PP is sister to in the tree.

H.   If the structure for (56) is the one drawn in (a), they like a house with both a porch and with rocking chairs and the rocking chairs can be anywhere in the house. If it is drawn as in (b), they like a house with a porch that has rocking chairs and the rocking chairs have to be on the porch:

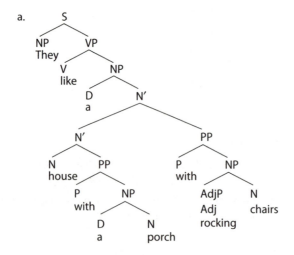

b.

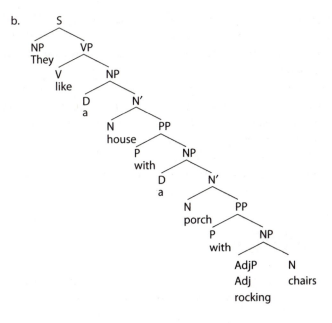

l.   Sentences (57) and (58) can be drawn with brackets as follows:

(57)   [[Tom] and [Jerry]] [make [[very good] ice cream]].
(58)   [They] [[washed [dishes]] and [cleaned [the sink]]].

As trees, they can be drawn as follows:

(57)

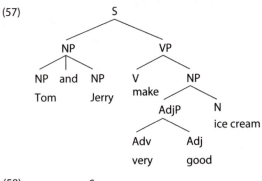

(58)

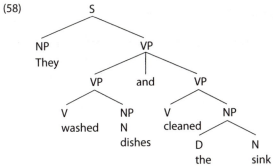

J.   In (51), *Dumbledore* is an NP because it can be pronominalized, i.e. replaced by *he*; it can be coordinated with another NP as in *Dumbledore and his accountant submit the forms on time*. It cannot be deleted or moved because it is the subject as we will see in Chapter 4. It can be questioned as in *Who submits the forms on time?*

Submits his tax-return on time every year is a VP since it can be pronominalized, i.e. replaced by *do so* as in *Dumbledore submits his tax-return on time every year and Hagrid does so too.* It can also be coordinated with another VP as in *Dumbledore submits his tax-return on time every year but neglects to renew his accident insurance.*

His tax-return is an NP since it can be replaced by *it*, can be coordinated as in *Dumledore submits his tax-return and insurance claims on time every year*, and moved as in *It is his tax-return that Dumbledore submits on time every year*. And so on…

Special topic: Negative concord

Unlike most of the special topics, Negative Concord does not supplement the material covered in the above chapter, but is an often debated issue. The prescriptive rule on multiple negation is as follows:

(62)   Two negatives in one sentence make the sentence positive.

Swan (1980: 182) says "[i]n standard English, *nobody, nothing, never* etc are themselves enough to make the sentence negative, and *not* is unnecessary".

We use certain types of multiple negatives in our utterances all the time, e.g. in (63) and (64b). In (63), the sentence expresses negation since the *no* is outside the clause and independent of the *I don't want to go*. In this sentence, the negatives do not cancel each other out, since the negatives are independent of each other, and the sentence is prescriptively correct. In (64b), an answer to (64a), *nothing* is negated and the sentence could be paraphrased as (65). In this sentence, the negatives cancel each other out:

(63)   **No**, I **don't** want to go.

(64)   a: I paid **nothing** for that.
        b: Five dollars is **not nothing.**

(65)   Five dollars is quite something.

Since (63) and (64) follow the rule, they are not objected to by prescriptive grammarians.

A sentence such as (66), however, is said to be incorrect if it means the same as (67) or (68):

(66)   They don't have no problems.
(67)   They don't have problems.
(68)   They don't have any problems.

Although two negatives are supposed to make a positive, most speakers understand (66) as a negative. This construction is referred to as Negative Concord, i.e. the two negatives work together to emphasize the negation rather than cancel each other out. Sentences such as (66) occur very frequently in spoken, informal English. However, the prescriptive rule is so well known that people often deliberately break it for impact. That may have been the reason a double negative is used in (69), a protest sign at the time that a student code of conduct was being considered at the University of Michigan in Ann Arbor:

(69)   WE DON'T
        NEED **NO**
        STINKIN
        CODE

Figure 3.2. Multiple Negation

Changes involving negatives follow a certain path, sometimes called the negative cycle. Thus, in Old English, there is a negative *no* or *ne*, as in (70). At some point, the negative weakens and contracts with the verb. That's the reason another negative is added in (71):

(70)   *Men ne cunnon secgan to soðe ... hwa*
        Man not could tell to truth ... who
        'No man can tell for certain ... who'. (*Beowulf* 50–52)

(71)   ***Næron ʒe noht** æmettiʒe, ðeah ge wel **ne** dyden*
        not-were you not unoccupied. though you well not did
        'You were not unoccupied, though you did not do well'. (*Pastoral Care,* 206).

At some point the *noht/not* itself weakens and we'd expect another negative. The prescriptive pressure of (62) stops this from happening, certainly in writing. There is the use of *never*, as in (72), however, as you can find when you google the sequence:

(72)   I **never** see him much these days. (meaning 'I don't see him often these days')

Review of Chapters 1–3

The first chapter shows that we know quite a bit about language intuitively without formal training and the second and third chapters make some of this knowledge more explicit. Chapter 1 examines two types of ambiguity, lexical and structural ambiguity, and the latter in particular has been helpful in showing the necessity for different tree structures in Chapter 3. Chapter 1 also explains prescriptive rules, examples of which are given in the special topics at the end of each chapter.

Chapter 2 lists the lexical (N, V, A, and P) and grammatical (D, AUX, C) categories we make use of in English. Tables provide the characteristics and examples of many of these. Several rules are also formulated to distinguish adjectives and adverbs in (12), determiners and adjectives in (37), and prepositions, complementizers and adverbs in (45). Pronouns are complicated because so many kinds exist. Personal pronouns function like entire phrases but have very little meaning. Other pronouns, e.g. possessives, are determiners.

Chapter 3 shows how sentences can be divided into phrases, each of which is centered around a noun, verb, adjective, adverb, or preposition. The NP and VP are the most complex since they can include an N′ or V′. These are intermediate categories, not quite full phrases (they lack something) but bigger than heads. Chapter 3 also suggests the S to represent the entire sentence and gives trees for coordinated phrases.

Exercises relevant to these chapters:

A.   List the lexical and grammatical categories in (1) and (2). Draw a tree for (1):

    (1)   The tortoise from Jupiter ate his food.

    (2)   Do not go gentle into that good night,
           Old age should burn and rave at close of day; …

B.   List the categories in (3), both lexical and grammatical. Give two reasons why *painted* is a verb:

    (3)   Zoya painted the chairs in the rain.

C.   Provide the tree for (3). The intended meaning for (3) is unambiguous: Zoya painted actual chairs while it was raining and she was out in it'.

D.   Draw trees for the phrases in (4) and (5) and for the sentences in (6) and (7):

    (4)   That sensitive poet from Shiraz
    (5)   noticed a hopeless sadness
    (6)   Vincent and his brother wrote many letters.
    (7)   We suggested those solutions quickly.

E.   Draw a tree for (8):

    (8)   The trees in the park are unhappy.

F.   How is the following sentence ambiguous?

    (9)   Outside of a dog, a book is a man's best friend. Inside a dog, it is too dark to read.

G.   Is there anything prescriptively incorrect in (10) and (11)? If so, say what?

    (10)   That`seemed logical enough.

    (11)   *ne durste þer **na man** speken; leste þe king hit wolde awreken*
            not dared there no man speak lest the king it wanted to-avenge
            'No one there dared to speak in case the king wanted to punish them.'
            (Layamon, *Brut* 12425)

Class discussion

H.   Please comment on 'You look real nice'. When would you say this; when might you say something else.

I.   Explain the difference between linguistic and non-linguistic knowledge.

J.   Briefly discuss the poem 'We Real Cool' by Gwendolyn Brooks in the light of either chapter 1 or 2 or both:

> We real cool. We
> Left school. We
>
> Lurk Late. We
> Strike straight. We
>
> Sing sin. We
> Thin gin. We
>
> Jazz June. We
> Die soon.

Keys to the exercises

A.   (1)   The (D) tortoise (N) from (P) Jupiter (N) ate (V) his (N) food (N)

(2)   Do (AUX) not (Adv) go (V) gentle (Adj) into (P) that (D) good (Adj) night (N), Old (Adj) age (N) should (AUX) burn (V) and (C) rave (V) at (P) close (N) of (P) day (N)

(1)

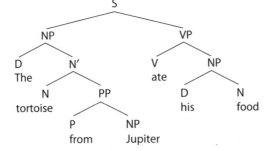

B.   Zoya: N   **C.**   (3)
painted: V
the: D
chairs: N
in: P
the: D
rain: N

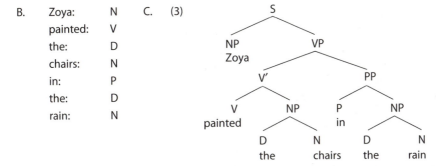

Painted is a verb because it shows past tense (morphological) and indicates an action (semantic). Sentence (3) is not ambiguous since *in the rain* is independent of *chairs*; it says something about where you painted them.

D.

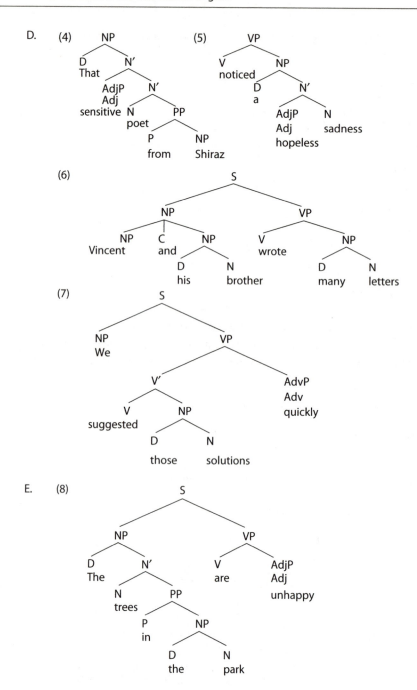

F. See the end of Section 2 (Chapter 3).

G. Sentence (10) is correct because *logical* is used as an adjective here. The multiple negation in (11) would not be correct in Modern English, but was in the 13th century.

Example of an exam/quiz covering Chapters 1 to 3

A.   Why is (a) prescriptively ungrammatical? What would you say in a formal situation instead of (a)?

  (a)   I would like to first make the point that bureaucrats don't think that way.

B.   Please list the category (N, V, etc) of each word in (b):

  (b)   The coyote evolved in North America alongside the wolf and expanded its range since they readily reproduce in metropolitan areas.

C.   Give two reasons why *evolved* in (b) is a verb.

D.   Draw tree structures (as in Chapter 3) for the phrases in (c) and (d):

  (c)   That careful driver in his Volvo

  (d)   heard a strange sound.

E.   Please draw tree structures (again as in Chapter 3) for the sentences in (e) and (f):

  (e)   Zoltan and Zoya read three books in a week.

  (f)   We rarely suggest useful solutions.

Keys to the exam/quiz

A.   Split infinitive (and contraction). Alternative: '… first like to make …(do not) …'

B.   The (D) coyote (N) evolved (V) in (P) North (Adj) America (N) alongside (P) the (D) wolf (N) and (C) expanded (V) its (D) range (N) since (C) they (Pron) readily (Adv) reproduce (V) in (P) metropolitan (Adj) areas (N).

C.   *Evolved* has an *-ed* ending and could be preceded by an auxiliary, e.g. *has*.

D.

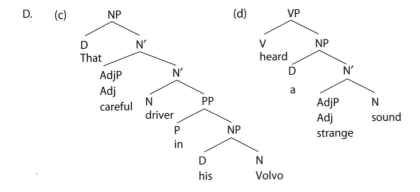

E.   (e)

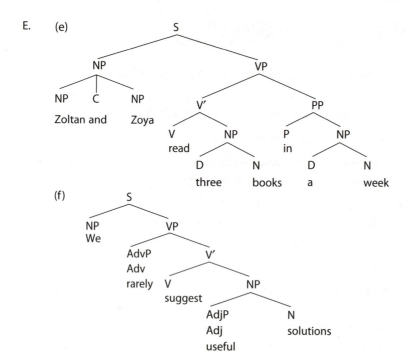

(f)

Chapter 4

Functions in the sentence

In Chapter 3, groups of words that go together were called phrases and labelled as NP, VP, AdjP, AdvP, and PP depending on what headed them. Phrases (and pronouns since they replace phrases) have functions in the sentence, e.g. subject, direct object, indirect object, and subject and object predicate. The name, label, or realization (e.g. NP) and the function itself (e.g. subject) should be kept separate.

As mentioned, we will not be putting functions in the tree structures since (most of) the functions follow from the tree structure. Certain functions such as subject and direct object occupy specific positions in the tree (daughter of S and sister of V respectively), and to label them would be redundant.

The four basic functions are subject, predicate, complement, and adverbial (see next chapter for adverbials). As explained in Section 1, a subject and predicate are needed in every sentence. Most verbs need complements as well, as Section 2 discusses. Complements come in different varieties; the ones dealt with in this chapter are direct object, indirect object, subject predicate, and object predicate. Some people equate object and complement, but technically complement is a broader category than object. In Section 3, verbs will be named depending on the type of complement they appear with. Section 4 provides trees for the different verbs, and Section 5 explores one additional verb type, the light verb.

1. Subject and predicate

Every complete sentence has a subject and a predicate. The subject is usually realized by an NP (sometimes by a clause, see Chapter 7), and the predicate is always realized by a VP. In (1), *the moon* is the subject and *has risen in the sky* is the predicate. The predicate says something about the subject:

(1)   [The moon] [has risen in the sky].

Other examples of subjects and predicates are given in (2). Note that subjects can be more than one or two words, as *their long-term survival in Florida* shows!

(2)   [Manatees] [are large, marine mammals]. [They] [can live up to 60 years and can weigh up to 1200 pounds]. [Their long-term survival in Florida] [is uncertain, however].

Typically, subjects start off a sentence, as in (1) and (2), but there are a number of constructions where they don't. For instance, in (3), the Adverb Phrase *fortunately for us* precedes the subject; in questions such as (4), the auxiliary verb does; and in (5), the sentence is a complex one and there are multiple subjects. (We'll go into complex sentences in more detail in Chapters 7, 8, and 10).

(3)   Fortunately for us, [she] managed to join the government.
(4)   Do [those people] like anything?
(5)   [He] made no answer, and [they] were again silent till [they] had gone down the dance, when [he] asked her if [she and her sisters] did not very often walk to Meryton. (Jane Austen, *Pride & Prejudice*, Chapter 18)

Since the subject is not always the initial word or phrase of the sentence, we need other ways to determine the subject. Table 4.1 lists three diagnostics for determining what the subject is.

Table 4.1. Subject tests (subject is in italics; verb is in bold)

a.   Inversion with the AUX in Yes/No questions
The pig from Malacandra **will** want to eat soon.
Will *the pig from Malacandra* want to eat soon?
b.   Agreement with the Verb/AUX
The pfiftrigg **is** nice.
The pfiftriggs **are** nice.
c.   Tag questions
The hross **is** nice, isn't *he*?

Let's apply these tests to (1). The first test of Table 4.1 shows that *the moon* is the subject since it can change places with *has*, as in the question (6):

(6)   Has [the moon] just risen in the sky?

The second test involves subject verb agreement. We discussed this rule in Chapter 3 because it is helpful in finding the head of an NP. The NP that determines agreement on the verb is the subject. In English, this marking is fairly limited. In (7) and (8), some instances of subject verb agreement are marked, which most of you know already. In English, the verb *be* shows the most inflection, as seen in (7), but most other verbs just show the singular third person, as in (8b), and leave the other subjects unmarked, as in (8a):

(7) a. **I am** happy.   (first person singular subject *I* with first person singular *am*)
     b. **You are** happy.   (second person subject *you* with second person *are*)
     c. **He/Matthew is** happy.   (third person singular subjectwith third person singular *is*).
     d. **We/they are** happy.   (plural subject with third person plural *are*).

(8) a. **I/you/we/they walk** regularly. (unmarked *walk*).
     b. **She/Emma walks** regularly.   (third person singular subject with third person singular verb)

Thus, to find the subject in (1), we could change its number (singular to plural or plural to singular) and see if that changes the form of the verb as well. In (1), the subject *the moon* is singular and, if we pluralize it to *the moons,* as in (9), the verb becomes plural as well (i.e. loses the third person singular ending):

(9) **The moons have** just risen in the sky.

This shows that the subject in (1) is indeed *the moon* (and in (9), it is *the moons* of course). Sentence (9) is a bit strange since there is only one moon surrounding earth. However, if we were on Jupiter, (9) would be appropriate. Hence, the strangeness is not caused by the grammar, but by our knowledge of the world.

The third test for determining the subject involves adding a tag question and seeing what the pronoun in the tag replaces. In (10), the *it* in the tag refers to *the moon* and not to *the sky* and that's why the former is the subject:

(10) The moon has just risen in the sky, hasn't **it**?

Having discussed three criteria for identifying subjects, I turn to a kind of subject that, at first, does not look like a subject, namely, *there* in (11):

(11) **There** are five unicorns in the parking lot.

If we apply the three tests of Table 4.1 to sentence (11), *there* and *five unicorns* each pass some, but not all, of the tests for subject. For instance, in a question *there* and *are* switch places; the tag will be formed with *there,* as in *aren't there*; but the agreement on the verb is determined by *five unicorns.* To account for this, we'll assume that both *there* and *five unicorns* function as the subject. *There* is called a dummy or pleonastic or expletive subject. It is used when no other subject occupies the position in the beginning of the sentence. A variant of (11) is (12), where *five unicorns* is in subject position and *there* is not needed:

(12)   **Five unicorns** are in the garden.

Turning to the predicate, we will just define it as everything in the sentence that is not the subject. In the tree, the predicate is always the VP that is under the right branch right below the S and the subject is the NP right below the branch off the S on the left side, as in (13).

(13)

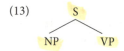

2.   Complements

A complement is what has to follow the verb. Complements come in different flavors, as direct and indirect objects and as subject and object predicates.

2.1   Direct and indirect object

A common function in the sentence is the direct object, usually realized as an NP, as in (14) (see Chapter 7 for the use of a clause as direct object):

(14)   a.   Harry Potter played [a game].
     b.   He read [the letter from Hogwarts].

Objects occur as sisters to the verb, as in (15), and can be turned into subjects in a passive construction, as in (16):

(15)

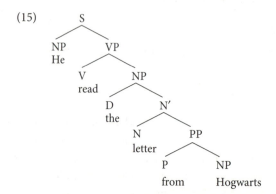

(16)   [The letter from Hogwarts] was read by him.

In (16), *the letter from Hogwarts* functions as the subject because, for instance, in a question it would switch with the auxiliary verb *was*. Make the subject in (16) plural and see what that shows!

Passive sentences are variants of non-passive or active ones and come about by switching the subject and the object and by adding a form of *to be* as in (17b), the passive variant of (17a). The subject of the active sentence (17a) becomes optional in the passive and, if expressed at all, is preceded by *by*:

(17) a. I saw him.   (active)

      b. He **was** seen (by me).   (passive)

Passives are useful when we don't know who the agent of the action is and they often occur when the object is more definite than the subject, as in (18), but this is a complex matter:

(18) **The decision** was made by **a small group of people**.
      (Talk of the Nation, 1998, COCA)

Passivization is a way to distinguish between objects (both direct and indirect) on the one hand and subject predicates, object predicates, and adverbials on the other, as we'll see in the next chapter.

The indirect object expresses the goal (*Santa* in (19a)) or the beneficiary of the action (*Harry* in (19b)):

(19) a. I gave Santa a letter.
      b. I made Harry some soup.

Indirect objects can be passivized as well, and in a sentence with both a direct and indirect object, it is the indirect object that becomes the subject. For instance, (20) is the passive counterpart of (19a), and the indirect object *Santa* becomes the subject, not the direct object *a letter*:

(20) [Santa] was given a letter by me.

Indirect objects can be preceded by the prepositions *to*, in the case of the goal, and *for*, in the case of a beneficiary, as in (21) and (22):

(21) I gave a letter **to Santa**.
(22) I made some soup **for Harry**.

When *to* and *for* are added the order of indirect and direct object switches, as you can see by comparing (18) with (21). Some grammarians call the PPs *to Santa* and *for Harry* indirect objects; others call them adverbials since they seem less important to the sentence (e.g. some can be left out) and they cannot become the subject of a passive sentence, as the unacceptable (23) shows:

(23) *Santa was given a letter to.

I will call the PPs in (21) and (22) indirect objects but am happy to listen to other views.

A list of verbs that take a direct object and those that take both a direct and indirect object is given in Table 4.2. In Section 3, we will label the former transitive verbs and the latter ditransitive. Many verbs have optional indirect objects. Table 4.2 is based on a limited search of the British Nation Corpus and the Corpus of Spoken American English; see Exercise N for more on this issue. You will have to decide each time you see them in a sentence if they have a direct or a direct and an indirect object.

Table 4.2. Verbs with direct and indirect objects

Verbs with only direct objects	with direct and mostly obligatory indirect objects	with direct and less obligatory indirect objects
see, eat, love, hit, hear, watch	give, teach, offer, tell, show, ask, lend provide, send, hand, promise, grant, award, begrudge, mail, throw	buy, bring, bake, read, pay, earn, build, cook, knit, prepare

Making this table, I was very surprised how few verbs only have a direct object. The reason is that we can imagine doing almost anything for the benefit of others, e.g. *running a mile for the ASPCA* and *reading someone a book*.

2.2 Subject and object predicate

The subject predicate is usually realized as an AdjP. It makes a claim about the subject, as in (24), and can also be an NP, as in (25), or a PP, as in (26) (see Chapter 7 for the use of a clause as subject predicate):

(24) He is [pleasant].
(25) He is [a nice person].
(26) He is [in the garden].

The verb used in sentences with a subject predicate is usually either *be* or *become* or can be replaced by it. Thus, in the first line of the poem by Dylan Thomas, discussed in exercise H from Chapter 2, the adjective *gentle* goes with the unexpressed subject and the verb *go* could be replaced by *become*. Other verbs that typically occur with a subject predicate are *feel, look, grow,* and *smell*, when used as in (27):

(27) a. This silk **feels** nice.
      b. That problem **looks** hard.
      c. The kitten **grew** tired.
      d. Those raspberries **smell** nice.

In (27abd), the verb can be replaced by a form of *be* and in (27c) by a form of *become*, with some loss of specific meaning. If you replaced the transitive verb in (13) and (14) with *be* or *become*, the results would be strange, to say the least.

As mentioned in the special topic to Chapter 2, many speakers overreact or panic when they produce an adjective right next to a verb, as in (27). The combination is correct, however, since the adjective modifies a noun (functioning as subject). It need not be changed to an adverb and in many cases it can't. A list of verbs that may have a subject predicate in English appears in Table 4.3.

Table 4.3. Examples of verbs with subject predicates

act, appear, be, become, get, go, grow, fall, feel, keep, look, remain, seem, smell, sound, stay, taste, turn

Most of the verbs in Table 4.3 can be used in other ways too and that's why it is important to think about the entire sentence and not just to look at the verb. For instance, each of the verbs in (27) can be used without a subject predicate, as (28) shows:

(28)   a.   He **felt** his pulse.
        b.   They **looked** around.
        c.   She **grew** strawberries in her garden.
        d.   I **smell** trouble.

In (24) and (27), the adjective functioning as a subject predicate says something about the subject, but an adjective can also say something about a direct object. The adjective then functions as an object predicate. There are relatively few verbs that take a direct object and an object predicate, so don't overuse the function in your analysis! It is safe to say that, if you see a verb such as *consider*, you need to think about the possibility of an object predicate, but not with verbs such as *see, read,* and *go*.

The object predicate is usually an adjective phrase, as in (29), but can also be an NP, as in (30), or a PP, as in (31):

(29)   The students found the exam [difficult].
(30)   Jane considers *Pride and Prejudice* [a classic].
(31)   She put the cup [on the table].

A few examples are given in Table 4.4.

Table 4.4. Verbs with direct objects and object predicates

consider	I considered Sabina very smart.
think	I thought Timber (to be) nice.
find	They found Einstein interesting.
know	I know Chandra to be nice.
put	She put snails on the table.
place	They placed a jar upon a hill.
call	They called the ship *The Lauderdale*.

Here too, it sometimes depends on your analysis whether you consider a phrase an object predicate or a direct object. For instance, *a good chairperson* in (32) can be an object predicate to the direct object *him*, in which case *to be* can occur between them, as in (33), and *him* is the same person as *a good chairperson*. Alternatively, *him* can be an indirect object and *a good chairperson* a direct object, in which case *for* can precede *him*, as in (34), and *him* and *a good chairperson* are not the same person. Hence, the verb *find* is ambiguous:

(32)   They found him [a good chairperson].   (ambiguous)
(33)   They found him to be [a good chairperson].   (Object Predicate)
(34)   They found for him [a good chairperson].   (Direct Object)

The terms for the two functions discussed in this section are much debated. Some grammarians call them subject and object complements; others subject and object predicatives; yet others call them subject and object attributives. I have chosen subject and object predicate to show that their function is similar to that of the VP predicate. It is as if the AdjP is more important than the verb in these constructions. That is the reason the verb in (24) to (26) can be left out in many languages and, in English, no verb appears to link object and object predicate, even though *to be* can be included in (33) and in (35):

(35)   Jane considers *Pride and Prejudice* to be [a classic].

Four suggestions on identifying the object predicate are as follows. (a) Only use this label if you have a (direct) object; (b) if you see the verb *consider*, it is a good candidate for having a direct object and object predicate; (c) if you leave out the object predicate, the sentence is incomplete or has a different meaning; and (d) don't overuse the function!

In short, some of the major functions of phrases in the sentence are subject, predicate, direct and indirect object, subject predicate and object predicate. There are special objects such as prepositional objects and objects of phrasal verbs. These will be dealt with in Chapter 5 together with the adverbial function.

3.   Verbs and functions

Verbs are distinguished depending on what objects or object predicates they select. Verbs that select objects are called transitive verbs and those that don't, as in (36) below, intransitive. If the verb selects one object, as in (13) and (14) above, it is (mono) transitive; if it selects two objects, as in (19), it is ditransitive. Verbs that select a subject predicate, as in (24) to (27), are called copula verbs or linking verbs and those that have both an object and an object predicate, as in (29) to (31), are called complex transitive. Two more types of verbs will be discussed in the next chapter: prepositional and phrasal verbs. Since adverbials can always be added to any verb, they do not play a role in the classification of the verb. I will now provide examples of each kind of verb.

Examples of **intransitives** are *swim, walk, arrive, cough, sleep,* and *sneeze.* They do not need a complement:

(36)   He sneezed and sneezed.

(37)   He slept during the meeting.

As mentioned before, you should look at the entire sentence before you can be completely sure of the classification of the particular verb. Thus, *walk* in *I walk the dog* is transitive, but in *I walked for hours* it is not. (In the next chapter, Section 5, I give some reasons why *during the meeting* in (37) is not an object but an adverbial).

Examples of **(mono-)transitives** are *eat, read, see, hear, plant, write, compose, paint, love, hate, drink, hit,* and *hug,* as in (38). They have a direct object complement:

(38)   He hugged the ball.

As also seen in Table 4.2, *give, tell, bake, cook,* and *play* are **ditransitives**. A typical ditransitive appears in (39). However, many transitive verbs have optional indirect objects as mentioned before. The example given in (40) contains a fairly optional indirect object *him*:

(39)   They told the public a lie.

(40)   I played (him) a tune.

If a verb selects a subject predicate, it is called a **copula or linking** verb. A number of copula verbs are given above in Table 4.3, namely *be, become, go, feel, look, grow, seem,* and *smell.* **Complex transitives** are verbs such as *consider, know, elect, keep, prove, deem, judge, reckon, make,* and *regard.* They have direct objects and object predicates as their complements. They are similar to regular transitives except that their object needs some modification. Please notice (again) that many verbs belong to more than one category. For instance, *make* can be a transitive, as in *I made a sweater,* or a complex transitive, as in *She made them happy,* or a ditransitive, as in *She made them a cake.*

Distinctions such as transitive and intransitive are useful to explain when to use verb forms such as *lay/lie, set/sit,* and *fell/fall.* The first verb in these three sets is the transitive one and the second is the intransitive. The verbs are irregular in that the normal rules for past tense (add *-ed*) and participle (add *-ed* or *-(e)n*) do not apply. Sentences (41a) and (42a) are in the present tense, (41b) and (42b) in the past tense, and (41c) and (42c) in the present perfect. (We'll discuss these terms in Chapter 6):

(41) a. This chicken **lays** an egg every day.   (transitive irregular)
      b. He **laid** that book on the table yesterday.
      c. I have **laid** the table like this for years.

(42) a. I **lie** down regularly.   (intransitive irregular)
      b. I **lay** down yesterday.
      c. I have **lain** here for hours.

One problem with these verbs lies in the past tense of the intransitive being the same as the present of the transitive. Both of these are irregular verbs since they are not predictable. In addition, there is an intransitive *lie*, meaning 'not telling the truth', that is regular in form, as (43) shows:

(43) a. They always **lie** under oath.   (intransitive regular)
      b. They always **lied** under oath.
      c. They have always **lied**.

This makes them really difficult to use!

To finish this section, I'll just again list some intransitive, transitive, and ditransitive verbs, as well as copulas and complex transitives with their complements. Seeing all together might give a better picture.

Table 4.5. Examples of the verb classes so far with their complements

Intransitive	no complement
walk, go, arrive, sneeze, go, lie (as in both *lie to congress* and *lie down*), *sit, die,* and *swim*	
Transitive	one (direct) object
see, eat, love, hit, hug, drink, break (as in *break the vase*), and *paint*.	
Ditransitive	one direct and one indirect object
give, teach, offer, tell, show, ask, lend, buy, bring, bake, read, provide, send, hand, promise, grant, cook, prepare, award, begrudge, mail, and *throw*	
Copula	one subject predicate
be, become, seem, appear, look, remain, keep, stay, fall, turn	
Complex Transitive	one (direct) object and an object predicate
consider, find, know, name (as in *name the ship the Albatros*)	

4. Trees for all verb types

As I have mentioned before, the tree structure reflects what the function of each phrase is. Thus, the subject and the predicate are the daughters of S, and the objects and subject predicate are sisters to V. The object predicate is a bit more complex but can be argued to be a sister of V too. The adverbial elements, as we'll see in the next chapter, are not sisters to V, but the prepositional objects and objects to phrasal verbs are.

Intransitives may occupy the entire VP, as in (44):

(44)

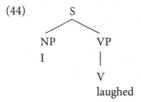

A structure for the (mono)transitive verb of (38) above is (45), and for the copula verb of (27a) above, it is (46):

(45)

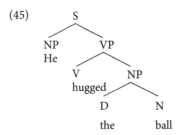

(46)

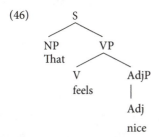

In general, we try to make trees show hierarchies, i.e. we seek to avoid triple branches in (47). However, to show that both the direct and indirect object in (47) are objects, I have drawn them as sisters to the V:

(47)

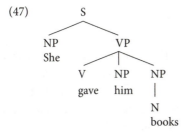

There are ways of expressing this in a non-flat/hierarchical structure but they are complicated and still controversial. Hence, this book will use (47), noting the problem of the flatness of the VP.

The other complement where flatness is a problem is the one to the complex transitive verb, as in (29) to (31) above. Since the object and predicate in some way form a unit (unlike the direct and indirect object), I'll represent it as in (48a), labeling the node above NP and AdjP a small clause (SC), i.e. a clause with the verb deleted. If the verb is present, the structure will look like (48b). More on (48b) in Chapter 8, however:

(48)   a.   b.

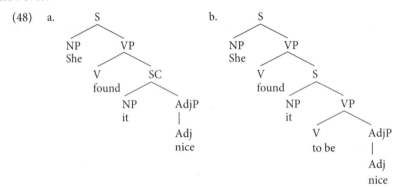

If the small clause in (48a) really has a *be* verb left out, we can think of the object predicate as a sister to V as well.

5.   Light verbs (optional)

This is an introductory grammar text, and hence not all kinds of verbs can be dealt with. To give an example of such a group, we'll look at light verbs, an interesting set of verbs in English that combines with mainly indefinite nouns (and sometimes prepositions also). Examples of light verbs with nouns are given in (49):

(49)   have a look, take a look, take a rest, take a tumble, take the initiative, take heart, take measures, give advice (on), make a decision (on), do a translation (of), do harm, give a hand, make trouble (for).

The verb and noun together have the meaning of a verb, e.g. *have/take a look* is similar to the verb *look*, *give advice* to the verb *advise*, and *make a decision* to the verb *decide*. With some, e.g. *do a translation*, the noun is still a real object and can be passivized, as in *A translation of Homer was done by that famous writer* although the indefinite subject sounds unusual; with some, e.g. *take a look*, the passive sounds ungrammatical, as in *A look was taken by me*. We won't draw trees for these or analyze them further.

6.   Conclusion

In this chapter, we have discussed six major functions for which phrases are used: subject, predicate, direct and indirect object, subject predicate, and object predicate. Particular functions are realized by particular phrases, e.g. the subject is often an NP. In Figure 4.1, a schematic representation for the functions of the phrases NP, VP and AdjP is given. Apart from VP, which is always a predicate (and the other way round), there is no one-to-one relationship between a phrase and a function. In Chapter 5, PPs and AdvPs will be discussed.

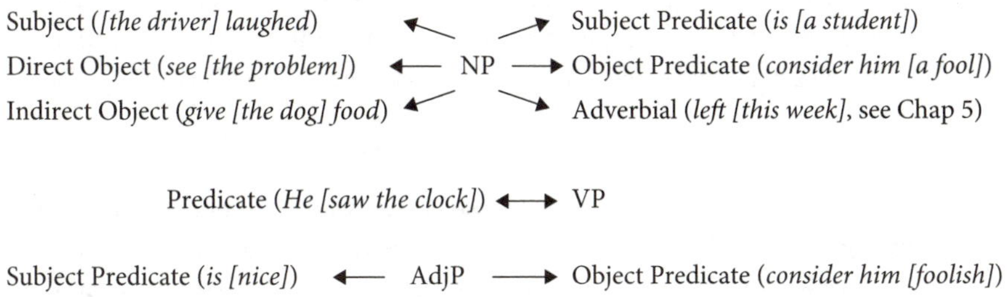

Subject (*[the driver] laughed*)   Subject Predicate (*is [a student]*)

Direct Object (*see [the problem]*)   ←—   NP   —→   Object Predicate (*consider him [a fool]*)

Indirect Object (*give [the dog] food*)   Adverbial (*left [this week]*, see Chap 5)

Predicate (*He [saw the clock]*) ←—→ VP

Subject Predicate (*is [nice]*)   ←—   AdjP   —→   Object Predicate (*consider him [foolish]*)

Figure 4.1.   A schema of the functions of NPs, VPs, and AdjPs

The classification of verbs is dependent on the kinds of objects and predicates they have. The obligatory elements following the verb are called complements. We have seen five classes of verbs. Intransitives have no objects, (mono)transitives have one, and ditransitives have two objects, a direct and an indirect. Copula verbs have a subject predicate and complex transitive verbs have an object and an object predicate. See what you find easier to recognize: the verb (as transitive or ditransitive) or the functions. Tree structures are also provided for each of these verbs with the complements as sisters to the V.

Key terms are the **six functions (subject, predicate, direct and indirect object, subject predicate and object predicate); and the classification of five verb types (intransitive, (mono)transitive, ditransitive, copula, and complex transitive). Be careful to keep function and phrase separate!**

Exercises

A.   Provide an example of each of the six functions we have discussed so far.

B.   Examples of subjects are given in brackets in (50), which is adapted from a wikipedia entry on javelinas. Do you agree with this selection of subjects?

(50)   [Peccaries] are medium-sized animals, with a strong superficial resemblance to pigs. Like pigs, [they] have a snout ending in a cartilagenous disc, and eyes [that] are small relative to their head. Also like pigs, [they] use only the middle two digits for walking, although, unlike pigs, [the other toes] can be altogether absent. [Their stomach] is non-ruminating, although [it] has three chambers, and is more complex than [that of pigs] is. (http://en.wikipedia.org/wiki/Peccary)

C.   Identify the subjects in the text used in Chapter 2, repeated here:

At last, we had begun filming. Should I say 'we'? I was living in the house and extremely curious about everything connected with the film. Fortunately, they let me hang around and even gave me a job. As an historian, I kept an eye on detail and did not allow the filmmakers to stray too far from the period of Louis Philippe. The project was to make an hour-long film about Houdin and it was decided to shoot the picture in Switzerland. This may have been a bad idea. It certainly mixed professional and domestic affairs.

D.   Identify the functions of the phrases in brackets in the sentences below:

(51)   [I] gave [him] [the ticket].
(52)   [They] [planted a dogwood].
(53)   [The trees in the park] are [unhappy].

E.   Identify the different kinds of complements (e.g. direct object, subject predicate) in (54) to (60):

(54)   They sold us their furniture.
(55)   Tom submits his tax-returns.
(56)   She seemed very happy.
(57)   He found it easy.
(58)   He took the early train.
(59)   The politician considered that argument invalid.
(60)   That sounds terrible.

F.   Provide the labels of the verbs in (54) to (60) (e.g. copula, ditransitive).

G.   Draw trees for sentences (54) to (60).

H. List all the functions and names/labels of the phrases in (61) to (64). To what categories do the following words belong: *helpful, from,* and *hard-working*?

(61) I considered the book very helpful.
(62) He baked Joan a cake.
(63) The pig from Mars left.
(64) The hard-working students seemed exhausted.

I. Read the first part of Mavis Gallant's short story "About Geneva":

Granny was waiting at the door of the apartment. She looked small, lonely, and patient, and at the sight of her the children and their mother felt instantly guilty. Instead of driving straight home from the airport, they had stopped outside Nice for ice cream. They might have known how much those extra twenty minutes would mean to Granny. Colin, too young to know what he felt, or why, began instinctively to misbehave, dragging his feet, scratching the waxed parquet. Ursula bit her nails, taking refuge in a dream, while the children's mother, Granny's only daughter, felt compelled to cry in a high, cheery voice, "Well, Granny, here they are, safe and sound!"

What kinds of verbs are *wait, look, feel,* and *drive* in this text? What is the function of *those extra twenty minutes, the waxed parquet,* and *small, lonely,* and *patient*?

J. Identify the subjects in (65) to (68). Provide two reasons why in each case:

(65) In the rain, it is sometimes hard to see.
(66) Only one of these people is happy.
(67) The book Chomsky wrote when he was young was reissued last year.
(68) Were the Wizard of Oz and Catweazle preparing to go to Alabama?

K. We reviewed the rule for *lay, lie,* etc in Section 3. State it in simple terms and then discuss what is happening in the cartoon?

Luann

Figure 4.2. *Lie ahead.* (Used with the permission of GEC, Inc. and United Media in conjunction with the Cartoonist Group. All rights reserved)

L.   Sentence is (69) is quite complex. What kinds of verbs are *grow* and *look*? What are their complements?

(69)   We must expect to see her grown thin, and looking very poorly. (Jane Austen, *Emma*, Vol 2, Chap 1).

M.   **Difficult.** The excerpt below is from Roethke's *Villanelle* 'I wake to sleep and take my waking slow', of which only the first six lines are given. Discuss the types of verbs that are used (intransitive, transitive, etc). If you are interested in literature, you may also look at the function of the adjectives and adverbs.

The Waking
I wake to sleep and take my waking slow.
I feel my fate in what I cannot fear.
I learn by going where I have to go.
We think by feeling. What is there to know?
I hear my being dance from ear to ear.
I wake to sleep and take my waking slow

Class discussion

N.   Find two intransitive verbs and two copula verbs (without looking directly in the book). Also, provide two sentences with only a direct object and two sentences with a direct and indirect object.

O.   Use the British National Corpus (BNC at http://www.natcorp.ox.ac.uk/) or the Corpus of Contemporary American English (COCA at http://www.americancorpus.org/) to see if any of your copula, transitive, and ditransitive verbs can be found with the complement you selected in the previous question.

Keys to the exercises

A.   Subject and predicate in [*He*][*left*]; direct object and direct object in *I gave [myself] [flowers]*; subject predicate in *Flowers are [nice]*; and object predicate in *I thought that [stupid]*.

B.   –*Peccaries* can be inverted in a question, as in *Are peccaries medium-sized animals, with a strong superficial resemblance to pigs?* It is a pretty obvious subject and if you made it singular, the verb would change, as in *A peccary is a medium-sized animal*. The third test would give you: *Peccaries are medium-sized animals, aren't they?*
    –The next subject *they* does not appear immediately at the beginning, but making *they* singular would have an effect on the verb, as in *Like pigs, it has a snout ending in a cartilagenous disc.*

–The third subject is trickier since we haven't talked about relative clauses yet. So, not to worry if you didn't see that. It wouldn't be on an exam at this point. The object *eyes* in this sentence is modified by *that are small relative to their head*. In that relative, *that* is the subject.

–The next *they* is pretty obvious again. You could make it singular, as in *Also like pigs, it uses only the middle two digits for walking.*

–*The other toes* and *their stomach* are obvious intuitively although the tests are a little hard to apply. You would have to change the sentences to make them into a single sentence question: *Can the other toes be altogether absent?* and *Is their stomach non-ruminating?*

–The next subject is *it* which if plural would cause the verb to be *have*.

–The last subject is again tricky. The original text didn't have the *is* following the NP *that of pigs*. After *than*, NPs on their own can be analyzed as subjects if you think there is a verb left out, and that's what I did.

C. *we, I, I, they, I, the filmmakers* (this will be clearer after Chapter 8), *the project, it, this, it.*

D. [I] gave [him] [the ticket]: S, IO, DO
[They] [planted a dogwood]: S, Pred
[The trees in the park] are [unhappy]: S, SuPred

E. (54) They sold **us their furniture**: IO DO

(55) Tom submits **his tax-returns**: DO

(56) She seemed **very happy**: SuPred

(57) He found **it easy**: DO, ObPred

(58) He took **the early train**: DO

(59) The politician considered **that argument invalid**: DO, ObPred

(60) That sounds **terrible**: SuPred

F. The verbs are ditransitive, transitive, copula, complex transitive, transitive, complex transitive, and copula.

G. (54)

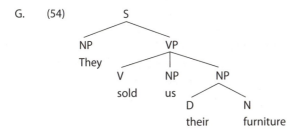

(55)

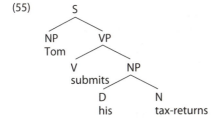

(56)

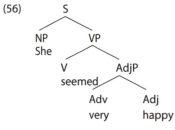

(57)

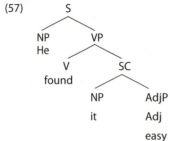

The tree for (58) is similar to the one for (55); the tree for (59) is similar to the one for (57); and the tree for (60) is similar to (56).

H.   Su:NP, Pred:VP, DO:NP, ObjPred:AdjP

Su:NP, Pred:VP, IO:NP, DO:NP

Su:NP, Pred:VP

Su:NP, Pred:VP, SuPred:AdjP

And the categories are: Adj, P, Adj

I.   *wait*: intransitive; *look*: copula; *feel*: copula; *drive*: intransitive (debatable).

those extra twenty minutes: Su; *the waxed parquet*: DO; *small, lonely, patient*: SuPred.

J.   In (65), *it*; in (66), *only two of those people*; in (67), *The book Chomsky wrote when he was young*; in (68), *the Wizard of Oz and Catweazle*. I'll give some reasons.

–   In (68), *Were the Wizard of Oz and Catweazle preparing to go to Alabama*, the subject and auxiliary have already inverted since it is a question. Thus, without having to invert the sentence yourself, you can see what the subject is, namely the phrase after the auxiliary. The agreement on *were* is plural which fits if the subject is the coordinated *the Wizard of Oz and Catweazle*. Notice that if you changed it to just *the Wizard*, the agreement becomes singular: *Was the Wizard preparing to go?* The tag question test doesn't work in a sentence that is already a question.

–   In the three remaining sentences, you could use tag-questions in some:

In the rain, it is sometimes hard to see, isn't it?

The book Chomsky wrote when he was young was reissued last year, wasn't it?

And Inversion would work as follows in the non-questions:

In the rain, is it sometimes hard to see?

Is only one of these people happy?

Was the book Chomsky wrote when he was young reissued last year?

If you changed the subject, the following would show the subject (this is hard to do with *it* in (65) though):

> *Two of these people are happy.*
> *The books Chomsky wrote when he was young were reissued last year.*

K. The funny aspect involves hypercorrection. The initial use of *lies* was correct. Since the future always lies ahead, the content is expressed in a redundant way that we often use. Some people pick on this.

L. In this sentence, the verbs *grow* and *look* are used as copulas since the adjective *thin* is used as subject predicate to modify *her* and *poorly* is used as subject predicate as well since it modifies the left out *her*. So, even though *poorly* looks like an adverb, it is an adjective (the *Oxford English Dictionary* says that the use of *poorly* as an adjective is somewhat rare, but it is quite frequent in Jane Austen). *Grow* can also be a transitive verb and *look* a prepositional object verb, but not in this sentence.

M. Many of the verbs are intransitive (*wake, sleep, fear, go, dance*) or used as intransitive (*learn, think, know*). This contributes to the apparent simplicity. The verb *take* is twice used as a complex predicate (although one could also argue it is light verb). There are two transitives (*feel, hear*) and one copula (*be*). There is only one adjective (*slow*), used twice. The adverbs are *-not, where*, and *there*.

An analysis:

Roethke's 'I wake to sleep and take my waking slow' is dominated by verbs. There is symmetry in the two sentences in that both start with similar sounding verbs (*wake* and *take*) and the first verb is repeated as a noun (*waking*). This focuses our attention on the waking and yet the author purports to be interested in sleeping.

As to the use of adjectives, only one is used (*slow*) and, on first reading, we might think this is incorrect and that it has to be an adverb (*slowly*). It is not incorrect and, moreover, using the adjective rather than the adverb focuses our attention on *waking* rather than on the verb *take*. Both the use of the verbs and the adjective contribute to making the poem puzzling since, if the poet really wanted to sleep, he should not want to be slow in falling asleep.

Special topic: Case and agreement

In this special topic section, we'll discuss case and agreement. Most of these rules have changed in the last 500 years and native speakers of English have lost their intuitions on case endings and agreement. Prescriptive rules die hard, however, so we'll discuss those and see how subject and object can be helpful here. One prescriptive rule can be formulated as (70):

(70) **Case in English:**
Subjects have **nominative** case. Direct and indirect objects have **accusative or objective** case. Prepositional objects also have **accusative or objective** case. Possessive nouns have **genitive** case.

In Modern English, cases are only visible on pronouns. For instance, in (71), the subject *she* is nominative and the direct object *him* accusative. *Me* has objective or accusative case because of the preposition *towards*. With full NPs, it is not obvious what the case is. Notice the lack of obvious case on *the garden*.

(71)　**She** saw **him** come towards **me** in **the garden**.

In (72), the demonstrative *this* doesn't show case, but *you* and *me* have accusative case since they are objects of the preposition *between*. In coordinates such as these, however, the rule is often broken in all stages of English. Thus, in (73) and (74), the nominative *I* is used rather than the accusative *me* and in (75), the nominative *he* is used where an accusative would be expected (prescriptively):

(72)　**This** (matter) is between **you and me**.

(73)　all debts are cleared between **you and I**. Shakespeare, *Merchant of Venice* III, 2, 321

(74)　If you are sick and tired of the way it's been going, …, you give **Al Gore and I** a chance to bring America back. (Bill Clinton, as reported in the New York Times in the 1990s)

(75)　In his speech, Mr. Giuliani said that one of the main differences between **he and Mrs. Clinton** was that "I'm in favor of reducing your taxes …" (again as reported in the New York Times, 8 April 2000).

In (76), the accusative *thee* (a special form for the second person, no longer used in Modern English) is used rather than the nominative *thou* (again no longer in use). The nominative would be expected since *the Diuell and thee* are the subject:

(76)　How agrees [the Diuell and **thee**] about thy soule?
　　　(Shakespeare *1 Henry IV* I, 2, 126)

Notice that in (76), the agreement on the verb is singular as well even though the subject is the plural *the Diuell and thee*. This 'mistake' happens often in coordinated subjects.

　　　With *wh*-questions, the case rule is also often broken. Thus, in (77), the use of *whom* in the first frame would sound very artificial even though, as the accusative or objective form, it is the correct form. *Whom cares* is not correct but completely appropriate in Figure 4.3.

(77)　**Who** shall I say is calling?

Figure 4.3. *Who* or *whom*? (Used with the permission of King Features Syndicate in conjunction with the Cartoonist Group. All rights reserved.)

Similarly, after copulas, many people insist on using the nominative. Before 1600 or so, in sentences with the copula verb *to be*, both subject and subject predicate have nominative case. Nowadays, this sounds overly formal.

The **genitive** case is used in cases such as (78) and (79). If the word does not end in *s*, an apostrophe and *s* are added, as in (78), but if it ends in an *s*, as in (79), either an apostrophe and *s* or just an apostrophe is added. Many people consider the ending in (79) pedantic and hence it often disappears altogether:

(78)   **Shakespeare's** works
(79)   **Employees'(s)** cafeteria

Turning to agreement, we can formulate the rule, as in (80). We have used it above to find the subject and the head of the NP that functions as subject:

(80)   **Agreement in English**
         The subject of a sentence agrees in person and number with the finite verb.

In Modern English, there is little agreement left on the verb. In standard English, apart from the verb *to be* (*I am, you are, s/he is, we are, you are*, and *they are* etc.), there is only a third person singular *-s* ending on verbs in the present tense (e.g. *I walk, you walk, s/he walks, we walk, you walk*, and *they walk*). Note that in some varieties of English, words such as *police* and *government* are singular, whereas in others, they are plural. In general, as long as you are consistent, either should be ok.

The difficulties with agreement usually occur with long subjects, as in (81), or with dummy subjects, as in (82):

(81)   [One of the problems that they worried about continuously] **were** solved rather quickly.
(82)   There**'s** some problems that they could not solve.

Prescriptively, (81) should have singular agreement, i.e. *was*, and (82) should be plural, i.e. *are*.

In earlier varieties of English, e.g. in 16th century English, there is much more agreement. For instance, in (83), the verb agrees with the second person singular *thou*. In some varieties of English, no agreement is left, as in (84), and in some, both singular and plural are possible, as in (85), from Hiberno-English:

(83)   Caes. What **sayst** thou to me now? Speak once againe.
         Sooth. Beware the Ides of March. (Shakespeare, *Julius Ceasar*, I, 2, 18)
(84)   The dog **stay** outside in the afternoon.
(85)   The boys **is/are** leaving.

Chapter 5

More functions, of prepositions and particles

This chapter deals with adverbials, i.e. the optional elements in the sentences that provide background information on when, where, why, and how the event described by the verb and its objects takes place. It is important to be aware that adverbials are not always realized as Adverb Phrases, but can also be realized as PPs or NPs (or as clauses, see Chapter 7). Note that the term 'adverb' refers to the category that heads the Adverb Phrase (AdvP) and that 'adverbial' refers to the function.

Prepositional objects are also discussed since they look like adverbials, but can be argued not to be. Objects to phrasal verbs are regular direct objects. They are discussed here rather than in Chapter 4 because they are easily confused with prepositional objects and include a preposition-like element called a particle. Finally, two other kinds of verbs are discussed involving particles and prepositions: the intransitive phrasal verb and the phrasal prepositional verb.

The main point of this chapter is to learn to distinguish between adverbials and objects. I'll provide some tests for this. When a sentence is passivized, the functions of subject and object may be reversed, i.e. an object then functions as a subject, whereas an adverbial can never function as a subject.

1. Adverbials

When adverbials modify verbs, they express when, where, how, and why the action takes place. So, they give background information on time, place, manner, and cause of the event. In the tree structure, we make a distinction between direct and indirect objects, subject predicates, and object predicates on the one hand (all referred to as complements) and adverbials on the other: objects, subject predicates, and object predicates are closer to the verb than adverbials. Even if in the tree the functions of the phrases are not indicated, you should be able to tell from the tree which phrase is the object and which is the adverbial, e.g. in (1):

(1)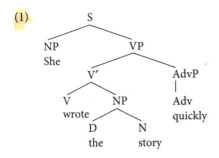

In (1), the NP *the story* is sister to the V *wrote* and is therefore the object; the AdvP *quickly* is sister to the intermediate V' *wrote the story*, and therefore modifies that. *Quickly* tells you how the story was written and is therefore an adverbial. Since the V' that represents *wrote the story* is intermediate inside the VP, we call it a V' ('V-bar').

When you draw the tree, perhaps look back to Chapter 3 (Section 5) and remember possible ambiguities, e.g. in (20) of Chapter 3. We'll go over how to construct the tree in (1) quickly (from top to bottom). First, you start with S, whose daughters are always NP and VP, as shown in (2a). The NP happens to be a pronoun, so nothing else needs to be done to the NP in terms of branches. The VP consists of a V *wrote*, an object *the story*, and an adverbial *quickly*. Be careful not to make the first branch to the left into a V because then you won't have space for all three. Instead, use the V', as in (2b), and then think what should be closest to the V, and fit them in, as in (2c). Remember the V' is a placeholder for lots of branches, a little VP so to speak, but still with the V as its head:

(2)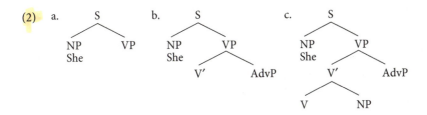

Now add the words to V and branches and words to the NP and AdvP and you have the finished tree of (1).

There is a difference between a VP-adverbial, e.g. *quickly* in (1), and a sentence adverbial, e.g. *fortunately, actually, indeed,* and *of course.* Sentence adverbials (or S-adverbials) do not modify the action of the VP but express the views and the mood of the speaker. Trees for a sentence-initial and sentence-final S-adverbial are given in (3). Duplicating the S intends to show that the adverbial is really outside the core sentence:

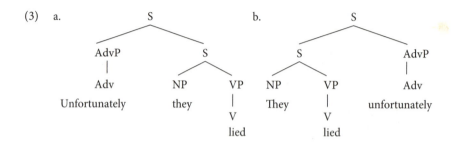

(3)   a.   b.

Certain adverbs can be both VP-adverbials and S-adverbials. For instance, *happily* has two interpretations in (4). One is where painting the pictures was a happy event, in which case *happily* is a VP-adverbial modifying *painted those pictures*, and the comma is less appropriate. A second interpretation is where the speaker expresses an opinion about the entire sentence (perhaps because the pictures turned out to be good):

(4)   **Happily**, they painted those pictures.

The same ambiguity exists for adverbs such as *wisely* and *clearly.* For most speakers of English, *hopefully* too is both a VP-adverbial and an S-adverbial, although for unclear reasons some people object to its use as an S-adverbial (see special topic to Chapter 2).

PPs that function as adverbials are typically VP-adverbials. They often provide background information regarding place, as in (5), and time, as in (6):

(5)

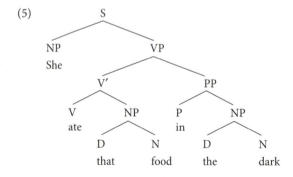

(6)

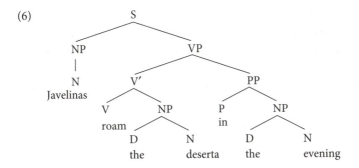

A sentence can have many adverbials (depending on the speaker's or hearer's patience). For instance, in (7), the speaker's feelings (the AdvP *unfortunately*), the time (the NP *that morning*), and place (the PP *to work*) of driving the car are given, as well as the reason for this action (the sentence *the bus had broken down*) and the way in which the action occurred (the PP *without glasses*):

(7)   [Unfortunately], he drove the car [to work] [that morning] [without his glasses] [because the bus had broken down].

It is possible to add more adverbials to this sentence, e.g. *quickly* or *recklessly*.

As can be seen in (7), adverbials are not only realized as AdvPs such as *quickly*, but also as NPs (*that morning*), PPs (*to work* and *without his glasses*), and clauses (*because the bus had broken down*, see Chapter 7). This means NPs function not only as subjects, indirect and direct objects, subject predicates and object predicates (see previous chapter), but also as adverbials. AdvPs on the other hand only function as adverbials. PPs function mainly as adverbials and subject predicates but, as we'll see in the next section, they also function as objects to certain verbs, namely prepositional ones (and, as we saw in Chapter 3 and will see in more detail in Chapter 9, they can also be modifiers inside a phrase). Identify the adverbials in Figure 5.1.

Beetle Bailey

Figure 5.1. Adverbials. (Used with the permission of King Features Syndicate in conjunction with the Cartoonist Group. All rights reserved.)

All adverbials used by Beetle are VP-adverbials, but one could imagine an S-adverbial, such as *unfortunately*, being used! Their realization is through an AdvP (*thoroughly, completely,* and *expeditiously*) and through a PP (*with gusto and verve, without delay,* and *with determination*).

We'll now turn to PPs that sometimes resemble adverbials but are actually objects.

2. Prepositional verbs

Prepositional verbs are verbs such as *abide by* in (8), *refer to* in (9), *glance at, lean against, add to, allow for, approve of, care for, insist on, resort to, apply for, account for, reply to, absolve from, long for, yearn for, result in, argue about,* and *defer to*. The P with the NP functions as an object:

(8)   They **abided** [by the contract].
(9)   He **referred** [to that article].

These verbs require a PP, i.e. (10) and (11) are ungrammatical, and that's why the PP is considered an object rather than an adverbial. *The contract* in (8) and *that article* in (9) can also be passivized, as in (12) and (13), and this test shows that they are real objects, as shown in (14), where the PP is sister to V:

(10)   *He abides.
(11)   *He refers all the time.
(12)   **The contract** was abided by.
(13)   **That article** wasn't referred to by him.

(14)

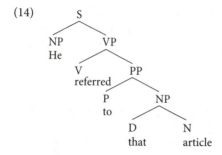

Native speakers of English know that verbs such as *refer* are combined with a certain preposition. Non-native speakers must learn the meanings of these verbs or look them up in a dictionary, e.g. *refer with, refer about, refer at* are not possible.

3. Phrasal verbs

Phrasal verbs must be distinguished from prepositional verbs and from verbs with an adverbial. Like prepositional verbs, they are listed separately in a dictionary since their combinations are somewhat idiosyncratic. Examples of phrasal verbs are *call up, bring up, cover up, look over, take away, turn in, put down, take off, put on, switch on/off, hand in, make out* (as in 'decipher'). Some example sentences are given in (15) to (19):

(15)   They **called up** the president.
(16)   They **covered up** the scandal.
(17)   Helen **turned in** her homework.
(18)   She **put down** the nasty people.
(19)   She **switched on** the light.

The prepositions *up, in, down,* and *on* accompanying these verbs have become particles rather than prepositions or adverbs since they no longer always express place or direction. The structure of a sentence such as (15) is therefore one of a verb with a particle, as in (20):

(20)

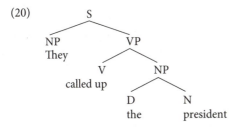

Thus, in (20), the verb and particle are placed in V together, whereas the object is a separate NP. We could represent the verb in (20) as a compound verb if you don't like two words under one category.

One of the easy (but not so well understood) criteria for determining if a verb is phrasal is whether the (pronominalized) object can be put between the verb and the particle, as in (21) to (25):

(21)   They called **him** up.
(22)   They covered **it** up.
(23)   She turned **it** in with many mistakes.
(24)   She put **them** down.
(25)   She switched **it** on.

This is not possible with prepositional verbs, as the unacceptable (26) shows:

(26)   *They abided **it** by.

The basic distinction, clear from (20), is that the V and particle form a unit and that the object is an NP, not a PP. This is so because (a) a pause can occur between the verb particle complex and the NP object, as in (27), but not between the V and the unit which is not a phrase as in (28); (b) the NP objects of a phrasal verb can be coordinated, as in (29), but the particle and NP cannot be coordinated with another particle and NP, as (30) shows; and (c) moving the NP object to the left by itself, as in (31), is ok, indicating the NP is a unit, but moving the particle and the NP together is not ok, as (32) shows, indicating they do not form a phrase:

(27)   She put down — the customers.
(28)   *She put — down the customers.
(29)   She put down the customers and the owner.
(30)   *She put down the customers and down the owner.
(31)   It was the customers she put down.
(32)   *It was down the customers she put.

In (33) and (34), examples are given of phrasal verbs without an NP object:

(33)   His career is **taking off**.
(34)   They finally **gave in**.

Because the verb and particle have lost their independent meanings in (33) and (34), just like the verbs in (15) to (25) above, they are referred to as phrasal verbs. Unlike the phrasal verbs in (15) to (25), the ones in (33) and (34) lack objects. Some other examples are *sleep in,* and *turn in*, as in (35):

(35)   Even though I **turned in** early last night, I **slept in**.

Figure 5.2 exemplifies a few more phrasal verbs. Calvin uses them intransitively, but some of these are also possible as transitive ones (*shut them up* and *mix them up*).

Figure 5.2. More Phrasal verbs (Reprinted with the permission of Universal Press Syndicate. All rights reserved)

    In Table 5.1, I am listing some phrasal verbs that just came to mind starting with the letter 'a', but there are thousands. For this reason, there are dictionaries of phrasal verbs in English (and some are online).

Table 5.1. Examples of phrasal verbs

Intransitive		Transitive	
add up	mean something	add up	calculate/add
drop out	stop participating	back up	put it in reverse
break down	experience a crisis	bring off	accomplish
catch on	(begin) to understand	bring out	publish
carry on	continue as before	bring up	raise (a child)
die out	diminish in intensity	drop off	deliver

Phrasal verbs are in general used in less formal styles; the synonyms in Table 5.1 are much more formal vocabulary choices.

4. Phrasal prepositional verbs (optional)

Constructions with phrasal prepositional verbs combine a verb, a particle, a preposition, and an NP. The object of such a verb is a prepositional object, as indicated with brackets in (36) and (37) for the verbs *put up with* and *come up with*:

(36)   Orrmm will not put up [with that noise].
(37)   Benji came up [with a new solution to Fermat's Theorem].

The reason the verbs are phrasal is that the verb and the particle have lost their independent meaning. They are, however, not very prepositional since the prepositional object cannot be passivized very well, as the awkwardness of (38) shows (and I indicate the awkwardness by means of a question mark):

(38)   ?That noise will not be put up with.

Other examples are *cut down on, catch up on, get away with, stand up for, face up to,* and *check up on.* Like phrasal verbs, phrasal prepositional verbs are very colloquial and are often avoided in formal writing. Could you think of a single verb that can replace the phrasal prepositionals in examples (36) and (37)?

5. Objects and adverbials

As a possible help in distinguishing the different functions, Table 5.2 is provided:

Table 5.2. Differences among objects, su/obj predicates, and adverbials

	Objects	Su/Obj Predicates	Adverbials
Obligatory	yes	yes	no: optional info on time, place, manner, etc.
Passive	yes	no	no

I have already mentioned that adverbials are optional but that objects and predicates are not. Thus, in contrast to prepositional objects, such as those in (10) and (11) above, an adverbial PP can be left out, as (39ab) shows.

(39)   a.   He slept [during the meeting].
       b.   He slept.

A second criterion for distinguishing the different functions is passivization. As mentioned, direct and indirect objects and the NP in the prepositional object can be passivized, e.g. (40), (41), and (42) respectively:

(40)   Emma was seen.   (active: Someone saw **Emma**.)
(41)   Walter was given a book. (active: Someone gave **Walter** a book.)
(42)   The article was referred to. (active: Someone referred to **the article**.)

After the direct, indirect, and prepositional objects are passivized, they of course function as subjects.

Not yet mentioned above is that objects of phrasal verbs can also be passivized, as expected if they are objects, as can objects of complex transitives. Respective examples are (43) and (44), where *the scandal* and *that math problem* are now the subjects:

(43)   The scandal was covered up immediately.
            (active: Someone covered up the scandal immediately.)
(44)   That math problem is considered unsolvable by many great minds.
            (active: Many great minds consider that math problem unsolvable.)

In (40) to (43), I have left the original subject unspecified (hence the 'someone' in the active); in (44), I have added *by many great minds. Many great minds* is the subject of the active sentence, but is optional in the passive. Hence, I would argue that the function of *by many great minds* is adverbial.

The NPs in adverbials, subject predicates, and object predicates cannot be passivized, as is shown for adverbials in (45) and object predicates in (46):

(45)   *The meeting was slept during.
(46)   *The chair was elected him. (passivized from the active *We elected him (to be) chair*)

As expected, the direct object in (46) can be passivized namely as *He was elected the chair*.

In the previous chapter, we discussed intransitive verbs such as *sleep, sneeze, go*, and *swim*. Now that we know there are PP objects as well as PP adverbials, how can we tell which is which using the criteria from Table 5.2, e.g. in sentences such as (47) and (48):

(47)   I went [to the library].
(48)   I swam [in the pool].

Some speakers regard the information contained in the PP as essential and others consider it less so. If the goal of the going is seen as obligatory in (47), one might call the PP an object, a prepositional object in this case; if the goal is seen as optional, the PP would be an adverbial. Hence, for sentences such as (47) and (48), there are two different analyses: the verbs can be intransitive ones with the PPs functioning as adverbials or the verbs can be prepositional ones with the PPs functioning as prepositional objects. Notice that these sentences differ as to whether or not they can be passivized, as shown in (49) and (50):

(49)   *The library was gone to.
(50)   ?The pool was swum in.

The results of passivization provided in (49) and (50) make the adverbial analysis plausible for (47) and the object analysis for (48). Those of you for whom (49) and/or (50) are ok consider both or one of the adverbials more like objects.

It could be that (50) sounds awkward because speakers feel ill at ease with the participle of the verb *swim*. Let's therefore try two other sentences and their passives:

(51)   He walked on the grass.
(52)   Washington slept in this bed.
(53)   The grass was walked on.
(54)   This bed was slept in.

Sentences (53) and (54) provide evidence that *the grass* and *this bed* are real objects in (51) and (52).

Two other frequently asked questions are (a) how the object predicate, as in (55) and (56), repeated from Chapter 4, differs from a modifier to a noun, e.g. *from Mars* in (57), or (b) from an adverbial in (58). I have indicated the most likely analyses by means of brackets:

(55)   Jane considers [*Pride and Prejudice*] [a classic].
(56)   She put [snails] [on the table].
(57)   I saw [a man from Mars].
(58)   I saw [a man] [in the garden].

The answer is that, in (57), *from Mars* forms part of the direct object (as indicated by the brackets) which can be replaced by a single element, as in (59). In a sentence such as (56), *on the table* is not part of the direct object since they cannot both be replaced by one element as the ungrammatical (60) shows:

(59)   I saw him.
(60)   *She put it.

The same is true for (55), since (61) has quite a different meaning than (55):

(61)   Jane considers it.

6. Conclusion

As a conclusion, I list instances of the eight types of verbs we have discussed in Chapters 4 and 5:

Table 5.3. Verb types and their complements

Name	Example	Complement	Sentence
intransitive	swim, arrive	–	She arrived (early).
(mono)transitive	see, eat, read, love	Direct Object	She saw me.
ditransitive	give, tell	Direct and Indirect Object	I gave him flowers.
copula	be, become	Subject Predicate	She is nice.
complex transitive	consider, know	Direct Object and Object Predicate	I consider her nice.
prepositional	refer, glance	Prepositional Object	He glanced at the book
phrasal	switch on/give in	Direct Object/ –	She turned off the light He gave in.
(phrasal prepositional	get down to	Prepositional Object	He got down to business).

Typically, the direct and indirect objects are realized as NPs and the subject and object predicates as AdjPs, but as was indicated above, there are other possibilities. The prepositional object is always a PP, but the reverse is not true since PPs can have many functions.

Adverbials are not relevant for the classification of verbs since they can always be added or deleted. As mentioned above, they are typically realized as PPs and AdvPs even though NPs and clauses are also possible. As an addition to Figure 4.1 where the functions of NP, VP, and AdjP are given, Figure 5.3 does the same for PP and AdvP:

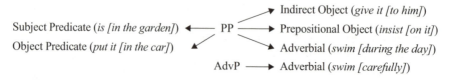

Figure 5.3. The functions of PPs and AdvPs

Passives are relevant since they allow us to find direct, indirect, prepositional, and phrasal objects. After being passivized, these objects of course function as subjects.

Key terms are **adverbial, prepositional verb, and phrasal verb**. Don't worry too much about phrasal prepositional verbs. Also relevant are **VP- and S-adverbials**.

Exercises

A.   Identify all the functions in (62) to (67). Draw trees for (62) and (65):

(62)   Fortunately, she found it easily.

(63)   I separated it carefully.

(64)   She found it easy.

(65)   He baked Zoya bread last night (i.e. he baked it for her).

(66)   Wisely, the pig from Mars left relatively early.

(67)   The hard-working students seemed exhausted after three weeks of classes.

B.   In the short text below, identify the underlined verbs (e.g. intransitive, complex transitive) and the function of the phrases in brackets:

I have [a shocking news item]. [This little-known tidbit] will stun some of you and put the rest [in a catatonic haze]. This is why I am warning you to brace yourselves. The Olympics are going on [right now].
(adapted from a piece by Steve Galindo in the State Press)

C.   Do the same in the text below. How would you analyze *deal* in the last sentence?:
Underground nitrogen leak shuts down roads in the city

A worker from T&T Construction punctured [a high-pressure nitrogen line] at about 7 a.m., shutting down [traffic] on the northeast side of town [all day]. The Police Department blocked off a large area because [it] didn't [initially] know what was leaking. "[It] could have been natural gas, so we had to be [careful]," [Tena Ray, a spokesperson], said. "Fortunately, we don't have to deal with things like this very often".
(adapted from a piece by Michelle Beaver in the State Press)

D.   Underline the PPs in the text below, and say which ones are adverbials.

In Rapid City, S.D., a buffalo escaped from an auction and ended up in a dressing room. It spent a couple of hours staring into a mirror at the Rushmore Plaza Civic Center. The buffalo jumped over a steel panel during the Black Hills Stock Show & Rodeo on Sunday morning, went down an alley and got into the dressing room reserved for visiting sports teams, said Brian Maliske, the civic center's general manager. "The door happened to be unlocked and he pushed the door open and went in," Maliske said. The crew conducting the Black Hills Classic Buffalo Sale decided to keep the animal locked in the dressing room for the rest of the auction. During its two hour stay, it reportedly became fascinated with the image it saw in a big mirror. When the sale ended, a rodeo crew member coaxed the buffalo out and into captivity.
(adapted from the *East Valley Tribune*, January 2005)

E.   Take a verb and combine it with different prepositions and explain what kind of verb is the result. For instance, take *sleep* and combine it with *in, during, off, around, over,* or *outside*.

F.   Make a sentence containing the verb *complain about*. What kind of verb is it? Do the same with *resort to, comment on* and *catch up with*.

G. Explain the ambiguity in the cartoon in Figure 5.4.

Figure 5.4. Glasses. (Used with the permission of the Thaves and the Cartoonist Group. All rights reserved)

H. How would you describe the difference between 'to visit with somebody' and 'to visit somebody'? Speakers of English use both. What would you say?

I. Find the adverbials in the text below (adapted from an Amnesty International document). How are they realized, i.e. what kind of phrases are they? Be careful not to list the phrases that modify nouns (*of the failure of justice*) or adjectives. This is a difficult text, I found, so don't get discouraged!

Human Rights and the Punjab
The organization provides a number of instances of the failure of justice in this report. The government authorities have failed to address the problem of 'disappearances' in Punjab. The government has not responded to any of the cases documented since December 1993. The practice of ignoring petitions continues.
The Supreme Court found the police guilty of abducting and killing people but grave concerns remain unaddressed. The report expresses concern about recent allegations in the press that hundreds of people have been killed in Punjab. Continuing allegations of 'disappearances' are indicative of the absence of a serious commitment by the state authorities.

J. Are there prepositional objects in the text of B? Are there phrasal verbs?

K. **(Difficult)** Please circle and label (transitive etc.) all lexical verbs in the text below.

Streets of Athens
My friends next door are some of the few Athenians who have not moved into a concrete block or sold local building contractors their family home for a handsome profit. The sprawling morass of concrete that spills into the Attica Plain surrounding the suburbs of Athens makes Europe's southernmost capital one of the world's most polluted cities. (adapted from The Guardian, June 1990)

Then, bracket and label all the direct/indirect objects, subject/object predicates, and adverbials of the text in K.

Class discussion

L.   What do (68) and (69) tell you about the type of verbs *switch on* and *look up* are respectively? One way to look at this is to focus on *the light* being preposed in (68) without taking *on* along. *Up the word* is not a unit in (69) since it cannot be coordinated with a similar unit:

(68)   It was the light he switched on.
(69)   *I looked up the word and up the quote.

M.   In connection with phrasal verbs, we discussed intransitive phrasal verbs, such as *take off* and *give in*, repeated here as (70) and (71). *Take off* can also be a transitive phrasal verb, as in (72):

(70)   His career took off.
(71)   They finally gave in.
(72)   She took off her glasses.

How would you analyze (73)? If you looked up *away* in a dictionary, it would tell you it derives from the PP *on way* and is now an adverb or preposition, just like *off* and *in*:

(73)   He went away.

One of the ways to solve this is to see if you can question where he went. If you could, that would mean *away* would be an adverb, and not a particle. It is not a likely P since it has no object (which we suggested in Chapter 2 was a way to differentiate between prepositions on the one hand and adverbs and particles on the other).

N.   A garbage collection company used (74) as one of its slogans. Explain the ambiguity in terms of verb type:

(74)   Our business is picking up.

O.   Identify the prepositions and particles in Figures 5.5 and 5.6.

Figure 5.5. *Put off until after*
        (The Born Loser: © Newspaper Enterprise Association, Inc.)

"I like writing on the computer.
If you make a mistake, you can
just back up over it."

Figure 5.6. *Back up over*
(FAMILY CIRCUS © 2005 BIL KEANE, INC. KING FEATURES SYNDICATE)

P. In the text in tree (20), I provide a tree for the phrasal verb when the object follows the verb and particle. Discuss some possible trees for sentences where the object intervenes between the verb and the particle.

Keys to the exercises

A. (62) Adv-ial Su Pred do Adv-ial
(63) Su Pred Do Adv-ial
(64) Su Pred Do ObjPr
(65) Su Pred Io Do Adv-ial
(66) Adv-ial Su Pred Adv-ial
(67) Su Pred SuPred Adv-ial

(62)   S   (It doesn't matter whether or not you connect AdvP and Adv with a line, as (62) shows)

```
                    S          (It doesn't matter whether or not you connect AdvP and
            ┌───────┴───────┐              Adv with a line, as (62) shows)
          AdvP              S
          Adv           ┌───┴───┐
        Fortunately    NP      VP
                       She   ┌──┴──┐
                            V'    AdvP
                          ┌─┴─┐    │
                          V   NP   Adv
                        found  it  easily
```

(65)

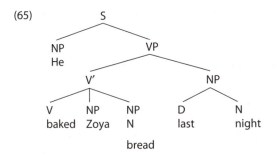

B.   I <u>have: transitive</u> [a shocking news item: DO]. [This little-known tidbit: SU] will <u>stun:</u>
     <u>transitive</u> some of you and <u>put: complex transitive</u> the rest [in a catatonic haze: ObjPr].
     This <u>is: copula</u> why I am <u>warning: transitive</u> you to <u>brace: transitive</u> yourselves. The
     Olympics are <u>going on: intransitive phrasal</u> [right now: Adverbial].

C.   A worker from T&T Construction <u>punctured: transitive</u> [a high-pressure nitrogen line: DO]
     at about 7 a.m., <u>shutting down: (transitive) phrasal</u> [traffic: DO] on the northeast side
     of town [all day: adverbial]. The Police Department <u>blocked off: (transitive) phrasal</u> a
     large area because [it: Su] didn't [initially: Adverbial] <u>know: transitive</u> what was <u>leaking:</u>
     <u>intransitive</u>. "[It: Su] could have <u>been: copula</u> natural gas, so we had to be [careful: SuPr],"
     [Tena Ray, a spokesperson: Su (appositive)], said. "Fortunately, we don't have to deal
     with things like this very often".

     Deal is a verb taking a prepositional object.

D.   <u>In Rapid City, S.D.</u>, a buffalo escaped <u>from an auction</u> and ended up <u>in a dressing room.</u>
     It spent a couple <u>of hours</u> staring <u>into a mirror</u> <u>at the Rushmore Plaza Civic Center</u>. The
     buffalo jumped <u>over a steel panel</u> during <u>the Black Hills Stock Show & Rodeo</u> <u>on Sunday</u>
     <u>morning</u>, went <u>down an alley</u> and got <u>into the dressing room reserved [for visiting sports</u>
     <u>teams]</u>, said Brian Maliske, the civic center's general manager. "The door happened to be
     unlocked and he pushed the door open and went in," Maliske said. The crew conducting
     the Black Hills Classic Buffalo Sale decided to keep the animal locked <u>in the dressing room</u>
     <u>for the rest [of the auction]</u>. <u>During its two hour stay</u>, it reportedly became fascinated <u>with</u>
     <u>the image</u> it saw <u>in a big mirror</u>. When the sale ended, a rodeo crew member coaxed the
     buffalo out and <u>into captivity</u>. The adverbials are all of the underlined or bracketed PPs
     EXCEPT *of hours* (goes with an N *couple*) and *of the auction* (goes with the N *rest*).

E.   *Sleep in* would be an intransitive phrasal, with *in* a particle, since *in* does not have it
     original (locational) meaning. *Sleep around* is similar. *Sleep off* is a transitive phrasal since
     one can say *sleep off a hangover* and *sleep it off*; *off* is a particle, because you would have
     to look up the meaning in a dictionary. *Sleep during* consists of an intransitive verb *sleep*
     and a preposition *during*. *During* is not a particle since *sleep it during* is ungrammatical,
     and it is not an adverb since it cannot occur independently of an NP, as in *I slept during*.
     Sleep outside contains an intransitive verb *sleep* and an adverb *outside*.

F.   She complained about the government; He resorted to violence; They commented on
     the book. They are all prepositional object verbs.

A sentence with the phrasal prepositional verb 'catch up with' is: They caught up with him.

G.   The question 'How do they look?' contains a copula verb, but the joke is that *look* can also be used in another way, namely as a prepositional verb. In this case, 'How do they see?' plays on that meaning.

H.   'To visit with somebody' is said to be American English, whereas 'to visit somebody' is said to be British English. The difference is that in the former case, *visit with* is a prepositional verb, whereas in the latter case, *visit* is a (mono)transitive verb.

I.   Adverbials in the first paragraph: *in this report*: PP and *since December 1993*: PP; in the second paragraph: *in Punjab*: PP.

J.   *Respond* could be argued to be prepositional; no phrasal ones.

K.   My friends next door (are) some of the few Athenians who have not (moved) into a concrete block or (sold) local building contractors their family home for a handsome profit. The sprawling morass of concrete that (spills) into the Attica Plain (surrounding) the suburbs of Athens (makes) Europe's southernmost capital one of the world's most polluted cities.

The names of the verbs are: copula, intransitive or prepositional verb, ditransitive, intransitive (possibly prepositional), transitive, and complex transitive.

The minimum you can do is as follows but that doesn't catch all complements: My friends next door are SuPr [some of the few Athenians who have not moved into a concrete block or sold local building contractors their family home for a handsome profit]. The sprawling morass of concrete that spills into the Attica Plain surrounding the suburbs of Athens makes DO [Europe's southernmost capital] ObjPr [one of the world's most polluted cities]. You could look inside these complements, as in:
[some of the few Athenians who have not moved Adv-ial or PO [into a concrete block] or sold IO [local building contractors] DO [their family home] Adv-ial [for a handsome profit]]. The sprawling morass of concrete that spills Adv-ial [into the Attica Plain surrounding DO [the suburbs of Athens]].

Special topic: The passive and 'dummies'

I consider the use or non-use of the passive a matter of style not of grammar (not even an issue of prescriptive grammar). In certain kinds of writing, the use of the passive can have advantages and, in others, it is better to be direct and to use the active. Sometimes, it is irrelevant to know who performed the action and then the passive is more appropriate.

Let me start off with some quotes against the use of the passive. George Orwell, in his 1946 essay 'Politics and the English Language,' is perhaps the strictest:

(70)   "Never use the passive where you can use the active."

Orwell was of course worried about political propaganda. Style books include similar statements:

(71) "Use the active voice. The active voice is usually more direct and vigorous than the passive" (Strunk *The Elements of Style* 1918; later Strunk & White 1959[2000]).

The Princeton Writing Center cautions against the use of the passive as recently as 2009 though it doesn't suggest getting rid of it altogether:

(72) "Remember: to use the passive voice effectively, use it sparingly. Otherwise, your writing may well evince the absurdity of this famous example …
`It was midday. The bus was being got into by passengers. They were being squashed together. A hat was being worn on the head of a young gentleman ….'"
(http://web.princeton.edu/sites/writing/Writing_Center/handouts/html/passivevoice.htm)

The passive has of course been in the English language since its beginning, as (73) shows, with the passive auxiliary and verb in bold:

(73) *Ða* **wæs** *gylden hilt gamelum rince*
then was golden hilt old man

harum hild-fruman on hand **gyfen**
grey war-chief in hand given

'Then was the golden hilt given into the old man's, the grey warrior's, hand.'
(*Beowulf* 1677–78)

Since passives use the auxiliary 'to be', rules such as (74) seem to include them:

(74) **Avoid the verb 'to be'.** "One of the most common stylistic mistakes aspiring writers make is to rely too much on the verb "to be." "To be" is the most basic verb in the English language, and writers can all too easily find themselves using it in almost every sentence." (http://www.essayforum.com/13_5678_0.html)

I think most of the time the copula 'to be' is meant when this rule is stated, but this rule may also contribute to the unpopularity of the passive.

Finally, the dummy subjects 'there' and 'it', also called pleonastics or expletives, are cautioned against by many style guides, as in the following quote from the Purdue University writing center:

(75) "Avoid overusing expletives at the beginning of sentences."
(http://owl.english.purdue.edu/owl/resource/572/04).

Many writers use these of course. Adam Smith's *Wealth of Nations,* a long text, contains 596 instances of *there*, many at the beginning of the sentence, and 4676 instances of *is*. Charles Dickens' *Bleak House*, a much shorter text, has 173 occurrences of *there* and 413 of *is*.

As with the passive, the frequent use of *to be, it,* and *there* is really a matter of style. Some authors like them, as reading the following adaptation from Ernest Hemingway's *Hills Like White Elephants* shows. I have put the forms of *to be* and the dummy subjects in bold:

(76)   The hills across the valley of the Ebro **were** long and white. On this side **there was** no shade and no trees and the station **was** between two lines of rails in the sun. Close against the side of the station **there was** the warm shadow of the building and a curtain, made of strings of bamboo beads, hung across the open door into the bar, to keep out flies. The American and the girl with him sat at a table in the shade, outside the building. **It was** very hot and the express from Barcelona would come in forty minutes. It stopped at this junction for two minutes and went on to Madrid.

Chapter 6

The structure of the verb group (VGP) in the VP

1. Auxiliary verbs
2. The five types of auxiliaries in English
3. Auxiliaries, 'affix hop', and the verbgroup (VGP)
4. Finiteness
5. Relating the terms for verbs (optional)
6. Conclusion

In this chapter, the verbs that can appear together in a VP are discussed in more detail. Most of the sentences we have talked about so far have contained one (finite and lexical) verb. In English, a VP can (in principle) have four auxiliary verbs and one lexical verb. English is quite unusual in this respect, compared to other languages that typically do not have this many auxiliaries. This complex of auxiliaries and the lexical verb will be called the Verb Group, abbreviated in the tree as VGP (and used when auxiliaries are present). English is also unusual in that if an auxiliary is not present and the sentence is negative or a question, a 'dummy' auxiliary *do* is needed.

In Section 1, the auxiliaries are defined and characterized in general terms. In that section, I also include auxiliaries as part of the (flat, non-hierarchical) Verb Group. We will label the auxiliaries as modal, perfect, progressive, passive, and dummy in Section 2. Auxiliaries are associated with a particular ending, i.e. affix, that appears on the verb immediately to their right. This process is called affix-hop and is discussed in Section 3. Section 4 provides rules for identifying finite verbs and for distinguishing them from non-finite ones. Section 5 is an optional section that reviews the terminology that is relevant to verbs and tries to justify the different classifications.

1. Auxiliary verbs

Verbs can be divided into **lexical** and **auxiliary verbs**. A VP contains one lexical verb and (optionally) up to four auxiliaries. Most of the VPs dealt with in the previous chapters consist of a single verb, and then they automatically are lexical verbs. Lexical verbs can be further divided into intransitive *arrive, walk,* copula *be,* transitive *see, eat,* etc, as we've seen. These verbs carry a real meaning and are not dependent on another verb. In addition to a lexical verb, the VP may contain auxiliaries which are then grouped together with the lexical verb in a Verb Group. Auxiliaries depend on another verb and add grammatical information. They are divided into different kinds in Section 2.

Auxiliaries are also sometimes called helping verbs since they help out other verbs. For instance, in (1), *has* does not mean 'possess'; it merely indicates that the action of the lexical verb *see* was in the past. In (2), on the other hand, *have* has a lexical meaning ('to possess') and there is no other lexical verb present. Its classification is transitive since it has a direct object (*a book on sentences*):

(1)   The Malacandran **has** seen the hross.   (perfect auxiliary *have* with lexical verb *see*)
(2)   I **have** a book on sentences.   (transitive verb *have*)

Unlike lexical verbs, auxiliaries invert in questions, as in (3), can precede the negative *n't* (i.e. the common form of *not*), as in (4), can be used in tag questions, as in (5), and can be used to emphasize that the action did indeed take place, as in (6):

(3)   **Has** she gone yet?   (perfect auxiliary *have*)
(4)   She **hasn't** done that yet.   (perfect auxiliary *have*)
(5)   She **hasn't** done that yet, **has** she?   (perfect auxiliary *have*)
(6)   She **HAS** actually said that!   (emphatic auxiliary)

If *n't/not* appears, as in (4) and (5), this adverb will be included in the Verb Group as well and will be abbreviated as 'neg' to save space in the tree. Table 6.1 provides some ways to recognize auxiliaries.

Table 6.1. Characteristics of auxiliary verb

---

a. They must be used with a lexical verb (unless the verb is elided).
b. They have little meaning; rather, they express tense, mood, and aspect.
c. They invert in questions, as in (3).
d. They occur before *n't*, as in (4).
e. They are used in tags, as in (5).
f. They are used for emphasis, as in (6).

The Verb Group will be represented as a flat tree structure, as in (7). As mentioned in Chapter 3, grammatical categories such as the auxiliary do not head their own phrase (in this book) and hence do not function at sentence level. Grammatical categories function inside a phrase or, in this case, as heads inside the Verb Group (if auxiliaries are present, VGP will be used; otherwise, V will suffice):

(7)

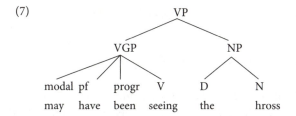

I use abbreviations for the auxiliaries for practical reasons: the full names are hard to fit in the tree otherwise. Let's now look at each of the auxiliaries in more detail.

2. The five types of auxiliaries in English

In this section, we'll discuss the auxiliaries as they appear if all are present in a sentence, namely modal, perfect (pf), progressive (progr), and passive (pass). When no auxiliaries are present, we need *do* in certain cases.

2.1 Modals

English is exceptional in the numbers of auxiliaries it has and the combinations it allows. Each auxiliary has its own name and position with regard to the others. Modals do not have agreement or tense endings (hence *he cans*; *I am canning to go*); they are the first to occur in a sequence of auxiliaries; and do not require an ending, i.e. affix, on the verb following them (*He can walk*, but not: *He can walked*). Thus, (8a) and (8b) are typical instances: the modals *might* and *could* are first and the verb following it does not have an affix:

(8) a. It **might** rain. (modal auxiliary *might*)
    b. Rigobertha **could** be going tomorrow. (modal auxiliary *could*)

There are nine modals in English: *can, could, may, might, shall, should, will, would*, and *must*. Modal auxiliaries express uncertainty, as in (8), necessity (*must, should*), ability, as in (9), or permission, as in (10):

(9) I **can** swim. (modal auxiliary *can*)
(10) You **may** go now. (modal auxiliary *may*)

Modals are also used where some languages would use the subjunctive mood. The Modern English subjunctive is very restricted and examples are given in (11a) and (12a). Alternatives using modals are provided in (11b) and (12b):

(11) a. They insisted that he **go**. (subjunctive mood)
    b. They insisted that he **should** go.

(12) a.   I wish it **were** Friday.   (subjunctive mood)
      b.   I wish it **would** be Friday

Since subjunctives are not common in Modern English, I will not go into this more deeply.

Modals are often used when we ask a favor of someone, as in (13), or when we want to be polite. The 'past' form (*could*) in (13) is seen as more polite than the 'present' form (*can*) in (14). Modals have lost the ability to express present and past tense, but they are finite. Thus, the difference between (13) and (14) is not related to when the action happened, but to how likely the event is to happen. *Could* is more polite since it expresses a more remote possibility; *can* is more direct and hence seen as less polite:

(13)   **Could** I borrow some money?   (modal auxiliary *could*)
(14)   **Can** I borrow some money?   (modal auxiliary *can*)

In English, the modal *will* (and *shall* in some varieties of English) is used to express future, as in (15) and (16), the latter of which is the contracted form:

(15)   He **will** go to Mars next year.   (future expressed by *will*)
(16)   She**'ll** walk on Jupiter in two years.   (future expressed by *'ll*)

There are special modals, called semi-modals: *dare (to), need (to), have to,* and *ought to*. They are seen as modals since they express obligation, ability, and necessity. *Used to* is sometimes added to this group, but it is much more a regular auxiliary expressing habituality. Semi-modals are in flux between auxiliary and lexical verb status. In (17), T.S. Eliot does not invert *dare* in a question (see test (c) of Table 6.1) and it therefore looks like a lexical verb, but in (18), acceptable for some speakers, *dare* is inverted and more of an auxiliary:

(17)   Shall I part my hair behind? Do I **dare** to eat a peach?   (semi-modal *dare*)
       (*The Love Song of J.A.P*, l 122)
(18)   **Dare** I eat a peach?   (semi-modal *dare*)

In English, only auxiliaries move, and if the sentence contains just a lexical verb, a dummy *do* will be used (see Section 2.5). Since *do* is used in (17), it is usually thought that *dare* in (17) is a lexical verb. The other semi-modals allow a variety of constructions as well. For instance, *ought* in (19) is very much an auxiliary since it moves, but in (20), it is not. Both occur in 19th century texts (see the *Oxford English Dictionary*):

(19)   How **ought** I address thee, how ought I revere thee?   (semi-modal *ought*)
       (Robert Browning, *Agamemnon* 796)

(20)   You did n't ought to have received 'em.   (semi-modal *ought*)
        (Charles Dickens, *Martin Chuzzlewit* 34, 403)

2.2   Perfect *have* (pf)

Have follows the modal if there is one. It is called the perfect auxiliary, and abbreviated as 'pf', though it does not make the meaning perfective or finished. It is used to indicate that a past action still has relevance and that mixture of tense and aspect is called the 'present perfect'. For instance, in (21), the speaker still lives 'here', whereas in the simple past tense, as in (22), the speaker no longer does:

(21)   I **have** lived here for ages.   (perfect auxiliary *have*, used in present perfect)
(22)   I **lived** here in the nineties.   (simple past)

There is currently a shift between British English and American English in that the former prefers the present perfect, as in (23), for the recent past, whereas the latter does the simple past, as in (24):

(23)   Well I've, **I've seen her today** but she said she'd er get me some socks and that...
        (BNC – informal conversations)
(24)   in fact, I **saw him today** at the airport (COCA – FOX TV)

When *have* is used, the verb following it is marked with an -*ed* ending (if it is regular), e.g. *lived* in (21). The form of the verb that is the result of 'affix-hop' is called the past participle, or -*ed* participle. Affix-hop is so called because the affix appears on the verb to the immediate right of the auxiliary it goes with: the affix 'hops' onto the next verb. In (25), the ending related to *have* appears on *be*, which is an irregular verb (like *see*, *go, do*, etc.) and therefore has an -*en* ending:

(25)   Zoltan may **have** been playing a terrible game.   (perfect auxiliary *have*)

The term past participle is perhaps somewhat confusing since the presence of the past participle does not make the entire sentence past tense. In fact, (21), (23), and (25) are in the present tense, and hence the name present perfect. There is a past perfect, as in (26), with the form of the auxiliary *have* in the past but otherwise similar. Its meaning is completion by a certain point in the past (in this case 'by five'):

(26)   He **had** done it by five.   (perfect auxiliary *had*)

In Figure 6.1, I provide (simplified) timelines for the different tense and aspect combinations, where S represents the time of speech and E the event. The present tense is used when the time of the event and the utterance are the same; the past is used when the event is at an earlier time; and the future is used when the event is at a later time. The present perfect is used when the event (represented by the arrow) started earlier but includes the time of speech and the past perfect is used when there is a reference time in the past, such as five o'clock, and the event occurred before that time. The future perfect has a time reference in the future by which time the event will have occurred.

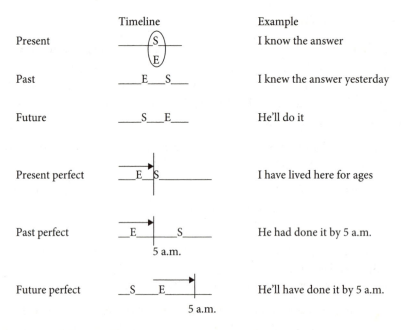

Figure 6.1. Timelines for tense and aspect

The exact order of S and E doesn't matter in the future perfect.

In Figure 6.2, we will list three progressives. If you are a native speaker, you know how to use these, but you might want to know terms such as present and past perfect since these are used. I don't think that you need to memorize the terms in Tables 6.1 and 6.2. I just want you to have a familiarity with the terms.

2.3   Progressive *be* (progr)

The progressive, abbreviated as 'progr', indicates that the action is or was in progress. This is the aspect of a verb, as opposed to the tense of a verb which tells you whether the action took place in the present, past, or future. In (27) to (29), the aspect is progressive, but the tense is present in (27), past in (28), and future in (29). Since the progressive indicates that an action is or was in progress, it is incompatible with verbs that express a state, as shown in (30) and (31):

(27)	Zoya **is** walking.	(progressive *be*)
(28)	Zoltan **was** playing the piano, when a noise disturbed him.	(progressive *be*)
(29)	He will **be** walking the dog.	(progressive *be*)
(30)	*He **is** knowing the answer.	(progressive *be*)
(31)	*The book **is** being blue.	(progressive *be*)

To form the progressive, a form of *to be* is used, as in (27). The verb that follows this auxiliary has an *-ing* ending through affix-hop. It is called a present participle, or *ing*-participle. Again, as in the case of past participles, the term is confusing since the present participle need not make the sentence into the present tense, as (28) shows.

In Figure 6.1, I showed simplified timelines for some simple tenses and the perfects. Figure 6.2 adds timelines for progressives. The present progressive expresses that the event is taking place for some time at the time of the utterance; the past progressive that it was taking place for some period in the past; and the future progressive that an event will be taking place in the future. A few more combinations can be added but I will leave that for the class discussion section (see Exercise G, Figure 6.5).

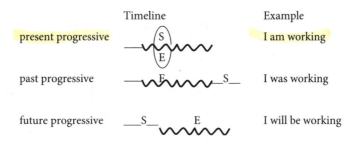

Figure 6.2. Three progressives

Some people argue that certain forms of *be* are not auxiliary verbs but lexical ones, and that the *-ing* forms are adjectives. I mention it here as a possible analysis in some cases. For instance in (27) above, one could argue *walking* is like *nice*, since like *nice*, it can be used to modify a noun in (32):

(32)   My nice **walking** shoes are very light.   (present participle used as adjective)

My own feeling is that *walking* in (27), where it refers to an action, is very different from *walking* in (32), where it describes the qualities of a noun. If we considered the distinctions made in Chapter 2, *walking* would be a verb in (27), but an adjective in (32). The same ambiguity occurs with passives, as will be shown next.

2.4   Passive *be* (pass)

As seen in Chapters 4 and 5, passive constructions, as in (33b), are made from active ones as in (33a) by switching the subject and the object around and by adding a form of *to be*. This passive auxiliary is abbreviated as 'pass' in the tree. The verb immediately following this *be* has a past participle ending, in this case *-en*, because of the affix 'hopping' from the auxiliary to the next verb:

(33)   a.   I see him.   (active)
       b.   He **is** seen by me.   (passive auxiliary *be*)

The stylistic effects of passives were discussed in Chapter 5. Here, we just discuss the form. In the active (34a), the Verb Group consists of a modal, a perfect, and a lexical verb. Because of the perfect *have*, the form of the verb *see* is a past participle. In (34b), the passive *be* is added and now its form is that of past participle (namely *been*) because it follows *have*. *Seen* appears as past participle as well because it follows the passive *be*. If this sounds too complex, just look at the ending of the verb on the immediate right of the auxiliary and Table 6.3 below:

(34)   a. Zoya **may have** seen Zoltan.   (modal *may* and perfect *have*)

   b. Zoltan **may have been** seen by Zoya. (modal *may*, perfect *have*, and passive *be*)

Passive participles can often be analyzed as adjectives (*known, mixed, written*) and are then not part of the Verb Group. Then, the form of *be* is not an auxiliary either, but a copula. It is up to the reader to decide whether *delighted* in (35) is a passive participle or an adjective. Most linguists would argue that (35) is not a passive construction since (a) adding a *by*-phrase, as in (36), is awkward, and (b) *delighted* appears after copula verbs such as *seem*, as in (37), which is typical of adjectives:

(35)   She **was delighted to** get chocolate.   (copula *be* and adjective)
(36)   *She was delighted **by Edward** to get chocolate.   (by-NP not possible)
(37)   She **seemed delighted** to get chocolate.   (*delighted* after *seem*)

The regular passive is constructed with the auxiliary *be* and that is the one you should probably use in formal writing. There is another passive auxiliary that I mention here but won't include in the Table or summaries, namely *get*, as in (38). According to the *Oxford English Dictionary*, the *get*-passive is first used in 1652. It seems more forceful than the *be*-passive:

(38)   Then he **got knocked** out.   (passive auxiliary *get*)
   (BNC, fiction)

As we'll see in the next section, if there are two *be* auxiliaries in a row, the first is the progressive and the second one is the passive auxiliary. Note that the passive auxiliary gets the affix of the preceding auxiliary through affix-hop, in this case that of the progressive. *Missed* is a past participle because of the preceding passive *be*:

(39)   Treatable chronic liver disease **may be being** missed in primary care …
   (google – medical site)

2.5   The 'dummy' *do*

Lexical verbs, such as *know* and *think,* cannot be used in questions and negative sentences in Modern English, as (40a) and (41a) show for *know*. Instead, a dummy *do* is used in (40b) and (41b):

(40) a. *Knows he the answer?
      b. Does he know the answer?
(41) a. *He knows not the answer.
      b. He doesn't know the answer.

Do does not appear together with the other auxiliaries but is only inserted in questions, as in (40b), or negative sentences with *n't/not*, as in (41b), or for emphasis, as in (42):

(42) Oh, but I DID know the answer.

In earlier English, dummy *do* does not appear in this way. In Shakespeare's time, for instance, it is optional, as (43) to (45) indicate:

(43) Or if it were, it **not belongs** to you. (*2 Henry IV*, IV, i, 98)
(44) **What meanes** your Lordship? (*Hamlet*, III, i, 106)
(45) What **does** this meane my Lord? (*Hamlet*, I, vi, 7)

Leaving the *do* out has an archaic effect, or just a playful one, as in Figure 6.3.

Figure 6.3. I think not. (© 2008 Jan Eliot. Reprinted with the permission of Universal Press Syndicate. All rights reserved.)

3. Auxiliaries, 'affix hop', and the verbgroup (VGP)

The auxiliaries dealt with in the previous section occur in a particular order: modal, perfect, progressive, and passive. Since dummy *do* only occurs if no other auxiliary is present, I will ignore it here. As mentioned, the verb that immediately follows a particular auxiliary bears the ending, also called affix, of that auxiliary. Since the affix associated with a particular auxiliary does not appear on the auxiliary but on the next verb, this process is called affix-hop. The auxiliaries and lexical verb go together in a verbgroup or VGP. As a summary of the auxiliaries and affixes, I list them in the table below.

Table 6.2. Auxiliaries and their affixes

Name of AUX	AUX	affix on the next verb	sentence	name of verb with affix
modal:	may, might, can, could, etc	–	He **may** go	infinitive
perfect:	have	-ed/-en	They **have** walk**ed** /seen/gone	past participle
progressive:	be	-ing	I **am** going	present participle
passive:	be	-ed/-en	They **are** loved/seen	past participle

A sentence that includes all four types of auxiliaries sounds a little contrived. Note the strict order (e.g. *have may* would be ungrammatical:

(46)   The woman made a 911 call from the trunk of a car [that] police believe she **may have been being** held in. (google – local news site)

In (46), there is a modal *may*, a perfect *have*, a progressive *be* marked with *-en* because of *have*, a passive *be* marked with *-ing* because of the progressive immediately to its left, and a lexical verb *held* that bears the affix of the passive auxiliary immediately to its left.

As shown in (7) above, the structure of a sentence with a number of auxiliaries is not very insightful, i.e. it is very flat, since all the auxiliaries are part of the Verb Group. The negative adverb *not* in English must be included in the Verb Group as well since it is an affix on the finite auxiliary. A structure for (47) is (48):

(47)   He **hasn't been doing** his homework.

(48)

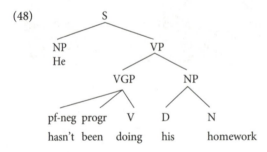

Other structures have been suggested with a less flat structure but they are still controversial and would lead us into a new set of arguments.

4.   Finiteness

The sentences we have discussed so far have been complete sentences, not sentence fragments. A complete sentence consists of a subject and a finite verb. A finite verb in English agrees with the subject (in the present tense) and indicates present or past. Its subject has nominative case, which can only be seen in the case of pronouns in Modern English, i.e. the subject pronoun of finite verbs must be nominative *I, you, he, she, it, we* and *they*, not accusative *me, him, her, us* or *them* (*you* and *it* are both nominative and accusative).

Finite sentences have a Verb Group with a finite verb as its first (or only) member. In (49), *have* is the finite verb that makes the entire Verb Group finite. As a result, the entire sentence is also finite:

(49)   I [**have** been going] there frequently. (finite *have* in a VGP)

Have is finite because it shows subject agreement (*have* rather than *has*, as in (50)), indicates present tense (*have* rather than *had*, as in (51)), and has a nominative subject (*I* rather than *me*, as in the ungrammatical (52)):

(50)   He has been going there frequently.
(51)   He had been going there frequently.
(52)   *Me have been going there frequently.

Note that in some varieties of English, sentences such as (52) are grammatical.

Modals, as in (53), are finite even though (for historical reasons) they never display subject-verb agreement:

(53)   I **might** have done that.

Only finite sentences are complete sentences. Most of us, however, use fragments in informal speech, in poetry, e.g. John Keats in the excerpt in (54), or even in formal writing:

(54)   *Ode on a Grecian Urn*
        Thou still unravish'd bride of quietness!
        Thou foster-child of silence and slow time,

        ...

        What mad pursuit? What struggle to escape?
        What pipes and timbrels? What wild ecstacy?

Nevertheless, incomplete sentences are generally frowned upon in formal writing. Sentence (55) below is not a complete sentence but is a sentence fragment. How can it be fixed?

(55)   Mentioning that point about finite sentences yesterday.

Sentence (55) can become a full sentence by adding a subject and a finite verb as in (56):

(56)   I was mentioning that point about finite sentences yesterday.

As will be shown in a later chapter, non-finite sentences can only be part of other sentences. It is always a good idea to count the number of lexical verbs. For instance, how many lexical verbs are there in (57)?

(57)   I have heard her sing too often.

In (57), there are two lexical verbs, *heard* and *sing*, but only the first Verb Group is finite since *have* is finite (e.g. the subject of *have* is nominative *I*). The Verb Group that *sing* is the sole member of is non-finite since its subject is accusative *her*.

Other sentences that include a non-finite Verb Group are (58) and (59), with the non-finite Verb Groups in bold. Note that the infinitive marker *to* is part of the Verb Group, and is abbreviated as 'inf':

(58)   **Seeing** the ordinary as extraordinary is something we all like to do.
(59)   She forgot **to google** them.

In (58), *seeing, is, like,* and *do* are lexical verbs, but only *is* and *like* are finite. In (59), *forgot* and *google* are the lexical verbs, but only *forgot* is finite.

A sentence can contain many Verb Groups, a (potentially) indefinite number if, as mentioned in Chapter 1, the speaker had enough energy and could continue. Sentences such as (60), containing more than one Verb Group, are discussed in Chapters 7, 8, and 10:

(60)   I noticed that she mentioned that he was saying that she should tell him …

Imperatives are used to order someone to do something. They often lack a subject, as in (61), but this need not be the case, as (62) shows:

(61)   Draw the trees for these sentences.
(62)   You, draw trees for this.

Imperatives are complete sentences and not sentence fragments.

5.   Relating the terms for verbs (optional)

In this section, I'll review all the terms we have used for verbs. First, we will discuss regular and irregular forms. These are relevant when forming a past tense or using a participle. When we use a participle, we may label its Verb Group as present, past, or future perfect. Then, we will see that the classification of verbs into e.g. transitive and of auxiliaries into e.g. modal belongs to a different type of classification. Finally, we add finiteness to the mix. This is quite a lot! So just try to read this section and don't worry too much about connecting all the terms.

We have briefly talked about regular and irregular verbs (end of Section 2 of Chapter 4). Regular verbs have a predictable form, as in *I walk, you walk, s/he walks, we walked*, and *they have walked*. If you are a native speaker of English, you know that third person singular present tense has *-s*, the past tense has *-ed*, and the past participle has *-ed* too. If you invent a new verb, you will use these endings without hesitation. Irregular verbs are unpredictable; they were once more regular but because of changes in the language, they now need to be learned, as Figure 6.4 shows.

Baby Blues

Figure 6.4. *Drawed* and *drew*. (Used with the permission of the Baby Blues Partnership and King Features Syndicate in conjunction with the Cartoonist Group. All rights reserved.)

Some people make a distinction between weak verbs (such as *walk*), strong verbs where the vowel changes in the past (such as *draw*), and irregular ones (such as *go*, with its past *went*). Many others just distinguish regular (the weak ones) from irregular verbs (the strong and irregular ones).

The ending is used to build the tense and aspect forms of English that we have seen in Figures 6.1 and 6.2. Thus the present perfect uses a present tense auxiliary (and *have* is irregular) and the past participle ending of another verb. The latter can be regular, as in the case of *walked*, or irregular, as in the case of *gone*. I list a few of the regular ones in (63a) and the irregular forms in (63b):

		present	past	past participle	
(63)	a.	walk(s)	walked	walked	(regular)
		love(s)	loved	loved	
		hike(s)	hiked	hiked	
	b.	go(es)	went,	gone	(irregular)[4]
		begin(s)	began	begun	
		sing(s)	sang	sung	
		write(s)	wrote	written	
		put(s)	put	put	

---

4.   Consult a dictionary (or the internet) for longer lists of irregular verbs.

I have suggested to not worry too much about the names of all the tense and aspect combinations (see Figure 6.5 below for even more names).

Whether a verb is regular or irregular or used as past or present is not connected to its classification as intransitive or transitive. We have divided verbs in Chapters 4 and 5 into intransitive, transitive, ditransitive, copula, complex transitive, phrasal and prepositional verbs. These can be either regular or irregular and most can be used in all the tense and aspect combinations discussed. Auxiliaries are irregular: modals only have one form, the progressive and passive auxiliary *be* is the most irregular, as is shown in (64a), and so is perfect *have*, as shown in (64b):

		present	past	past participle
(64)	a.	am, is, are	was, were	been
	b.	has, have	had	had

The copula *be* and transitive *have* work the same way of course.

Finally, we have used finite and non-finite to label verbs. The present and past forms of verbs (*am, was, sings,* etc) are always finite and the past participle (*been*) and present participle (*being*) always non-finite. Sometimes, it is hard to distinguish the simple past (e.g. *had*) from the past participle (e.g. *had*) and you have to look at the sentence. Remember that as long as one finite verb is present, the entire VGP is finite, as is the entire sentence.

6.   Conclusion

In summary, this chapter has classified the different kinds of auxiliary verbs: the modal, perfect, progressive, and passive which occur in this order; *do* is added in questions and negative sentences when an auxiliary is not available. Several names for tenses, such as the present perfect and past progressive, are also provided. I would suggest that, unless you are going to teach them, to just ignore the names and have some sense for these terms and what they mean on timelines (see also Exercise G).

Finiteness is also discussed: a verb is finite if it agrees with the subject and if this subject bears nominative case. Since finite verbs and their relationship to lexical and auxiliary verbs are often challenging, I end with a list of examples in Table 6.3. The clauses are indicated by brackets but their use will not be explained till the next chapter. For now, remember that if you have a lexical verb, there is a clause.

Notice that each sentence has at least one finite verb in Table 6.3.

Table 6.3. Some finite (in **bold**), lexical, and auxiliary verbs (<u>underlined</u>)

1.	[Those people	**<u>could</u>** AUX modal	<u>have</u> AUX perfect	<u>been</u> AUX progressive	<u>goofing</u> off]. lexical phrasal

1. [Those people **<u>could</u>** <u>have</u> <u>been</u>   <u>goofing</u> off].
   AUX   AUX   AUX   lexical
   modal   perfect   progressive   phrasal

2. [He   **<u>has</u>** <u>been</u>   <u>wanting</u>   [to <u>go</u> there for ages]].
   AUX   AUX   lexical   lexical
   perfect   progressive   transitive   intransitive

3. [I **<u>mentioned</u>** [that it   **<u>had</u> been**   <u>said</u> [that she **<u>wished</u>** [to <u>leave</u>]]]].
   lexical   AUX AUX   lexical   lexical   lexical
   transitive   perfect passive   transitive   transitive intransitive

4. [I **<u>saw</u>** [him <u>giving</u> her a present]].
   lexical   lexical
   transitive   ditransitive

5. [[<u>Feeling</u> fine], he **<u>left</u>** early   [to <u>put</u> dinner on the stove]].
   lexical   lexial   lexical
   copula   intransitive   complex transitive

Key terms are **auxiliary and lexical verb; affix; participle; modal, perfect, progressive, and passive; regular and irregular verbs; finite and non-finite; nominative case, and tense.**

Exercises

A.   Identify the auxiliary/ies in (65) to (68), e.g. are they passive, or modal? List the finite
verbs as well:

(65)   Rigobertha has been meeting Carlos.
(66)   Belo and Horta were awarded the Nobel Peace Prize.
(67)   Indonesia was not too happy with the decision.
(68)   They may be bringing about a peaceful solution in East Timor.

B.   Identify the auxiliaries (e.g. modal, passive) in the passage from Chapter 2, repeated here.
Again, list the finite verbs as well:

Granny was waiting at the door of the apartment. She looked small, lonely, and patient,
and at the sight of her the children and their mother felt instantly guilty. Instead of
driving straight home from the airport, they had stopped outside Nice for ice cream.
They might have known how much those extra twenty minutes would mean to Granny.

C.   Think up a sentence with a perfect and a passive auxiliary.

D.   Add a progressive auxiliary to: *He might go.* Now add a perfect as well.
Take out the perfect in *He could have been going.*

E.   Read the two poems below. Then, compare the use of the verbs: lexical as opposed to
auxiliary, and finite as opposed to non-finite. What is the effect of this different verb use?

As the cat	Fire and Ice
climbed over	
the top of	Some say the world will end in fire,
	Some say in ice.
the jamcloset	From what I've tasted of desire
first the right	I hold with those who favor fire.
forefoot	
	But if it had to perish twice,
carefully	I think I know enough of hate
then the hind	To say that for destruction ice
stepped down	Is also great
	And would suffice.
into the pit of	
the empty	Robert Frost (1874–1963); www.bartleby.com
flowerpot	

william carlos williams (1883–1963)

Optional (Section 5)

F.   In the following list of verbs, identify the irregular ones:
     wait, become, see, look, take, lead, grow, hang, light, run, garden, paint, and *drive.*

Class discussion

G.   In Sections 2.2 and 2.3, I have given simplified timelines to the different tenses and
     aspects. There are a few more possibilities that I have added together with the previous
     ones in Figure 6.5. Discuss these in class and perhaps draw some of your own timelines.

H.   If you have access to the internet in class, search for some sites with irregular verbs. They
     vary enormously in number. What is the largest number you can find.

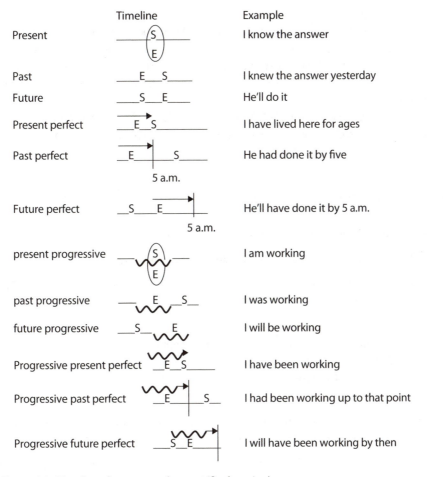

Figure 6.5. Timelines for tense and aspect (final version)

Keys to the exercises

A.   *has* (perfect) and *been* (progressive) in (65); *were* (passive) in (66); no auxiliaries in (67); *may* (modal) and *be* (progressive) in (68).
Finite verbs: in (65), *has*; in (66), *were*; in (67), *was*; in (68), *may*.

B.   Granny was (progressive) waiting at the door of the apartment. She looked small, lonely, and patient, and at the sight of her the children and their mother felt instantly guilty. Instead of driving straight home from the airport, they had (perfect) stopped outside Nice for ice cream. They might (modal) have (perfect) known how much those extra twenty minutes would (modal) mean to Granny.
Finite are: was, looked, felt, had, might, would

C.   He has been seen.

D.   He might be going.
He might have been going.
He could be going.

E.   In the first poem, there are 2 finite lexical verbs; in the second, there are 12 lexical and 4 auxiliary verbs, and only 1 Verb Group is non-finite. Note also that in the second poem, a number of nouns are somewhat verbal, e.g. *hate, destruction, fire,* and *desire*. They are either based on a verb or can be used as a verb. Discuss the effects of the verb use on the tone of the poems.

F.   Irregular are: *become, see, take, lead, grow, hang* (can also be regular), *light* (can also be regular), *run,* and *drive*. You can tell this by thinking of the past and participle forms, e.g. *become* has *became* and *become* respectively.

Special topic: Reduction of *have* and the shape of participles

The prescriptive rule against contraction can be formulated as follows:

(69)   In formal writing, **do not contract auxiliaries and negatives**.

Most people do not fully spell out the auxiliaries in speech or informal writing. Thus, *have* in (70) becomes *'ve* or *a*, as in (71), or even *of*, as in (72):

(70)   I **should have** done that sooner.

(71)   Now, that's someone who they **shoulda** kept out the sun.
(COCA-Fiction 2008)

(72)   He **should of** said something.
(COCA-fiction 1994)

Reduction of *have* is typically done by speakers when *have* is in fact an auxiliary as in (71) and (72), not when it is a main verb, as in (73), formed from (74):

(73)   *He shoulda books in his office.

(74)   He should have books in his office.

Reduction of auxiliaries has occurred since medieval times. Sentences (75) to (79) are from the 15th and 16th centuries, where the reduced forms of *have* are in bold:

(75)　*it xuld **a** be seyd*
　　　'It should have been said'. (*Paston Letters*, #131 year 1449)

(76)　*3e wold **a** be plesyd*
　　　'You would have been pleased'. (*Paston Letters*, #176 year 1464)

(77)　*there xuld not **a** be do so mykele*
　　　'There should not have been done so much.' (*Paston Letters*, #205 year 1469)

(78)　So would I **ha** done by yonder Sunne.
　　　(Shakespeare, *Hamlet*, IV, 5, 65 First Folio Edition 1623)

(79)　I know you **ha'** practised vpon the easie-yeelding spirit of this woman.
　　　(Shakespeare, 2 Henry 4, II, 1, 126)

Hence, even though the reduction of *have* to *of* and *-a* is common in speech nowadays (and was common in writing in earlier times), it is 'not done' in formal writing. Since perfect *have* is weakening, we find sentences such as (80):

(80)　I feel that American Express **should of not have** paid once they received my call and emails of the merchandise not working. (google – complaints site)

As mentioned, the perfect auxiliary *have* and the passive auxiliary *be* are followed by a past participle. This rule is often violated. Remember the discussion of *lie* and *lay* (with participles as *lain* and *laid* respectively) in Chapter 4? Other instances are the past participles *bitten* and *gone*. They are often replaced by the past tense, as in (81) and (82), but this use is not prescriptively correct in Modern English even though it occurs in writers such as Milton, as in (83), Dryden, Pope, Addison, and Swift:

(81)　Some mosquito **has bit** me.

(82)　I **should have went** to Medical School at the U of A. (overheard on ASU campus)

(83)　According to his doom: **he would have spoke**,
　　　But hiss for hiss return'd with forked tongue. (Milton, *Paradise Lost*, X, 517–8)

Two other comments can be made about the forms of the participle. First, in earlier stages of English, the affix was often not present, as in (84) and (85). It is not clear what caused that absence:

(84)　What have I **do**? (Chaucer, *Miller's Tale*, 3739)

(85)　If I so ofte myghte have **ywedded be**. (Chaucer, *Wife of Bath's Prol.* 7)

Secondly, the present participle is preceded by the auxiliary *be*, as we have seen in Section 2.3, but in many varieties of English, this participle has a prefix, as in (86). Most frequently, the verb preceding it is *go*, as in (87) from an English folksong, or *keep*:

(86)　He **was a**-working

(87)　A Frog he **went a**-courting.

The *a*-prefix is the remnant of an older *on* that marked the progressive.

Review of Chapters 4–6

I'll start with Chapter 6. In this chapter, the Verb Group (VGP) is examined more carefully: a Verb Group contains at least a lexical verb but can also contain one or more auxiliaries. Verbs (and Verb Groups) are either finite or non-finite. If verbs express tense and have a nominative subject, they are finite; if not, they are non-finite. Some verbs are irregular in form. That affects the shape of, for instance, their simple past and present perfect.

In Chapters 4 and 5, functions at sentence level are discussed: subject, predicate, direct object, indirect object, phrasal object, prepositional object, subject predicate, and object predicate. These are obligatory parts of the sentence. Verbs are classified in terms of whether or not they have obligatory complements: intransitives do not but transitives, ditransitives, copulas, complex transitives, phrasal and prepositional verbs do.

In contrast to complements, adverbials function to add background and can be added to a sentence optionally and without limitation (except for the speaker's and hearer's level of patience and memory). The difference between direct object, indirect object, phrasal object, and prepositional object on the one hand and subject predicate, object predicate, and adverbial on the other is that the former can be passivized. As a reminder, I'll provide a list of the major verb types with a simple tree for each. Review the Tables of Chapters 4 and 5 as well.

(1)   **Intransitive: no objects**

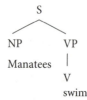

(2)   **(Mono)transitive: one direct object**

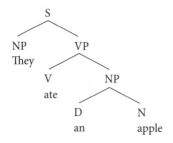

(3)   **Ditransitive: one direct and one indirect object**

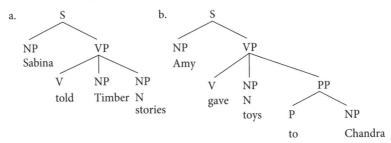

(4)   **Copula: one subject predicate**

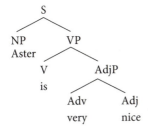

(5)   **Complex Predicate: one direct object and an object predicate**

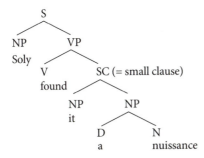

(6)   **Prepositional object verb: one PP object**

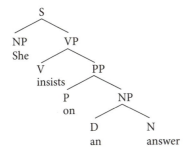

(7)   **Phrasal: no object if intransitive, as in (7a); one direct object if transitive, as in (7b).**

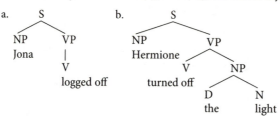

Examples of midterm exams covering Chapters 4 to 6

Example 1

A.   In Text A, list (or underline) the lexical verbs and label them as e.g. transitive, complex transitive, or phrasal verb.

B.   List the adverbials, subjects, and direct objects in paragraph 1 of Text A.

C.   List the auxiliary verbs in paragraph 2. Are they modal, perfect, progressive, or passive?

D.   Circle the finite verbs in the complete text.

E.   Are any of the verbs irregular?

F.   Draw a tree for:

(8)   Spain was the target at the end of the century

Text A (adapted from: *The Good Neighbor*, by G. Black).
Ever since the US Civil War, the countries of Central America and the Caribbean have occupied a special place in the American psyche. Cuba, Nicaragua, Panama and their neighbors have been a magnet for adventurers and pioneers, a proving ground for grand abstractions of democracy and freedom, and frequently they have given scoundrels a refuge. For most of the twentieth century people knew them as "banana republics"; by the 1980s, a chain of clothing stores serving affluent customers in today's travel-mad world had adopted that name.

This was frontier territory, a land where the whim of the adventurer was often the only law, where Americans had limitless prerogatives, and where people considered outside intruders malicious. Senator Hannegan of Indiana saw something else. He saw Britain hastening 'with race-horse speed' to seize all of Central America. Spain was the target of similar suspicion at the end of the century, but was succeeded in turn by Germany, Mexico and the Soviet Union. Each of these foreign powers was charged with importing ideologies alien to the natural order of the region.

Example 2

A.   Find all the lexical verbs and classify them (monotransitive, phrasal, etc.) in Text B, a text from a few years ago, but in many respects still relevant.

B.   Find all the complements and classify them (direct object, indirect object, subject predicate, etc.). How are they realized (NP, PP, AdvP, etc.)?

C.   Point out the auxiliary verbs and classify them. Also circle or list the finite verbs.

D.   Are *result*, *kill*, and *carry* regular or irregular verbs?

E.   Draw a tree for:

(9)   Continued hostilities have resulted in terrible abuses inside Afghanistan.

Text B. Afghanistan troubles
Continued hostilities have resulted in catastrophic human rights abuses inside Afghanistan. All warring factions have carried out attacks against residential areas. The factions have targeted civilians. They have killed tens of thousands of people in various parts of the country. The vast majority of the victims have been Kabul residents. Previous attacks against Kabul stopped when the Taleban forces entered Kabul about five months ago. Now, Taleban has threatened a bombardment. This will leave many people dead and many more wounded.

(adapted from an Amnesty International document)

Example 3

A.   List or circle the finite verbs in the second paragraph of Text C.

B.   List and identify the lexical verbs (transitive, intransitive, etc.) and the auxiliary verbs (passive, perfect, etc.) in the first paragraph.

C.   Draw a tree for (10). First, indicate the functions and names/labels by means of brackets.

(10)   They met in Paris at the beginning of the 20th century.

D.   What is the function and name/label (i.e. realization) of the following phrases in the sentences in which they occur:

(11)   a brilliant success (first paragraph).
(12)   Picasso's arrival (second paragraph).

Text C (adapted from an article in Arizona State University's *State Press*)
Imagine if Steve Martin wrote a comedic concept play with the entirely possible idea that Pablo Picasso and Albert Einstein could have met in Paris at the beginning of the twentieth century in a small bistro. He has succeeded, and the Arizona Theatre Company's production of *Picasso at the Lapin Agile* is a brilliant success. Martin has created a hilarious and thought provoking look at two geniuses.

The play begins with Einstein and several other patrons discussing the probability that Picasso would venture into the bistro. Einstein is anticipating Picasso's arrival. The players discuss everything from physics to the letter 'E'. The play abounds with Steve Martin's bizarre philosophies and even stranger sense of humor.

Questions that are not related to the text:

E.　Explain (using terminology used in class and in Chapter 5) why the following sentence is ungrammatical:

(13)　*Down the president she ran.

F.　Add passive auxiliaries to the following sentences (and make the appropriate changes):

(14)　Picasso may have played a part.
(15)　Einstein is looking at Picasso.

Key to example 1

A.　The lexical verbs in the first paragraph are *occupied* (transitive), *been* (copula), *given* (ditransitive), *knew* (complex transitive), *serving* (transitive; this is tricky), *adopted* (transitive) and in the second paragraph: *was* (copula), *was* (copula), *had* (transitive), *considered* (complex transitive), *saw* (transitive), *saw* (transitive), *hastening* (intransitive), *seize* (transitive), *was* (copula), *succeeded* (transitive, but here passivized), *charged* (complex transitive, but passivized), and *importing* (transitive).

B.　The adverbials are: *Ever since the US Civil War, (in the American psyche), frequently, For most of the twentieth century, by the 1980s, (and in today's travel-mad world)*. The PPs in parentheses could also modify *place* and *customers* respectively.
　　The subjects are: *the countries of Central America and the Caribbean, Cuba, Nicaragua, Panama and their neighbors, they, people,* and *a chain of clothing stores serving affluent customers (in today's travel-mad world)*. The direct objects are: *a special place (in the American psyche), a refuge, them,* and *that name* and the sole indirect object is *scoundrels*. The only subject predicate is long: *a magnet for adventurers and pioneers, a proving ground for grand abstractions of democracy and freedom* and the object predicate is: *as "banana republics"*.

C.　The auxiliaries are *had* (perfect), *was* (passive), and *was* (passive).

D.　The finite verbs are: Ever since the US Civil War, the countries of Central America and the Caribbean (have) occupied a special place in the American psyche. Cuba, Nicaragua, Panama and their neighbors (have) been a magnet for adventurers and pioneers, a proving ground for grand abstractions of democracy and freedom, and frequently they (have) given scoundrels a refuge. For most of the twentieth century people (knew) them as "banana republics"; by the 1980s, a chain of clothing stores serving affluent customers in today's travel-mad world (had) adopted that name.
　　This (was) frontier territory, a land where the whim of the adventurer (was) often the only law, where Americans (had) limitless prerogatives, and where people (considered) outside intruders malicious. Senator Hannegan of Indiana (saw) something else. He (saw) Britain hastening 'with race-horse speed' to seize all of Central America. Spain (was) the target of similar suspicion at the end of the

century, but (was) succeeded in turn by Germany, Mexico and the Soviet Union. Each of these foreign powers (was) charged with importing ideologies alien to the natural order of the region.

E.   The irregular verbs are auxiliaries *have* (three times), *had, was* (twice), and copula *be* (four times), the ditransitive *give*, the complex transitive *know*, the transitive *see* (twice).

F.

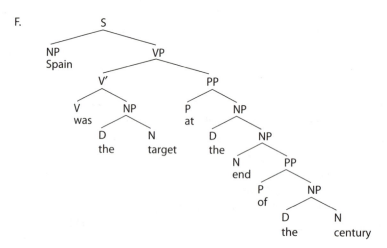

Key to example 2

A.   *resulted*: prepositional verb; *carried out*: phrasal; *targeted*: transitive; *killed*: transitive; *been*: copula; *stopped*: intransitive; *entered*: transitive; *threatened*: transitive; and *leave*: complex transitive.

B.   *in catastrophic human rights abuses (inside Afghanistan)*: prepositional object/PP; *attacks against residential areas*: phrasal object/NP; *civilians*: direct object/NP; *tens of thousands of people*: direct object/NP; *Kabul residents*: subject predicate/NP; *Kabul*: direct object/NP; *a bombardment*: direct object/NP; *many people*: direct object/NP; *dead*: object predicate/AdjP; *many more*: direct object/NP; and *wounded*: object predicate/AdjP.

C.   Auxiliaries: five instances of *have* (perfect), one *has* (perfect), and one *will* (modal). The finite verbs are five instances of *have*, one *stopped, entered, has* and *will*.

D.   regular.

E.

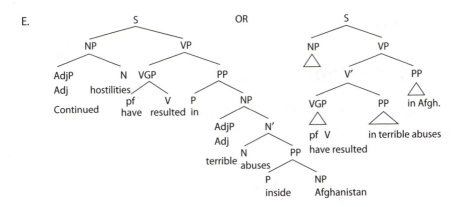

Key to example 3

A.   The finite verbs are: *begins, would, is, discuss,* and *abounds.*

B.   *Imagine*: transitive, *wrote*: transitive, *met*: (here) intransitive, *succeeded*: intransitive, *is*: copula, and *created*: transitive.

C.

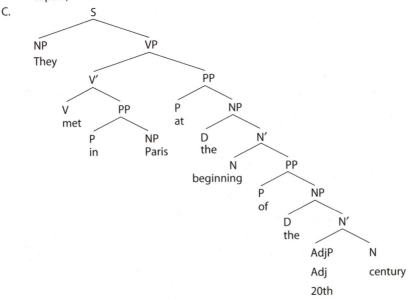

D.   SuPr: NP; DO: NP

E.   The *run down* in *She ran him down* is a phrasal verb and the particle cannot be separate from the verb.

F.   A part may have been played by Picasso; Picasso is being looked at by Einstein.

Chapter 7

Finite clauses
Embedded and coordinated

1. Sentences and clauses
2. The functions of clauses
3. The structure of the embedded clause:
   The Complementizer Phrase (CP)
4. Coordinate sentences:
   The Coordinator Phrase (CP)?
5. Terminological labyrinth and conclusion

So far, the sentences we have focussed on have included one lexical verb and one or more auxiliaries. These are simple sentences. This chapter gives examples of sentences that include more than one lexical verb, which means that they are composed of more than one clause. Sentences that are part of another sentence, i.e. that have a function in that sentence, are often referred to as embedded clauses, where the embedded clause is seen as subordinate to the other.

There are also coordinated clauses. They involve at least two clauses (and two lexical verbs) that are joined by *and* (or another coordinator) and both coordinated clauses are of (almost) equal importance. Both embedded and coordinated constructions enable us to make very long sentences (infinite if we have the energy) and ones we had never heard before.

Section 1 provides some examples of complex clauses and Section 2 discusses functions, such as subject, object, and adverbial, as they relate to clauses. In Section 3, I introduce the structure of the embedded clause, making use of the grammatical category complementizer and the Complementizer Phrase (abbreviated as CP). In Section 4, I do the same for coordinated clauses by using the coordinator to form a Coordinator Phrase (also abbreviated as CP). Section 5 reviews some of the terminology.

1.   Sentences and clauses

A simple clause contains one lexical verb. Hence, if there are two lexical verbs, there are two clauses. For instance, in (1), the lexical verbs are *noticed* and *like* and hence, there are two clauses: the main clause (*I should have noticed that Zelda doesn't like Zoltan*) and the embedded one (*Zelda doesn't like Zoltan*). This can be indicated by means of brackets:

(1)   [I should have **noticed** [that Zelda doesn't **like** Zoltan]].

In determining the clauses in a text, it will be helpful to first identify the lexical verbs and then to draw the brackets around the clauses.

The embedded clause in (1) is part of the main clause. We could split it up into two clauses, as in (2), but that is awkward:

(2)   I should have noticed it. Zelda doesn't like Zoltan.

Auxiliaries, such as *should* and *does* in (1) and (2), are not relevant for determining the number of clauses or sentences; only lexical verbs are. How many main verbs are there in the middle frame of Figure 7.1?

Figure 7.1. A pony (Used with the permission of the Baby Blues Partnership and King Features Syndicate in conjunction with the Cartoonist Group. All rights reserved.)

If I counted right, there are ten. If you really want a pony, that may not be so many!

In a coordinated sentence, there are also two lexical verbs (or more, if more clauses are coordinated or if one of them contains an embedded clause) but they are joined by a coordinator. Thus, in (3), we have the main verbs *arrived* and *ate* and the coordinator *and*:

(3)   [The food **arrived**] and [they **ate**].
       (COCA – fiction 1995)

As we'll see, it is easier to divide (3) into two separate clauses than (1) and that is because coordinated clauses have a looser connection.

Some linguists call the larger sentence in (1) the sentence or main clause and the smaller sentence the embedded sentence, dependent, or subordinate clause. In Section 5, I list some of these terms. I will use both clause and sentence interchangeably to indicate a unit that contains a lexical verb. The complementizer *that* in (1) functions to link the embedded sentence to the main clause, but can often be left out in English. Try that in (1). For a list of complementizers, look back to Chapter 2, Table 2.5.

In (1), both clauses have a VP containing a finite verb, i.e. *should* and *does* (remember auxiliaries can be finite), but embedded sentences can be non-finite as well. In this chapter, I discuss the clauses with finite VPs and in the next chapter those with non-finite VPs. Be careful not to confuse finite verbs, such as *should* or *does*, with lexical verbs, such as *noticed* and *like*: each clause must have a lexical verb, but each clause need not have a finite verb.

2.   The functions of clauses

As mentioned, embedded clauses function inside another clause as subject, direct or phrasal object, subject predicate, or adverbial. For instance, in (1) above, the embedded clause functions as direct object; in (4), it is a subject; in (5), a subject predicate; in (6), a phrasal object; and in (7), an adverbial. The embedded clauses are indicated by means of brackets here:

(4)   [That she left] was nice.   (embedded subject)
(5)   The problem is [that she reads junk].   (embedded subject predicate)
(6)   I figured out [that it didn't work].   (embedded phrasal object)
(7)   He read books [because it was required]. (embedded adverbial)

Embedded clauses do not function as indirect objects or as objects of prepositional objects. They do not function as object predicates either. Inside an NP or AdjP, clauses function as modifiers (e.g. relative clauses) or complements (e.g. noun complements). Examples of relative and complement clauses will be given in Chapter 10.

Coordinated clauses have no function in another clause. They are on an equal footing, most argue, with each other. In (3), this means that you could even make them into two independent clauses, as in (8), and although that sounds very 'choppy', it is still better than (2):

(8)   The food arrived. They ate.

We'll now turn to the tree structures.

3. The structure of the embedded clause: The Complementizer Phrase (CP)

As mentioned, embedded sentences have complementizers that connect the embedded clause to another clause. These complementizers are sisters to S and a sentence with a complementizer is a Complementizer Phrase, abbreviated as CP. The CP, as in (9), expresses that there is a sentence S that can be independent, i.e. occur on its own but, when it functions in another sentence, it is glued to that sentence by the C. The C determines the nature of the phrase above the C and S, namely the CP:

(9)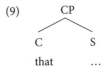

Unlike the S, the CP cannot appear on its own, since a sentence such as (10) is a fragment:

(10)   That he went to the store.

Using CP, C, and S, a sentence such as (1), has a structure as in (11). I have slightly simplified (1) by taking the auxiliaries out:

(11)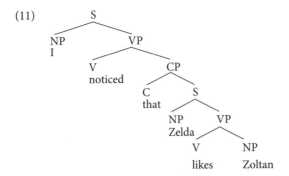

Using a CP makes it possible to include the complementizer in the sentence and link the embedded S to the main S. In (11), the embedded CP is the sister to *noticed*, which means that it functions as the direct object to *noticed*.

There are also embedded clauses that express questions. In these, the C position can be occupied by *if* or by *whether*, as in (12). The CP here, as in (11), functions as a direct object:

(12)

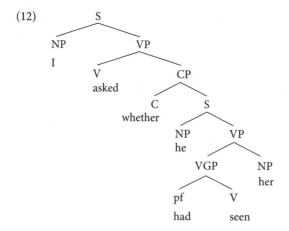

Trees for a CP as subject and a subject predicate clause are given in (13) and (14) respectively:

(13)

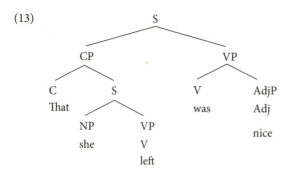

(14)

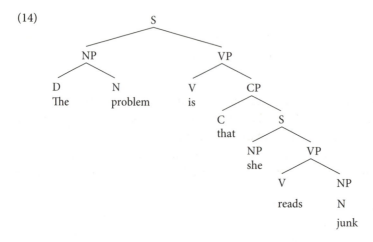

Other examples of complementizers are *because, before, after, unless*, and *since*. These particular complementizers are often used to introduce adverbial clauses. An example of an embedded adverbial is given in (15):

(15)

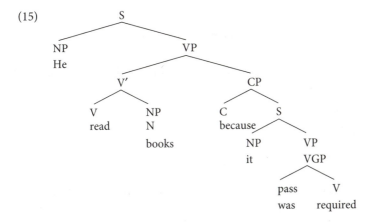

The position of clauses functioning as adverbials, like that of non-clausal adverbials, is very flexible. For instance, in a sentence such as (15), the *because*-clause can also precede *he read books*, as in (16):

(16)   Because it was required, he read books.

We will assume that the tree structure for this is as in a sentence with an S-adverbial, discussed in Chapter 5, namely, as in (17). However, other trees are possible:

(17)

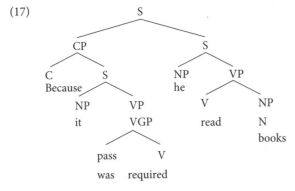

Sentences containing embedded subjects, such as (4) above, are often changed into extraposed sentences, such as (18). The reason for the extraposition of the subject clause is that speakers do not like to have embedded sentences in the beginning or middle of the main clause. The dummy subject *it* takes the place of the extraposed clause:

(18)   It was nice [that she left].

I'll refrain from drawing a tree here, but if you want to draw one, attach the extraposed CP as if it were an S-adverbial.

After seeing a C and CP, some of you might have wondered if there is a C′ as well. There is, and we will briefly mention this in Chapter 11. Until then, we will draw the CP with just a C and S. Now, we'll continue with the structure of the coordinate clause.

4.   Coordinate sentences: The Coordinator Phrase (CP)?

As in the case of coordinate phrases (discussed in Chapter 3), there is a debate over how best to represent coordinate sentences, such as (3) above. I think (3) is similar to (19) in that there is a connection between the two clauses. In (20), on the other hand, the two clauses have no causal relationship (at least not one obvious to me):

(19)   [She arrived] and [he left].
(20)   [Phoenix is a city in Arizona] and [the moon is made of cheese].

We could argue that sentences that are more closely connected have a coordinator *and* that really means 'and then'. Then, the second clause is subordinate to the first and the structure of (19) would be similar to the adverbial clause in (15) above. I have represented that as (21), where *and he left* would function as an adverbial to the main clause:

(21)

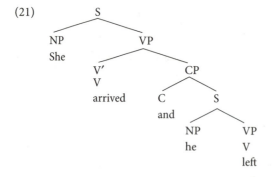

In (20), neither clause is subordinate to the other. This could be represented as (22):

(22)

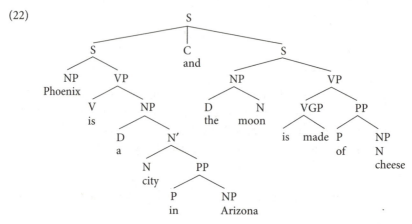

I leave it to the reader to decide whether (21) or (22) is more appropriate for (19) and (20) (see Chapter 3, Section 4, for more arguments).

Coordinated structures, especially the ones with a closer connection between the clauses, often leave out the second subject if it is identical to the first, as in (23). This is analyzed as ellipsis, i.e. deletion, of the second subject. In a tree, you could leave this as a blank space. It is possible to repeat the subject, as in (24), or use a pronoun but this is only done if you want to emphasize the subject:

(23)   [Streams of people arrived] and [ate arctic anchovies].
(24)   [Streams of people arrived] and [streams of people ate arctic anchovies].

As an alternative to analyzing (23) as a case of ellipsis, you could argue that it involves the coordination of two VPs, as in (25). Again, I leave that to you to decide:

(25)

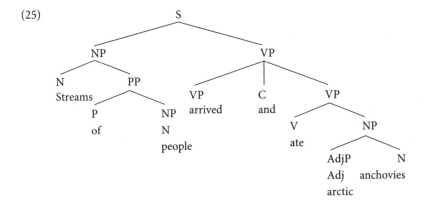

In this section, I have used the coordinator *and* since that is the most frequent. In some kinds of writing, it is the third most frequent word (after the articles *a* and *the*, and usually in competition with the prepositions *to* and *of*). Other, less frequent coordinators are *(n)or, (n)either, so* and *but*.

5.   Terminological labyrinth and conclusion

In this concluding section, I will list some synonyms or near synonyms for terms related to clauses that are used in the grammatical tradition. Remember that, in this book, the terms clause and sentence are used interchangeably. Grammar has existed for thousands of years and hence there are many terms that have come to be used. I am sorry about that. We need a United Nations decision on this but, for the moment, perhaps Table 7.1 helps.

Table 7.1. Terms for clause

sentence = main clause = matrix clause = independent clause = superordinate clause = S
clause = embedded clause/sentence = dependent/subordinate clause = CP (Complementizer Phrase)
complementizer = subordinating conjunction = subordinator = C
clause = coordinated clause = coordinated sentence = CP (Coordinator Phrase)
coordinator = coordinating conjunction = C

Note that a main clause always has to be finite but that an embedded clause can be finite or non-finite.

In conclusion, this chapter discusses sentences that contain more than one lexical verb. These are of two types, embedded and coordinated. Embedded clauses are part of another clause and typically function as subject, direct object, or adverbial in that clause. Examples are given of all the functions that clauses have as well as of their trees. There can be more than one embedded clause in a main clause, and sometimes clauses are extraposed. We represent embedded clauses as CPs (Complementizer Phrases), and these consist of a complementizer C and an S.

Coordinated sentences are like independent sentences but are combined with a coordinator, such as *and*. Two possible structures are suggested, one when the two clauses are dependent on each other and another when that's not the case. The reader is invited to choose for him- or herself depending on the kind of sentence. There is also a brief discussion of subject ellipsis which may occur when the subject in coordinate sentences is identical. Here too, there is an alternative analysis.

Key terms are **clause and sentence; main clause/sentence; embedded and coordinate, CP, S, and C; complementizer; coordinator; ellipsis;** and **extraposition.**

Exercises

A.   Find the lexical verbs in the sentences below (adapted from the *London Times*, http://www.timesonline.co.uk/tol/news/uk/article509889.ece). After that, put brackets around the clause that goes with each of these verbs.

(26)   Mr. Bell, the Chief Inspector of Schools in England, finds that classroom discipline is worse since the current government took office several years ago.

(27)   The proportion of secondary schools with good pupil behavior has fallen from three quarters to two thirds, while 9 per cent have serious discipline problems.

(28)   The Chief Inspector worries that so many of the 60 per cent of youngsters from non-professional backgrounds lack the ambition or qualifications to go to university a quarter of a century after he became the first in his family to do so.

(29)   Access to good schools is the key. Mr. Bell highlights unacceptable levels of variability in the performance of state schools.

(30)   He focuses particularly on the 10 per cent that make little or no improvement between inspection visits.

(31)   Because children in these schools are effectively being written off, it is little wonder that many suffer the greatest problems with discipline.

B.   Underline the lexical verbs and put brackets around the clauses that go with them in the following text, adapted from http://www.eva.mpg.de/psycho/dogs/dogs_research.html.

One aim of the Department of Comparative and Developmental Psychology is the investigation of the evolution of different cognitive processes. The comparative approach includes the study of a variety of animal species. Although most of our work is done with the great apes, we also investigate other species such as goats, seals, and dogs. For a number of reasons, the domestic dog (*Canis familiaris*) is a very interesting model for investigating different questions regarding the evolution of cognitive abilities. The fact that dogs have been living with humans for at least 15.000 years may have led to the selection of cognitive abilities by humans or even the co-evolution of dogs' cognitive abilities with those of humans. We know from different studies that dogs are sensitive to the attentional state of humans. We also know that dogs understand communicative cues. Those abilities have not been found in nonhuman primates and wolves.

C.   Draw trees for:

(32)   Zelda noticed that candies disappear.
(33)   They suggested that the sketch was done by daughters of the architect.
(34)   They fussed that the unpleasant computer was down again.
(35)   They purified books because they didn't like them.

(36)   I heard that a manuscript has been stolen.

(37)   Amir didn't know if Zoya was unhappy.

(38)   He left the party because she arrived.

D.   And for:

(39)   Fortunately, Zelda discovered that Zoltan missed her.

(40)   Because the snow was bad, the traffic on that street became impossible.

(41)   Zoltan mentioned that Bela had gone to the library without his rain jacket.

(42)   That two paintings were stolen from the Munch Museum is so sad.

(43)   I wondered whether that would happen.

E.   List the functions of the embedded clauses in (32) to (43).

F.   Draw trees for (44) and (45). The latter is a non-finite and this construction will be discussed in the next chapter:

(44)   I wonder what he saw.

(45)   He told us where to go.

G.   There are a few special types of sentences that we haven't had a chance to talk about above, namely (46) and (47):

(46)   If he was rich, (then) he would own an island.

(47)   He did that task as well as he could.

We won't draw trees for these, but think about the structures. They are very different from each other.

Class discussion

H.   Sentences such as *I mentioned that Sue won the Nobel Prize yesterday* are ambiguous. How are they (draw trees) and how would you change them if you wanted to avoid ambiguity?

I.   Find the lexical verbs in:

> We the People of the United States, in Order to form a more perfect Union, establish Justice, insure domestic Tranquility, provide for the common defence, promote the general Welfare, and secure the Blessings of Liberty to ourselves and our Posterity, do ordain and establish this Constitution for the United States of America. (The Preamble to the Constitution of the United States)

J.   How might you bracket the long sentence in Figure 7.1?

Keys to the exercises

A. The lexical verbs are underlined and the clauses surrounded by brackets:

(26) [Mr. Bell, the Chief Inspector of Schools in England, <u>finds</u> [that classroom discipline <u>is</u> worse] [since the current government <u>took</u> office several years ago]].

(27) [The proportion of secondary schools with good pupil behavior has <u>fallen</u> from three quarters to two thirds, [while 9 per cent <u>have</u> serious discipline problems]]. (I think in this sentence, we could argue that *while* is a coordinator).

(28) [The Chief Inspector <u>worries</u> [that so many of the 60 per cent of youngsters from non-professional backgrounds <u>lack</u> the ambition or qualifications [to <u>go</u> to university a quarter of a century [after he <u>became</u> the first in his family to <u>do</u> so]]]]. (The clause around *go* should get clear in the next chapter; don't worry about that now).

(29) [Access to good schools <u>is</u> the key]. [Mr. Bell <u>highlights</u> unacceptable levels of variability in the performance of state schools].

(30) [He <u>focuses</u> particularly on the 10 per cent [that <u>make</u> little or no improvement between inspection visits]].

(31) [[Because children in these schools are effectively being <u>written</u> off], it <u>is</u> little wonder [that many <u>suffer</u> the greatest problems with discipline]].

B. [One aim of the Department of Comparative and Developmental Psychology <u>is</u> the investigation of the evolution of different cognitive processes]. [The comparative approach <u>includes</u> the study of a variety of animal species]. [[Although most of our work is <u>done</u> with the great apes], we also <u>investigate</u> other species such as goats, seals, and dogs]. [For a number of reasons, the domestic dog (*Canis familiaris*) <u>is</u> a very interesting model for [<u>investigating</u> different questions regarding the evolution of cognitive abilities]]. [The fact [that dogs have been <u>living</u> with humans for at least 15.000 years] may have <u>led</u> to the selection of cognitive abilities by humans or even the co-evolution of dogs' cognitive abilities with those of humans]. [We <u>know</u> from different studies [that dogs <u>are</u> sensitive to the attentional state of humans]]. [We also <u>know</u> [that dogs <u>understand</u> communicative cues]]. [Those abilities have not been <u>found</u> in nonhuman primates and wolves].

C. (32)

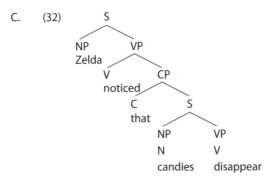

(33)

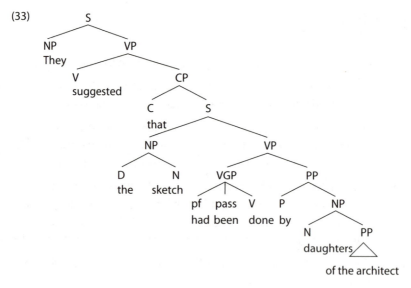

(34)

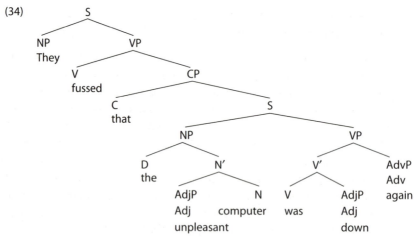

(35)

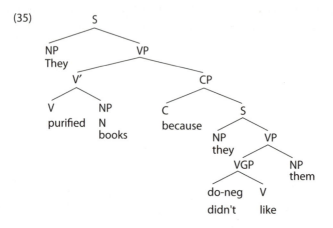

Sentence (36) involves an embedded object and is similar in structure to (32), (33), and (34). Sentence (37) is similar too, except that *if* is in the C. Sentence (38) has the same structure as (35).

D.   (39)

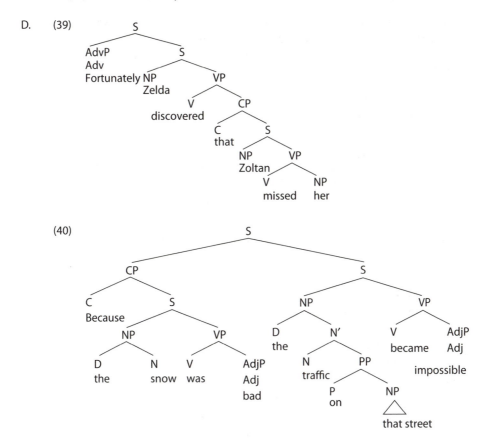

(40)

Sentence (41) is similar to the above embedded objects, and so is (43), except that *whether* is in C. The structure of (42) is as below, with the embedded clause as subject:

(42)

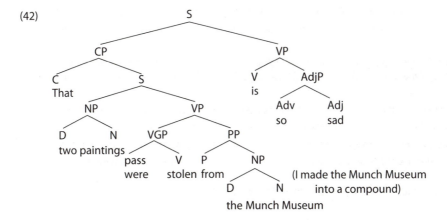

E. In (32), (33), (34), (36), (37), (39), (41), and (43) it is a Direct Object; in (35), (38), and (40) an Adverbial; and in (42), it is a Subject.

F. In (44), the object of the embedded clause *what* is used as complementizer. We can represent that by saying that *what* moved to the C position.

(44)

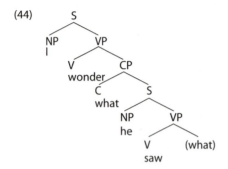

The same is true in (45): the adverb *where* is used as complementizer:

(45)

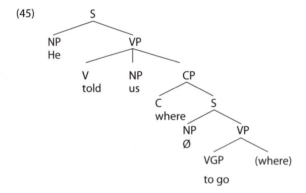

G. In (46), the two clauses are coordinated since one is not subordinate to the other. In (47), *as well as he could* is an adverbial, and one could argue that the head is the adverb *well*, so that it is an AdvP in form. The head *well* is modified by a clause *as he could* that is dependent on the adverb *as*, a discontinuous modifier. This is quite a complex construction.

Special topic: Preposition or complementizer: The 'preposition' *like*

Especially since the 1980s, *like* has expanded its uses tremendously. It is sometimes claimed that it is the most frequent word in the speech of certain groups of speakers (see cartoon below). Prescriptive grammarians are not too pleased with this development, but tend to focus on the use of *like* as a complementizer. This prescriptive rule goes as follows:

(48)   *like* is a preposition and not a complementizer.

That means that *like* can introduce an NP but not a clause. Instead of *like*, *as* is used to introduce a sentence. Fowler (1926 [1950]: 325ff.) is not too clear in the following excerpt but is not happy with the use of *like* except as preposition. He writes:

> It will be best to dispose first of what is, if it is a misuse at all, the most flagrant & easily recognizable misuse of *like*. A sentence from Darwin quoted in the OED [Oxford English Dictionary] contains it in a short & unmistakable form: *Unfortunately few have observed like you have done.* Every illiterate person uses this construction daily; it is the established way of putting the thing among all who have not been taught to avoid it … in good writing this particular *like* is very rare.

Swan (1980: 73) is more low-key and says that "[i]n informal American English, *like* is very often used as a conjunction instead of *as*".

According to prescriptive authorities, we should allow *like* as a preposition as in (49), but not as a complementizer as in (50) to (54):

(49)   Certainly, he is not **like** Mr. Knightley.
       (Jane Austen, *Emma*, Vol 1, chap 4)

(50)   "When we open up our hearts and our minds to those who may not think precisely **like** we do, or believe precisely what we believe, that's when we discover at least the possibility of common ground." (President Obama, 17 May 2009, Commencement Speech Notre Dame University)

(51)   Shop **like** you mean it. (advertisement)

(52)   I felt **like** I could tell you anything. Now I don't feel **like** I can anymore. (quoted in Tannen's *That's not what I meant*).

(53)   Winston tastes good **like** a cigarette should. What do you want: Good grammar or good taste? (an ad in the 1960s that caused much controversy)

(54)   She forgot all about the library **like** she told her old man now. (*Beach Boys*' Song)

Except as complementizer and preposition, *like* is often used to mark direct speech, as in (55), focus, as in (56), or to soften a request or demand, as in (57). These uses are not accepted in formal speech either, even though some are old, as (58) and (59) show, quoted in the OED:

(55)   So the other girl goes **like**: 'Getting an autograph is **like**, be brave and ask for it'. So I got it. I just went up to him and he **like**. 'O.K …

(56)   I couldn't get to class because, well, **like** I had this accident on the freeway.

(57)   Stephanie, you, **like**, still owe me that $10.

(58) 3on man is **lyke** out of his mynd.
(Dunbar Poems, xix, 19)

(59) all looking on, and **like** atonisht staring
(Spenser, *Fairie Queen*, iv, x, 56)

Figure 7.2. Quotative 'like'
(Reprinted with the permission of Universal Press Syndicate. All rights reserved.)

Chapter 8

Non-finite clauses

1. Non-finite clauses
2. The functions of non-finites
3. The structure: CP
4. Coordinating non-finites
5. Conclusion

Chapter 7 deals with finite embedded and coordinated clauses, i.e. those sentences or clauses that contain finite verbs. The present chapter deals with non-finite sentences (or clauses), i.e. those that contain only non-finite verbs. Non-finite sentences can only function as parts of another sentence; they are not considered well-formed sentences on their own in formal writing but are seen as sentence fragments. Since they are not complete sentences, they cannot be coordinated unless that coordinated structure is itself embedded. Remember from the last chapter that one lexical verb means one clause, two such verbs two clauses and so on. This holds for non-finite lexical verbs too!

In Section 1, I list the three kinds of non-finite clauses and review the general characteristics of non-finites. Then, in Section 2, I will briefly illustrate the functions that non-finite clauses have. Tree structures are provided in Section 3 and using a CP with empty positions is justified. In Section 4, we'll consider coordinated non-finites.

1. Non-finite clauses

There are three kinds of non-finite clauses, namely those whose verb groups contain infinitives, or present participles, or past participles. We'll first consider infinitives.

In (1), there are two lexical verbs, *expected* and *go*. This means there are two clauses, which I have put brackets around. The non-finite clause *her to go* is the object of *expected*. This non-finite clause can of course be rephrased by means of a finite clause, as in (2):

(1) [I expected [her **to go**]].
(2) [I expected [that she would go]].

The infinitive implies something uncertain or something that will happen in the future perhaps. The corresponding main clause therefore has a modal *would*, expressing a similar uncertainty.

There are two types of infinitives: one with *to*, as in (1), and a bare one, without *to*, as in (3). The bare infinitive lacks the uncertainty:

(3)   She made [him **leave**].

The bare infinitive in (3) occurs only as the object after verbs such as *make, see, hear*, and *feel*. The *to*-infinitive is much more frequent. It occurs as object to many verbs, as subject, subject predicate, and adverbial, as we'll see.

The infinitival clause with *to* frequently has a *for* as complementizer, as in (4), or an *in order*, as in (5), that connects the infinitival clause to the main clause:

(4)   I expected [**for** him to be scared …]
      (from the catsite.com)
(5)   [**In order** to understand the legislative process], it is necessary first of all to know something about the nature of the lawmaking body itself. (from an Alabama Senate document)

As we'll see when we draw the Verb Group for the non-finite clause, *to* will be put inside this Verb Group since it is similar to a modal. If you want to name it, call it an infinitive marker. I abbreviate it as 'inf'.

Apart from infinitives, there are two other kinds of non-finite Verb Groups, usually referred to as participles. They involve the present participle ending in *-ing*, as in (6), and the past participle ending in *-ed* or *-en*, as in (7). Again, I have bracketed the clauses these verbs go with:

(6)   [**Walking** down Rural Road], he was bothered by the traffic lights.
(7)   [**Kidnapped** last night], he is in Central Asia right now.

The form of *kidnapped* is a regular past participle because it ends in *-ed*. However, past participles, like simple past tenses, can have irregular endings. The participle clause in (6) can have *while* as a complementizer.

As mentioned in Chapter 6, non-finites fail to express tense. Thus, in (8), the non-finite *to walk* in the subordinate clause is neither past nor present nor future. Instead, the finite verb *is/was/will be* in the main clause determines the tense. The same is true for the non-finite in (9):

(8)   [**To walk** in the Superstition Mountains] is/was/will be nice.
(9)   [**Walking** in the Superstition Mountains] is/was/will be nice.

In addition, the verb in non-finite clauses displays no person or number marking, as is shown by the ungrammaticality of *walks* in (10):

(10)   *[For him to **walks** in the Superstitions] is nice.

A third characteristic of non-finites is that the subject is not nominative. Thus, (11) and (12) are grammatical with the subject of the infinitive as *him*, i.e. accusative. Sentence (13) with a nominative *he* as subject of the non-finite is not:

(11)   I want [**him** to go].
(12)   I heard [**him** playing a song].
(13)   *I want **he** to go.

If the subject of the non-finite clause is not a pronoun, the accusative or objective case on this subject is of course not visible, as (14) shows:

(14)   She couldn't bear to see [**Edward** suffering].

The non-finite verb *suffering* in (14) can also be a verbal noun, as in (15a), and then the subject has genitive case, namely *his* or *Edward's*, rather than the accusative *him* or *Edward*. In (14), *suffering* is a verb but in (15a) it is a noun because it is preceded by a possessive. Note that you could replace the possessive by an article, as in (15b):

(15)   a.   She couldn't bear to see [**his/Edward's** suffering].
        b.   She couldn't bear to see [**the** suffering of him/Edward].

Prescriptive grammarians object to (12) and (14), and prefer (15), known as gerund. We will come back to gerunds as a special topic. I like to think of present participles as a hybrid category, in between nouns and verbs, and prefer to avoid the term gerund.

As we saw in the previous chapter, finite embedded clauses, as in (16a), can become independent from the main clause by leaving the complementizer *that* out, as in (16b). A non-finite clause, as in (17a) can be the object inside another clause but, on its own, as in (17b), it is not a complete sentence:

(16)   a.   I know [that he left].
        b.   He left.
(17)   a.   I want [him to go].
        b.   *Him to go.

We'll now turn to the functions of the non-finite clauses.

2.   The functions of non-finites

The functions of non-finite clauses are similar to those of finite ones. They function at sentence level as subject in (18), direct object in (19), adverbial in (20), and subject predicate in (21):

(18)   [Eating pancakes] is a pleasant thing.
(19)   I love [eating pancakes].
(20)   They went there [to eat fry bread and chocolate].
(21)   The problem is [to decide on what to eat].

The present participle clause, as in (18) and (19), and the *to*-infinitive clause, as in (20) and (21), are the most versatile in function. This is indicated as 'broad' in Table 8.1. Past participle clauses, as in (7), are more restricted in that they usually function as adverbials and bare infinitives are mostly objects of certain verbs. This is indicated in the table as 'narrow'. I think the functions of non-finites are not difficult but, just as a review, see if you can identify the functions of the clauses in (1) to (9).[5]

Table 8.1 lists the different kinds of finite and non-finite clauses, with examples, their complementizers, and in how many functions they are used.

Table 8.1. Embedded clauses

		Example	C	Function
Finite		(2)	*that, because*, etc	broad
Non-Finite	infinitive	(1)	sometimes: *for*, as in (4); *in order*, as in (5)	broad
	bare-infinitive	(3)	no	narrow
	present participle	(6)	*while, after, before*	broad
	past participle	(7)	*when, where*	narrow

In Chapter 10, finite and non-finite clauses will be shown to function inside phrases as well.

3.   The structure: CP

I represent a non-finite clause by means of a CP, as in (22), the structure for (17a). This captures that the non-finite clause is fairly similar in structure to the finite clause but, as we'll see, it is a little more reduced and therefore can have more empty positions:

(22)

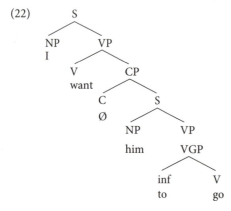

---

5.   In (1) to (4), these clauses function as objects, in (5) and (7) as adverbials, and in (6), (8) and (9) as subjects.

In (22), I have put in an empty complementizer. This C position can be filled by *for* in a number of cases, e.g. in (23). I like to use the C position, even if it is empty, because it shows that the non-finite clause is embedded:

(23)   I want [**for** you to do your homework].

Non-finite clauses need not include a subject. The subject may be understood, as in (24). Since the subject is understood, I will add a subject position, with an empty subject, as in (25), as well as an empty C since there is no complementizer:

(24)   To hike around Weaver's Needle is pleasant.

(25)

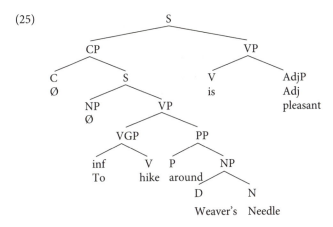

We could add the subject and complementizer in (25) and the reason I prefer (25) is that it is pleasant for **someone** to walk around Weaver's Needle; the tree expresses that there is a subject even if this subject is left out.

The infinitive marker *to* adds some uncertainty, as we have seen comparing (1) and (3). I think it is somewhat similar to a modal and have therefore placed it in the Verb Group. Be careful in recognizing this *to*: it goes before a verb. A preposition goes before a noun or pronoun, as in *to us*.

Sentences such as (6) and (7) above can also be represented using a CP, as (26) and (27) show:

(26)

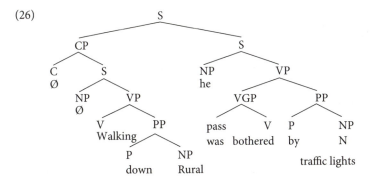

(27)

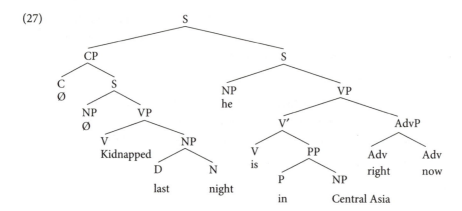

As in the case of infinitives, there are people who prefer a structure with fewer empty positions. I like seeing which clause is embedded and which clause has a potential subject. This comes in handy with dangling modifiers, for instance, as we'll see in the special topic to this chapter.

In the previous chapter, I mentioned extraposed finite clauses. Extraposition is possible with non-finites as well. For instance, (24) might be rendered as (28):

(28)   It is nice [to hike around Weaver's Needle].

In (28), the infinitival clause that functions as the subject of the entire sentence has been moved from the beginning to the end of the sentence.

Table 8.2 gives examples of some non-finite Verb Groups that have a full CP, an empty C, an empty subject, and an empty C as well as empty subject.

Table 8.2. The non-finite CP

	To-infinitive	Present participle
Full CP	I want [for her to do well].	—
Ø C	I want [Ø her to do well].	I saw [Ø him crossing the street].
C Ø NP	*I want [for Ø to do well].[6]	[While Ø doing that], she fell.
Ø C Ø NP	I want [Ø Ø to do well].	I like [Ø Ø doing well].

4.   Coordinating non-finites

Non-finite clauses can be coordinated, as in (29). Note that the coordinated non-finite clauses *gossiping about Zelda* and *chewing gum* function as subject to the verb *is*. (Speakers differ as to whether the verb is *is* or *are*):

(29)   [[Gossiping about Zelda] and [chewing gum]] is hard to do at the same time.

---

6.   Note that most varieties of English do not accept *for to* here but that certain varieties do.

Other examples of coordinated non-finites are given in (30) to (32):

(30)   She could not think of [[Emma losing a single pleasure], or [suffering an hour's ennui]]. (adapted from Jane Austen's *Emma*)

(31)   But Emma, in her own mind, determined that he did not know what he was talking about, and that he shewed a very amiable inclination [[to settle early in life], and [to marry]].
(*Emma*, Vol 2, Chap 6)

(32)   The point is [[to watch the whales], and [to participate in fun]] ...

The coordinated non-finites function as the object to *think* in (30), as the complement to *inclination* in (31) (this will get clearer in Chapter 10); and as the subject predicate in (32). So, coordinated non-finite clauses always function as a unit inside another clause.

I will suggest (33) as a tree for coordinated non-finites functioning as a subject. I leave it to your imagination what the verbs are:

(33)

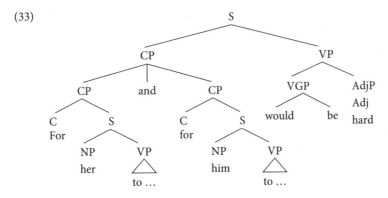

Note that I am using 'coathangers' in (32). That means that I am not indicating that the VPs can be divided into a V (or VGP), an NP. and a PP. It shows that in this particular tree, we are not really interested in the structure of the VP. However, I have tried to avoid using coathangers in this book.

5.   Conclusion

In this chapter, non-finite clauses are discussed. Their structure and function is quite similar to that of finite clauses. They are CPs and function inside another clause as subjects, objects, adverbials, and subject predicates.

They differ from finite clauses in that the complementizer often does not appear and the subject can be absent. They also cannot stand on their own. If they are coordinated, they have to function together as an embedded clause.

Key terms are **non-finite Verb Group, infinitive, bare infinitive, present participle, past participle, gerund, CP, empty C,** and **empty subject.**

Exercises

A.   Please find the non-finite clauses that function as direct objects and adverbials in the sentences below, adapted from an article in the *East Valley Tribune* (4 April 2005, by Jason Emerson). You might try to locate the lexical verbs first.

(34)   Arizona State University wants to make wholesale changes to the undergraduate curriculum.

(35)   The effort is still in the early stages but could result in a fundamental shift in the knowledge and skills gained from a university education.

(36)   The discussion intends to transform ASU into what President Crow calls the "New American University."

(37)   Changing a university's curriculum is often controversial. It can erupt into full-blown controversies, as Stanford University discovered in the 1980s when faculty members voted to replace a number of books that had been considered part of the Western Canon.

(38)   The task force is focusing on what the ideal ASU student should know upon graduation.

(39)   The task force hasn't talked yet about specific changes. But some early ideas include adding interdisciplinary classes and continuing them over four years until graduation. Now, general studies are clustered in the first two years.

(40)   Carlson said the task force continues to debate how to make undergraduate education more meaningful.

B.   Are there any coordinated sentences? Is there ellipsis?

C.   Draw trees for the following sentences:

(41)   Drawing trees is easy.

(42)   Emma wanted to do that.

(43)   For Ed to be resigning from that job is stupid.

(44)   Anselm made Vicky read the paper.

(45)   I saw turkeys crossing the street.

(46)   Santa set the alarm to be on time.

D.   In the text below, find the non-finite clauses.

When movie producers for *Star Trek III* needed someone to produce alien-sounding dialogue for the Klingons, they turned to Marc Okrand, a linguist who has done scholarly work on Native American languages. Okrand, however, didn't limit himself to creating lines of dialogue. He also developed a language, complete with phonological, morphological, and syntactic rules, in addition to vocabulary. His hard work paid off not only by giving him subsequent film work, but also by making him a sort of celebrity among *Star Trek* fans across the world, who are studying Klingon. These fans are also teaching their children to speak it, and are translating major works into Klingon. Any short sentence will show you the complexities of Klingon. All nouns may be followed by one or more suffixes divided into five types. If there are two or more suffixes, the suffixes must occur in a specific order.

E.   Construct a sentence with two embedded sentences, one of which must be a non-finite clause functioning as direct object.

F.   Construct a sentence with three non-finite clauses.

Class discussion

G.   The following sentences are ambiguous. Why?

(47)   Flying planes can be dangerous. (from Chapter 1)
(48)   Visiting aliens should be amusing on a Monday morning.

H.   Bracket the clauses in the sentence in Figure 8.1.

Figure 8.1. Embedded sentences
(Pardon my planet (I need help) © 2008 Vic Lee. King Features Syndicate)

I.   Read Keats' poem "To Autumn" and circle/list the finite verbs in the first two stanzas. Discuss the difference between the two paragraphs in class.

> To Autumn
> Season of mists and mellow fruitfulness,
> Close bosom friend of the maturing sun,
> Conspiring with him how to load and bless
> With fruit the vines that round the thatch-eaves run;
> To bend with apples the mossed cottage-trees,

And fill all fruit with ripeness to the core;
To swell the gourd, and plump the hazel shells
With a sweet kernel; to set budding more,
And still more, later flowers for the bees,
Until they think warm days will never cease,
For summer has o'er-brimmed their clammy cells.

Who hath not seen thee oft amid they store?
Sometimes whoever seeks abroad may find
Thee sitting careless on a granary floor,
Thy hair soft-lifted by the winnowing wind;
Or on a half-reaped furrow sound asleep,
Drowsed with the fume of poppies, while thy hook
Spares the next swath and all its twined flowers:
And sometimes like a gleaner thou dost keep
Steady thy laden head across a brook;
Or by a cider-press, with patient look,
Thou watchest the last oozings hours by hours.

Where are the songs of spring? Ay, where are they?
Think not of them, thou hast thy music too, –
While barred clouds bloom the soft-dying day,
And touch the stubble-plains with rosy hue;
Then in a wailful choir the small gnats mourn
Among the river sallows, borne aloft
Or sinking as the light wind lives or dies;
And full-grown lambs loud bleat from hilly bourn;
Hedge-crickets sing; and now with treble soft
The red-breast whistles from a garden-croft;
And gathering swallows twitter in the skies.

J. Make up some sentences with an infinitival and participial object, as in (49) and (50).
Try to think about the difference between the use of infinitive and present participle.
You might look back to Table 8.2 as well:

(49)   I want to visit Iceland, Israel, India, and Indonesia.
(50)   I like traveling.

This is quite complex and has to do with *to*. I think verbs with the present participle as
complement are more auxiliary-like and the two clauses are not as independent as when
an infinitive is involved. What do you think?

Keys to the exercises

A. The lexical verbs are underlined and the non-finite clauses functioning as objects and adverbials are indicated by brackets:

(34) Arizona State University <u>wants</u> [to <u>make</u> wholesale changes to the undergraduate curriculum]. (=Object, DO)

(35) The effort <u>is</u> still in the early stages but could <u>result</u> in a fundamental shift in the knowledge and skills <u>gained</u> from a university education. (coordinated clause and reduced relative)

(36) The discussion <u>intends</u> [to <u>transform</u> ASU into what President Crow <u>calls</u> the "New American University]." (=Object, DO)

(37) [<u>Changing</u> a university's curriculum] <u>is</u> often controversial. It can <u>erupt</u> into full-blown controversies, as Stanford University <u>discovered</u> in the 1980s when faculty members <u>voted</u> [to <u>replace</u> a number of books that had been <u>considered</u> part of the Western Canon]. (=Adverbial)

(38) The task force is <u>focusing</u> on [what the ideal ASU student should <u>know</u> upon graduation]. (=Object)

(39) The task force hasn't <u>talked</u> yet about specific changes. But some early ideas <u>include</u> [[<u>adding</u> interdisciplinary classes] and [<u>continuing</u> them over four years until graduation]]. (=Object that consists of coordinated non-finite clauses). Now, general studies are <u>clustered</u> in the first two years.

(40) Carlson <u>said</u> [the task force <u>continues</u> [to <u>debate</u> [how to <u>make</u> undergraduate education more meaningful]]]. (=Object three times, DO)

B. Coordinated clauses occur in (35), since *but* can be seen as a coordinator. There is ellipsis of the subject before *could*. In (39), two present participle clauses are coordinated and form a complement.

C. (41)

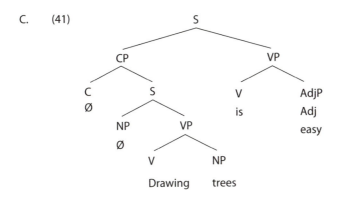

(42)

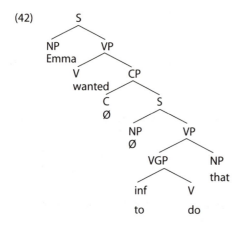

(43)

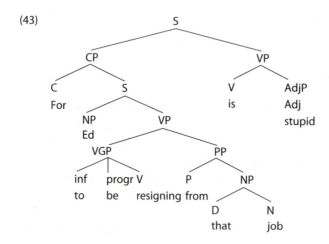

(44)

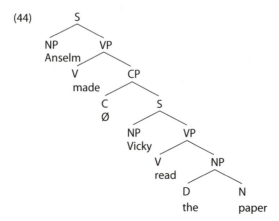

Sentence (45) has the same structure as (44).

(46)

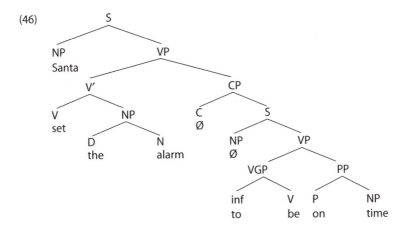

D.   Non-finite clauses are in brackets: When movie producers for *Star Trek III* needed [someone
      to produce alien-sounding dialogue for the Klingons], they turned to Marc Okrand, a
      linguist who has done scholarly work on Native American languages. Okrand, however,
      didn't limit himself to [creating lines of dialogue]. He also developed a language, complete
      with phonological, morphological, and syntactic rules, in addition to vocabulary. His hard
      work paid off not only by [giving him subsequent film work], but also by [making him a
      sort of celebrity among *Star Trek* fans across the world, who are studying Klingon]. These
      fans are also teaching [their children to speak it], and are translating major works into
      Klingon. Any short sentence will show you the complexities of Klingon. All nouns may be
      followed by one or more suffixes [divided into five types]. If there are two or more suffixes,
      the suffixes must occur in a specific order.
E.   Kim and Paul hoped [to see unicorns in the parking lot] [because they had studied
      their habits].
F.   They intend [to find out if [looking out the window more often] makes [them work better]].

Special topic: Dangling participles and gerunds

There are two topics discussed here that involve the present participle. Both have been much
criticized by prescriptivists.

   As we have seen in Chapter 3, PPs can go with a noun (e.g. *woman* in *the woman with
glasses*) or with a verb (e.g. *saw* in *saw her with glasses*). Sometimes, it is hard to tell. In this
special topic, we'll look at non-finite adverbial clauses that are misplaced and often result in a
funny reading. There are prescriptive rules about how to place the modifier. In (51), there is one
relevant for a non-finite clause:

(51)   **Avoid Dangling Participles**
       The subject of a clause with a participle in it (i.e. without a subject of its own) must
       be the same as the subject of the main clause.

Swan (1980: 455) provides the following rule: "It is usually considered a mistake to make sentences like these in which the subjects are different: *Looking out of the window of our hotel, there were lots of mountains* … However, there are some very common expressions which break this rule. *Generally speaking,* … *Judging from his expression,* … *Considering,* …". Fowler (1926 [1950]: 675) says that "it is to be remembered that there is a continual change going on by which certain participles or adjectives acquire the character of prepositions or adverbs, no longer needing the prop of a noun to cling to". Hence, neither Swan nor Fowler are very critical of the use.

'Incorrect' uses are given in (52) to (56). Some of these are funny because we automatically think of the participles as having the same subject as the main clause:

(52)   Running down the street, the house was on fire.
(53)   Referring to your letter of 5 September, you do not state …
(54)   Although spoken in Shakespeare's First Folio, we do not speak that way today.
(55)   Lying in a heap on the floor, she found the clothes.
(56)   Being a student, the challenges are many.

Sometimes, the left out subjects seem to be able to refer to the subject of the main clause, or to the closest NP, or to neither. The first meaning we come up with in (57) is the one where the waiter is drenched in syrup:

(57)   The waiter brought the waffles to the table drenched in maple syrup.

Misplaced participles are not new. An example from Shakespeare appears in (58). I have put brackets around the participle:

(58)   It's giuen out, that [sleeping in mine Orchard], A Serpent stung me: so the whole eare of Denmarke, Is by a forged processe of my death Rankly abus'd: But know thou Noble youth, The Serpent that did sting thy Fathers life, Now weares his Crowne. (*Hamlet* I, v, 35)

The gerund was mentioned in section 1. Many grammarians avoid the term 'gerund'; I mention it in this book since it seems to be a pervasive term among my audience. It is a present participle that looks either as a noun or as a verb, as in (59) and (60) respectively:

(59)   I like [his **doing** that].
(60)   I like [him **doing** that].

Fowler calls the present participle used as a verb the 'fused participle' (1926 [1950]: 206), probably because it gets the same case as the noun preceding it. He calls the one used as a noun the gerund. In the *Modern English Usage*, Fowler doesn't quite define the fused participle, except by providing examples, as in (61):

(61)   [Women having the vote] reduces men's political power.

About its users, Fowler says "[i]t need hardly be said that writers with any sense of style do not, even if they allow themselves the fused participle, make so bad a use of the bad thing as is shown above to be possible" (1926 [1950]: 207).

In conclusion, the dangling participle, as in (52) to (58), can result in amusing ambiguity; the present participle used as a verb, as in (60), has been denounced for centuries (without much success).

Review of Chapters 7 and 8

Chapters 7 and 8 cover embedded and coordinated sentences. If a sentence contains more than one lexical verb, it contains multiple sentences or clauses. An embedded clause functions (as subject, object, adverbial, or subject predicate) inside another clause. This is true for finite and non-finite embedded clauses. The finite embedded clauses discussed in chapter 7 all contain a finite verb and a complementizer that is optional in some cases. The non-finite clauses come in a number of shapes, as infinitives, present participles, and past participles. They are 'smaller' in that the complementizer and subject need not be present.

A coordinated clause can be split into two independent clauses but only if its clauses are finite. Coordinate finite sentences can leave the second subject out after a coordinator, and that is called ellipsis. Some coordinated sentences are borderline embedded sentences since the second clause can be seen as an adverbial.

The structure of the embedded sentence is a CP which accommodates the complementizer C and the S. A typical embedded clause is given in (1), with the CP embedded in the main S as sister to the V:

(1)

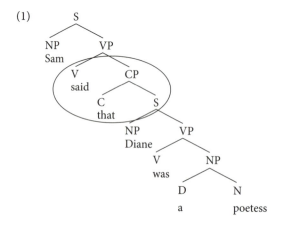

In a non-finite clause, some of the positions in (1) would be empty; see (26) of Chapter 8.

The structure of coordinate sentences is also a CP with a coordinator C and S. Subjects and complementizers can be absent in the non-initial coordinated clause. We discussed two possible structures.

Exercises

A.   In the following sentences, please identify by means of brackets and labels the finite and non-finite clauses that function as subjects, direct objects, subject predicates, and adverbials:

(2)   Some linguistic historians prefer to believe that languages live and die by social evolution.

(3)   They saw him cross the street without looking.

(4)   It is gratifying to see that idea becoming more accepted.

(5)   Since the advent of printing, the standard language may have developed that way because of increased standardization.

(6)   The president that founded this organization was arrested twice before he was replaced.

B.   Which are the lexical verbs in (2) to (6) and which are the finite Verb Groups (i.e. a VGP containing a finite verb)?

C.   Draw a tree for (7):

(7)   Poirot thought that he had sufficient evidence to solve the mystery.

Keys to the exercises

A.   (2)   Some linguistic historians prefer [OBJECT: to believe [OBJECT: that languages live and die by social evolution]]. Note that I consider 'live and die' as coordinated verbs not as separate clauses.

(3)   They saw [OBJECT: him cross the street [ADVERBIAL: without looking]].

(4)   It is gratifying [(extraposed) SUBJECT: to see [OBJECT: that idea becoming more accepted]].

(5)   Since the advent of printing, the standard language may have developed that way because of increased standardization. NOTHING

(6)   The president that founded this organization was arrested twice [ADVERBIAL: before he was replaced]. Note that this sentence also contains a relative clause. Relative clauses modify a N and do not function independently. For more on this, see Chapter 10.

B.   In (2), *prefer, believe, live, die* are lexical. In (3), *saw, cross,* and *looking* are; in (4) *is, see, becoming*; in (5), *developed*; in (6), *founded, arrested, replaced* are.

Finite VGPs in (2) are *prefer, live* and *die*; in (3), *saw*; in (4), *is*; in (5), *may have developed*; and in (6), *founded, was arrested, was replaced*.

C.   (7)

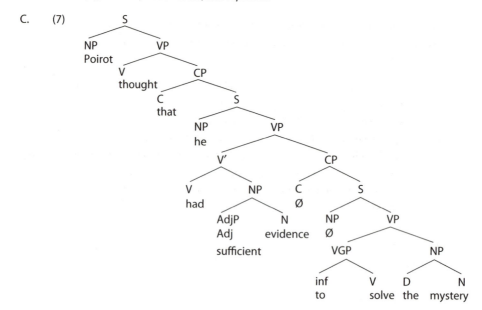

Sample quiz/exam, covering Chapters 7 and 8

A.   What is prescriptively wrong with sentence (1)? Provide the name of this phenomenon and explain why it is wrong.

(1)   Although spoken by Shakespeare, we don't speak that way today.

B.   Identify the (main and subordinate) clauses by means of brackets in the short text below. Indicate which clauses are finite:

The future of 100,000 refugees was dealt another blow this week after the Bhutanese government rejected a UN formula. Bhutan and Nepal started negotiations to solve the problem of the people in refugee camps in 1992. Since then 9 high-level meetings have taken place without resulting in a solution, however.

C.   Draw trees for (2), (3) and (4):

(2)   Those Martians decided that they would take along some chickens on their trip.
(3)   They wanted to see him before leaving Malacandra.
(4)   For us to accompany penguins on that trip is a wonderful opportunity.

Keys to the Quiz/Exam

A.   The subject of the main clause (*we*) and that of the embedded clause (a hidden subject that is probably *language/English*) are not the same. That's why the prescriptive problem is that of a dangling participle.

B.   The clauses are bracketed and the finite clauses have FIN marking that:
FIN[The future of 100,000 refugees was dealt another blow this week FIN[after the Bhutanese government rejected a UN formula]]. FIN[Bhutan and Nepal started negotiations [to solve the problem of the people in refugee camps in 1992]]. FIN[Since then 9 high-level meetings have taken place [without resulting in a solution, however]].

(2)

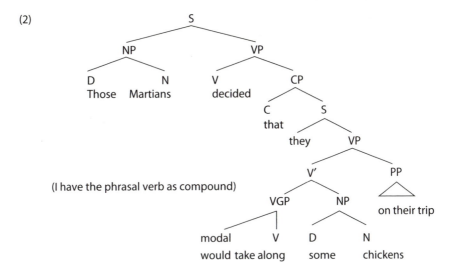

(I have the phrasal verb as compound)

(3)

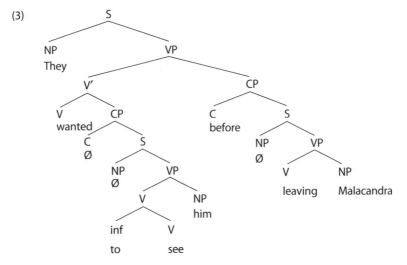

(4)

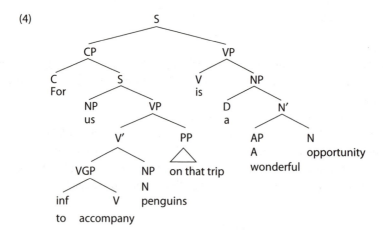

Chapter 9

The structure of the PP, AdjP, AdvP, and NP

1. The structure of the PP, AdjP, and AdvP and the functions inside
2. The structure of the NP and the functions inside
3. Arguments for distinguishing complements from modifiers (Optional)
4. Conclusion

Up to now, we have mainly seen phrases function at sentence level (as subjects, direct objects, subject predicates, adverbials, etc.). In this chapter, examples are given where phrases function inside other phrases, as modifiers and complements to the heads of these phrases. Grammatical categories, such as the determiner, also function inside phrases, whereas auxiliaries function in the Verb Group (see Chapter 6) and complementizers link one sentence to another.

Some of the structure of the NP, AdjP, AdvP, and PP has already been provided in Chapter 3. There, we noted that PPs could be modifiers to a noun (or adverbials in a sentence). In this chapter, we discuss the modifier function in more detail and add the complement. The four possible functions inside a phrase are determiner, head, modifier, and complement. There can be more than one modifier in a phrase, but not more than one complement or determiner.

In Section 1, I review the structure for the simple phrase, the PP, AdjP, and the AdvP, and examine the components of each of these phrases. In Section 2, we discuss the NP. It can have a modifier as well as a complement and a determiner. The distinction between modifier and complement is elaborated on Section 3. This distinction can be skipped depending on how much detail you want (or have time) to explore.

1.   The structure of the PP, AdjP, and AdvP and the functions inside

The structure of the Prepositional Phrase is relatively straightforward, with a P head and an NP complement, as in (1a). The PP can of course be longer, as in *on the roof of the very fancy gingerbread house*, with a tree as in (1b):

(1)   a.   PP   b.   PP

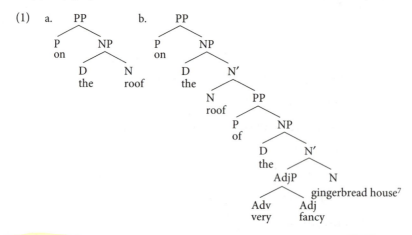

The preposition is the head of the PP and the NP that follows always functions as complement. There are a limited number of modifiers to PPs, e.g. *right* and *straight*, as in *right to school*. We won't draw a tree including those here.

Instances of Adjective Phrases are *very fancy* in (1b), *blatantly illegal* in (2), *perfectly safe, nice, interesting,* and *too good*:

(2)   That was [blatantly **illegal**].

These phrases are called AdjPs because their heads are adjectives, i.e. *illegal* in (2). A structure for an AdjP would be as in (3), where *illegal* is the head and the adverb *blatantly* modifies it:

(3)   AdjP

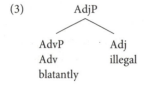

The adverb *blatantly* expresses the manner of the illegality. I have made it into an AdvP because you can expand it into *very blatantly*, but most modifiers to adjectives are degree adverbs, so just Adv.

Thus, (3) contains an Adj head and an AdvP modifier. In very rare cases, there can be a complement to the adjective as well (not to the adverb though). For instance, in

---

7.   I treat gingerbread house as a compound noun.

(4a), *of his catch* does not describe the manner or the place of being proud but what someone is proud of, i.e. *of his catch* is the complement of *proud* (inside the VP we'd call it a direct object). The same is true of *about that waste* in (4b):

(4)   a.   He was [blatantly proud of his catch].
      b.   There is something that is [very illegal about that waste].

A tree for the AdjP in (4b) is given in (5). I have indicated the different functions of the elements of the phrase. As in the case of VPs where objects are sisters to V, the complement *about that waste* is sister to the Adjective. In (5), I have put in the (intermediate) label Adj′ (pronounced 'Adjective-bar'). In Chapters 3 and 5, we mentioned intermediate nodes in connection with the NP and the VP. As mentioned, as much structure as in (5) is unusual for an AdjP:

(5)

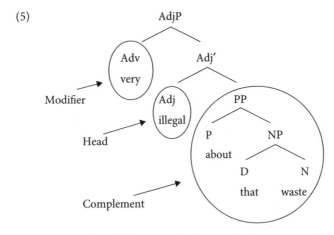

Some other examples of adjectives that have complements are *able, afraid, aware, conscious, fond, glad, happy, mad, proud, reasonable*, and *successful*.

Very frequently, adjectives are 'stacked', as in (6), which is a bit exaggerated:

(6)   The **beautiful, large, fast, young, spotted** leopard jumped out of nowhere.

Adjectives occur in a particular order that native speakers don't even pay attention to, but that is very complex to work out. Try ordering the adjectives in (6) in a different way and see how that works out. If you are curious about the order and the tree for (6), look at question D and its answer.

AdvPs have a simple structure. The ones listed in (7) came up after a search for *happily* in the *British National Corpus* (all from written non-fiction):

(7)   a.   One day he will **happily** walk along a busy road.
      b.   I'd **happily** buy her this.
      c.   It is a contradiction which thousands **happily** go along with because they are keen to advance up the social ladder.
      d.   He was a gentle man, **happily** dominated by his competent wife.
      e.   I turned to find the young Mr. Cardinal beaming **happily** at me.

So, these have just a head, as in (8a), or as I often put them, as in (8b):

(8) a.   AdvP   b.   AdvP
          | Adv
          Adv   happily
          |

          happily

The AdvPs can be expanded by a modifier that precedes the head, e.g. by the degree adverb *very* in *very happily* in (9), also from the *BNC* non-fiction collection, with the AdvP drawn in (10):

(9)   The majority of popular community fish will survive **very happily** on this diet.

(10)   AdvP

          Adv   Adv
          very   happily

The adverbs that modify adverbs are few in number. Some examples are *very, so, too, extremely, really*, and *quite*. They are all degree adverbs and cannot be expanded. That's why they do not head their own AdvP, but are represented as just an Adv in (10). A summary table is provided.

Table 9.1. Components of the PP, AdjP, and AdvP

PP	P head and NP complement	(*on the roof*)
AdjP	Adv(P) modifier and Adj head and occasional PP complement	(*very proud of his mother*)
AdvP	Degree Adv modifier and Adv head	(*very happily*)

When drawing a tree, you need not put the functions in, just use D, Adj, N, PP, etc.

2.   The structure of the NP and the functions inside

Typical instances of NPs are provided in (11a) and (11b):

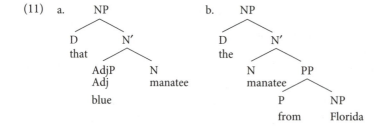

(11) a.   NP   b.   NP
          D   N'   D   N'
          that   the
                 AdjP   N   N   PP
                 Adj   manatee   manatee
                 blue   P   NP
                                                    from   Florida

In (11a), the AdjP *blue* modifies the head in that it describes a quality or characteristic of the manatee. We can add many such modifiers, e.g. where the manatee comes from, if it is fast or slow, and whether we think it is nice or not. *From Florida* in (11b) modifies the head as well since it tells you where the manatee is from. So modifiers can precede or follow the head: AdjPs precede and PPs follow. Hence, they are sometimes called pre-modifiers and post-modifiers respectively. Determiners function as pointers: *that* points to a particular *manatee* and *the* makes it a specific manatee. In (12a) and (12b), I repeat these structures with the functions added, but we don't usually clutter up the tree that way since the functions are predictable from the tree.

(12)   a.

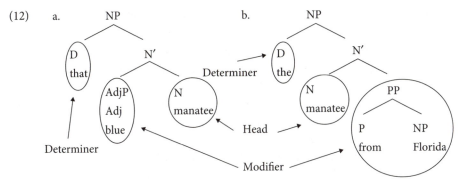

An NP in English can also contain what is called a complement to the noun. Unlike objects in the VP, complements to N and Adj are optional and that's what makes it hard to distinguish between modifiers and complements. See how helpful the following discussion and that in Section 3 are and decide if the distinction is important or interesting for you.[8]

Examples of NPs with complements to the head nouns are given in (13) to (16), with the complement in brackets:

(13)   The teacher [of Martian]
(14)   Their discussion [about genetics]
(15)   The student [of elephants]
(16)   Your reply [to my letter]

The nouns that can have complements are verb-like. One way to check if a PP is a complement is to make the noun into a verb. If you change the nouns into verbs in (13) to (16), the complements change into direct objects in (17) to (19) and into prepositional object in (20). The type of object they become depends on the verb:

(17)   You teach [Martian].
(18)   They discussed [genetics].
(19)   She studied [elephants].
(20)   You replied [to my letter].

---

8.   From my own experience, this is difficult material and, since it is less crucial to the understanding of the NP (and AdjP), I sometimes skip complements to nouns.

The NPs in (13) to (16) change into full sentences in (17) to (20) as well. A table with typical PP modifiers and complements to nouns is given as Table 9.2.

Table 9.2. Examples of nouns with modifiers and with complements

Modifiers	Complements
the manatee [from Florida]	the teacher [of English]
the student [with red hair]	the student [of physics]
a boy with [with green hair]	an appeal [to reason]
a book [on the table]	the investigation [of corruption]
a glass [on the table]	the allegations [of murder]
green tea [from Korea]	recruitment [of new staff]
a computer [with sound]	his attack [on that celebrity]

Modifiers are quite free, e.g. *with red/green hair* and *on the table* can occur with many nouns. Complements are more restricted and only go with certain nouns, e.g. *student, teacher, discussion, disgust* and *investigation*. Adding *of physics* to *teacher* and *student* is fine but adding it to *boy* results in a very strange phrase!

As in the case of objects inside the VP (Chapter 4), complements to the N can be represented in the tree as sisters to the head, in this case N, as in (21) and (22):

(21)
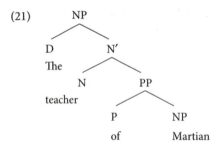

(22)
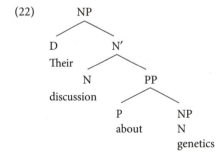

So far, we have seen that the elements of an NP in English function as determiner, head, modifier, and complement. This is summarized in Table 9.3. The name (i.e. label

or realization) of each of these functions is listed underneath the function. Note that there can be many modifiers but only one determiner and one complement.

Table 9.3. Functions inside the NP (the '∧' indicates that there can be more than one)

determiner	modifier∧	head	complement	modifier∧
D	AdjP∧	N	PP	PP∧
the	nice	student	of chemistry	from Macedonia
several	interesting	discussions	about politics	at night
a	delicious	pie	–	from my friend
those	noisy	teachers	of linguistics	from outer space

In tree form, the expanded NP in the first example of Table 9.3 looks like (23):

(23)

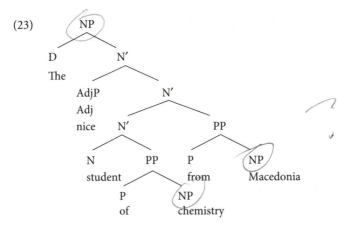

As indicated by the ∧∧ in Table 9.3, modifiers can be repeated on both sides of the noun. Multiple modifiers often result in ambiguities, as in (24) and (25):

(24)   On a menu: 'Vegetarian Chicken Soup'.   (Was the chicken vegetarian?)
(25)   An o/Old English French teacher.(When spoken, the punctuation doesn't appear!)

In this section, we have spent most time on the head, the modifier, and the complement. The determiner is relatively easy. Check Chapter 2 for a list of determiners. If the D is there, it appears right underneath the NP, as in (26):

(26)

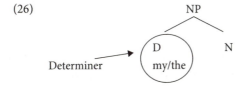

The determiner is special in that it is both an umbrella category name, which includes articles, quantifiers, demonstratives, possessives, etc. (see Chapter 2), as well as a function name.

As you may remember from Chapter 2, the pre-determiner may be added as a function inside the NP. In (27), three quantifiers that function in this way are given. In a tree, they would precede the D, but I won't go into this here:

(27)   **All** the nice books; **half** the people; **both** my pictures.

The last element we are adding to the NP is the focusser or emphasizer, but these are relatively rare. Some of the ones that occur in English are *just, only, especially,* and *even*, as in (28). Most of these are tricky in that they can be used in other ways too, e.g. *even* and *just* are also adjectives, and most are adverbs as well:

(28)   then it will perhaps gravel [**even** a philosopher] to comprehend it.
(George Berkeley, *Treatise* 97)

3.   Arguments for distinguishing complements from modifiers (Optional)

As was mentioned in the previous section, inside the NP, some elements are more closely related to the head N than others. We can refer to these as complements and modifiers respectively. They can be compared to the objects (even though the latter are more obligatory) and the adverbials in the VP. Above, I have suggested that, if you can change the noun into a verb (*discussion* into *discuss*), the PP complement will change into an NP object (or PP object depending on the verb). To me, that is the most crucial argument. In this section, I provide several additional arguments (summarized in Table 9.4) for distinguishing complements from modifiers and provide trees that show the distinction.

3.1   Complement and modifier follow the head N

The NP in (29) has a modifier *from England* that tells you where the teacher is from and a complement *of physics* that tells you what the teacher teaches:

(29)   A teacher of physics from England.

In the tree structure, we represent the difference between the complement and the modifier by having complements be sisters to N and modifiers sisters to N'. For instance, in (30), *of physics* is sister to N and is therefore the complement, whereas *from England* is a sister to the N′ and is therefore the modifier:

(30)

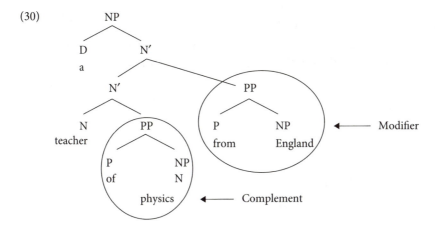

There can only be one complement and the order between complement and modifier cannot be reversed as the ungrammaticality of (31) shows:

(31)   *A teacher [from England] [of physics].

The impossibility of complement modifier reversal is the first argument that you can use to distinguish between complements and modifiers.

Apart from word order (complement is closest to the head), there is a second way to distinguish complements from modifiers and it involves determining what pronoun one can use to pronominalize certain parts of the NP. In (28), *teacher of physics* and *teacher of physics from England* are N′s. The N′ can be replaced by *one*, but the N (and NP) cannot be replaced by *one*. In (32), *one* replaces *teacher of physics*, i.e. an N′, and the sentence is grammatical; in (33), *one* replaces *teacher*, i.e. an N, and this results in an ungrammatical sentence:

(32)   I know the [teacher of physics] from England and the **one** from France.
(33)   *I know the [teacher] of physics from England and the **one** of chemistry.

These sentences provide evidence for the special status of the intermediate category N′ in that it can be replaced by *one*, as in (32), unlike the N in (33).

3.2   Complement and modifier precede the head N

Complements and modifiers can also precede the N, as in (34). The modifier *English* again says something about the teacher, i.e. where he or she is from, and the complement *physics* clarifies what the teacher teaches:

(34)   That English physics teacher.

There can be many modifiers, as (35) shows, but there can only be one complement connected to the noun, of course, as (36) shows:

(35)   That [nice] [intelligent] teacher [with purple hair].
(36)   *That [physics] teacher [of chemistry].

Again, the complement is closer to the head than the modifier, as (34) shows. The complement is sister to the N whereas the modifier is sister to the N′:

(37)

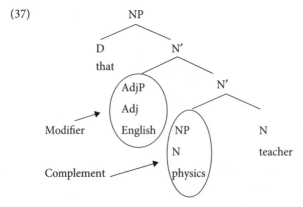

The same arguments to distinguish complements and modifiers hold as in the case of (29). First, their order cannot be reversed, as the ungrammaticality of (38) shows, and there can only be one complement but many modifiers, as in (39):

(38)   *That physics English teacher.
(39)   That nice, patient, English [chemistry] teacher.

Secondly, replacement by *one* of the N′ *physics teacher* in (34) is possible. See (40). The N *teacher* cannot be replaced. See (41):

(40)   That English one.
(41)   That English physics one.

The N′ *English physics teacher* can also be replaced of course.

So far, I have only drawn trees with the modifiers and complements either preceding or following the noun. Tree (42) has modifiers on either side as well as a complement preceding the head:

(42)

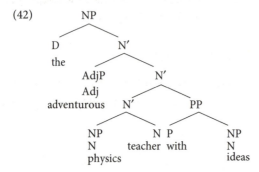

The complement *physics* in (42) is sister to the N *teacher* and the two modifiers are sisters to N'.

A question that often comes up in class is what the category of some of these pre-nominal modifiers and complements is. When complements precede the head, it is unclear what the category is, an N or an Adj. For instance, *English* in (37) is a clear adjective when it tells you where someone comes from. However, it looks like a noun when the teacher teaches the English language, as in the ungrammatical (38). I will treat it as a noun when it is a complement and an adjective when it is a modifier.

In this section, I have shown that there is evidence that complements and modifiers are distinguished in an NP: their order, coordination, and pronominalization by *one* differ. I will finish by summarizing the differences that are the easiest to use, and among these it is (a) and (b) that may be clearest. See also Table 9.2.

Table 9.4. Modifiers and complements to N: a summary

	Modifiers	Complements
a	All Ns may have modifiers	only certain Ns have complements: those Ns that are verb-like
b	gives general background information	gives information pertinent to the N
c	position is relatively free	occurs either right before or right after the N
d	more than one are possible in one NP	only one per NP

4. Conclusion

In this chapter, we have discussed the different functions of elements inside the AdjP, AdvP, PP, and NP. The functions include head, determiner, modifier, and complement. Not all phrases include all these functions, only the NP does. The other phrases are less complex. The PP has a head and a complement, the AdjP a head, a modifier, and a complement, and the AdvP just a modifier. The most important part is to recognize a phrase and its head and to be able to draw a tree.

The functions of modifier and complement are similar to the functions of adverbial and object in the VP, discussed in Chapters 4 and 5, with the exception of the names given and their optionality. This is not something you need to think about further if it makes the matter more complex. The adverbial of the VP is called modifier when it occurs in the AdjP, AdvP and NP, and the different kinds of objects in the VP are not differentiated but just called complements in the AdjP, PP, and NP. The NP may also contain a determiner where the VP has a subject. The complements in the NP and AdjP are usually optional, whereas objects and predicates in the VP are obligatory.

Key terms in Sections 1 and 2 are **determiner, modifier, head, and complement;** in Section 3, they are **complement as opposed to modifier; word order; pronominalization; and coordination.**

Exercises

A. In the sentences below, adapted from *The Death of Ivan Ilych* by Leo Tolstoy, find the PPs that function as modifiers inside phrases, i.e. as modifiers to nouns or adjectives:

(43) During an interval in the Melvinski trial, the members and public prosecutor met in Ivan Egorovich Shebek's private room, where the conversation turned on the celebrated Krasovski case.

(44) On receiving the news of Ivan Ilych's death, the first thought of each of the gentlemen in that private room was of the changes and promotions it might occasion among themselves or their acquaintances.

(45) Leaning against the wall in the hall downstairs near the cloak-stand was a coffin-lid covered with cloth of gold, ornamented with gold cord and tassels.

B. Provide a tree structure for the following NPs (use NP, AdjP, D, etc.). Also list the functions of the different elements.

(46) one of their irrational responses

(47) the attack on the conclusions of that report

(48) a hilarious look at two geniuses

(49) four fluffy feathers on a Fiffer-feffer-feff (from Dr. Seuss's *ABC*)

C. Provide a tree structure for the following sentences:

(50) This wonderful fridge is available in Montana.

(51) A very curious, red book with ink stains was found.

(52) He hides behind the pile of books on his desk.

(53) The lovely pig from Wyoming told the bureaucrat in Washington the story of his life.

Optional (Section 1)

D. In (6) above, repeated here as (54), we saw five adjectives in a row. Try to see how the classes listed in (55) are ordered in relation to each other:

(54) The **beautiful, large, fast, young, spotted** leopard jumped out of nowhere.

(55)
opinion	size	appearance	speed	age	shape	color	origin	material
pretty, ugly	large	soft, sweet	fast	old	round	pink	Israeli	golden

Now try to draw a tree for (54).

Optional (Section 3)

E. Try to draw trees for (56) and (57) expressing the difference between complements and modifiers. Which PPs and NPs are complements? Provide reasons for your answer:

(56) Canadian students of English

(57) a French Old English student.

Class discussion

F. My own favorite ambiguous NP is given in (58):

(58) The chocolate toy factory.

I can think of three interpretations and a few trees. Two of my favorite trees are as follows. Discuss the difference!

(59)

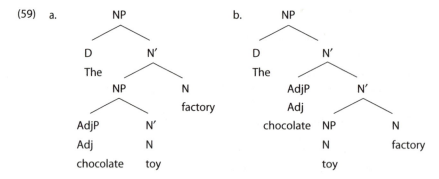

Remember that sisters to N categories are complements, so that the NP complements to the N *factory* would be the products of the factory, and that sisters to N′ nodes describe physical properties of the factory.

G. The first sentence of Exercise A is actually as in (60). Do you think there is ambiguity? Is the *trial* modified by the PP that follows, or is that PP an independent adverbial?

(60) During an interval in the Melvinski trial in the large building of the Law Courts the members and public prosecutor met in Ivan Egorovich Shebek's private room, where the conversation turned on the celebrated Krasovski case.

H. Compare the NP in (61a) with the S in (61b). What are the similarities/differences?

(61) a. Stella's destruction of that awful set of dishes.
b. Stella destroyed that awful set of dishes.

Keys to the exercises

A.   The below PPs all modify an N:

(43)   During an interval [in the Melvinski trial], the members and public prosecutor met
in Ivan Egorovich Shebek's private room, where the conversation turned on the
celebrated Krasovski case.

(44)   On receiving the news [of Ivan Ilych's death], the first thought [of each [of the
gentlemen [in that private room]]] was of the changes and promotions it might
occasion among themselves or their acquaintances.

(45)   Leaning against the wall [in the hall downstairs] (could also be Adverbial) near the
cloak-stand was a coffin-lid covered with cloth [of gold], ornamented with gold
cord and tassels.

B.   The structure for (46) is as follows, with *one* as the head and *of their irrational
responses* as the modifier. In this phrase, the determiner *one* is functioning as noun
head (see Chapter 2 for other determiners that do this). A test for picking the head is
making the phrase into a subject and then checking the agreement on the verb (*One
of their responses was to ...* and not *One of their responses were...*):

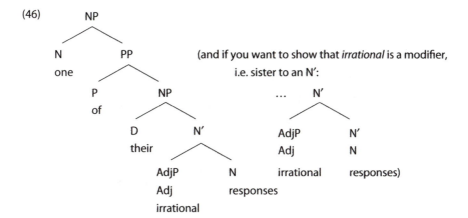

In (47), *the* is the determiner, *attack* the head, and the rest is the complement (because *attack* is
a verb-like noun):

(47)

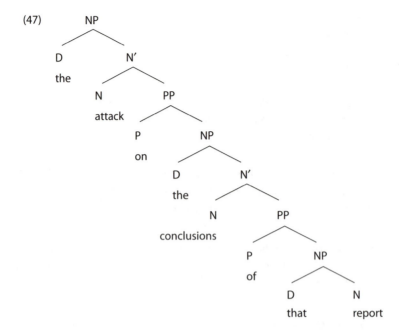

In (48), *a* is the determiner, *hilarious* the modifier, *look* the head, and the PP the complement:

(48)

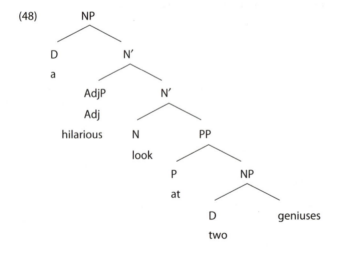

In (49), *four* is the determiner, *fluffy* is the modifier, *feathers* the head, and the PP is the (post-) modifier. I could have shown that the PP is the modifier by making it a sister to an N' but haven't:

(49)

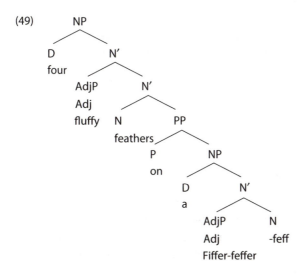

C.   (50)

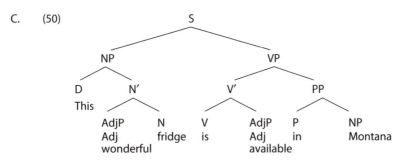

(51)   a.

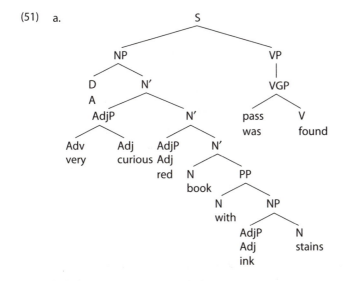

There are other correct trees for (51). You could put *red* and *book* more closely together than *book* and the PP, as I've done above. Also, if you wanted to express that the PP in (51) is a modifier not a complement, you could make it sister to N′ rather than N, as in:

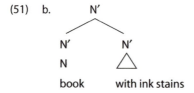

A structure for (52) is as follows. There are again other possible trees for (52), e.g. one could indicate that the PPs are modifiers by making them sisters to N′. Notice in (52) that *on his desk* is modifying *the pile of books*. If it were an independent adverbial, it would mean that he hides on his desk behind a pile of books:

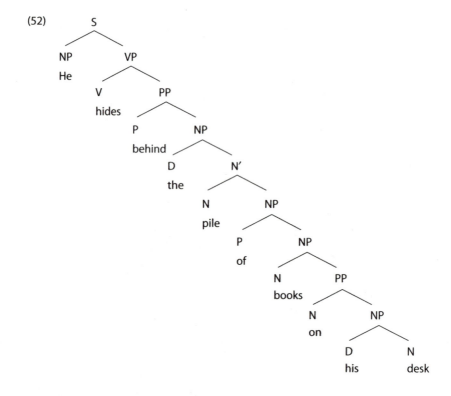

A tree as in (53) is a challenge if you don't have enough space. Doing it by hand (in draft form) will save you a lot of time over drawing it using a computer. Note that I could have made the PPs *from Wyoming* and *from Washington* sisters to an N′, showing their modifier status:

(53)

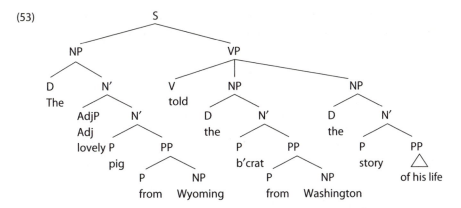

D.   The adjectives are usually seen as ordered in the way that I have listed the types in (55). In (54), *tall* is an adjective of dimension, *thin* of physical characteristic, as is *strong*, *young* is age-related, and *clever* expresses a value. The tree for the NP in (54) is as below (and of course the last AdjP could be sister to an N′ too):

(54)

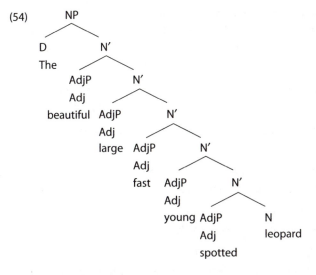

E.   The structure for (56) is as in (38) above, with *Canadian* as modifier and *of English* as complement. One of the reasons is that you can say *The Canadian one*, but not *the one of English*:

(56)

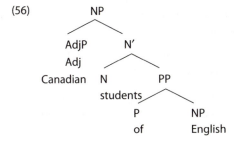

In (57), since *Old* is capitalized, it goes with *English*, and I have made it into a D, but modifier would be ok too. The modifier is *French* and the complement is *Old English*:

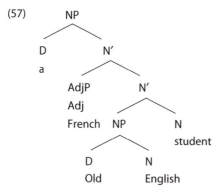

(57)

Special topic: Pronoun resolution

In this special topic, we'll look at some problems that speakers and writers encounter when they are deciding on which pronoun to use. The choice of the pronoun, of course, depends on the antecedent, the phrase that the pronoun refers to. Some are easy, as in (62), but some are ambiguous, e.g. the *he* in (63) could in principle go back to Obama or to Putin:

(62)   I noticed **a woman** in that store. **She** was wearing a greenish purple jacket.

(63)   Obama met Putin at the Kremlin. **He** wanted to discuss Afghanistan.

Writers are usually advised, as in (64), not to be ambiguous and sentence (63) would be clearer using *the former* or *the latter* rather than *he*:

(64)   **Avoid ambiguity:** "There should not be two parties justifying even a momentary doubt about which the pronoun represents." (Fowler 1926 [1950]: 464)

The use of the plural *they* and *their* to refer to a singular antecedent is still frowned upon. The prescriptive rule could be formulated as (65) and an example appears in (66):

(65)   Avoid 'singular *they*': do not use *they, them,* or *their* to refer to a singular antecedent.

(66)   **The student** should be aware not to leave **their** computer unattended in the library.

'Singular *their*' in (66) is of course used because English lacks a gender-neutral third person pronoun.

The *OED* is not prescriptive on this topic and lists the following function of *they*. It also cites examples of this use from the 16th century:

(67)   *They:* "Often used in reference to a singular noun made universal by *every, any, no,* etc., or applicable to one of either sex (= 'he or she')."

There are many other rules to help writers decide on the use of pronouns. In Chapter 10, we'll discuss, as special topic, the prescriptive rules for which relative pronoun to use for which antecedent.

Chapter 10

Clauses as parts of NPs and AdjPs

1. Relative clauses (RC)
2. Inside the NP: Relative and complement clauses
3. NPs as compared to AdjPs, AdvPs, and PPs
4. More on RCs
5. The structure of modifiers and complements (optional)
6. Conclusion

In Chapters 7 and 8, the functions of finite and non-finite clauses are discussed at sentence level (e.g. as subjects or objects). The present chapter shows that clauses can also function inside the phrase as modifiers or complements. Traditionally, modifier clauses are called relative clauses and we'll continue that practice. Relative clauses come in many kinds, as we'll see.

In Section 1, I provide a brief introduction to the shape and function of relative clauses. In Section 2, examples are given of relative clauses and complement clauses inside the NP. The non-finite reduced relative is also discussed. These two first sections are the most important. In Section 3, we look at the internal structure of phrases other than the NP, and in Section 4, we explore some different types of relative clauses. In Section 5, we examine the tree structure.

1. Relative clauses (RC)

Throughout the book, we have seen that PPs can function as adverbials and as modifiers. A PP used as modifier has a function very similar to that of a relative clause, as (1) and (2) show:

(1) The student [from Zombie Island] has yellow hair.   (modification by PP)
(2) The student [who is from Zombie Island] has yellow hair. (modification by RC)

A relative clause (RC) typically starts with a *who, which,* or *that* relative pronoun and provides further information about a noun.

Let's look at the short text in (3), from the *Times of London,* and see where the RCs are:

(3)   "Changes have to be made," said a 34-year-old political activist [who asked to remain anonymous]. Her first target would be headscarves, [which are mandatory in Iran]. "The least of the freedoms [we need] is the ability to choose what to wear. For women this is really an issue. Whenever you go out, you have to be vigilant because the moral police may not think it is appropriate and they may even take you to jail. A woman's integrity is judged by the colour of your dress – well, isn't that stupid?"

As you can see, I have put brackets around the three relative clauses. The first modifies the noun *an activist,* the second *headscarves,* and the third *freedoms.* The third one has the relative pronoun *that* or *which* left out, but you could always add it. When you look at the entire text, there are lots of other clauses that are not relative, e.g. *whenever you go out* is a finite clause functioning as adverbial and *it is appropriate* is a finite clause functioning as direct object. So, be careful when you see a clause!

2.   Inside the NP: Relative and complement clauses

In this section, we will divide the finite relative clauses into restrictive and non-restrictive. We also add the complement clause and the non-finite reduced relative.

2.1   Relatives

Clauses that modify nouns, such as the one in (4), are referred to as relative clauses because the noun they modify (*stories* in this case) plays a role (has a function) in the RC. The RC is related to the noun by means of *which*:

(4)   The stories [which he repeats often] are boring.

The element that connects the noun and the clause, i.e. *which* in (4), is called a relative pronoun. In (4), the relative pronoun functions as the direct object of *repeat.* Relative pronouns can also function inside the relative clauses as subjects, as in (2), or have other functions. The first two relative pronouns in (3) are subjects. The third one lacks a relative pronoun but, if we added *which,* it would function as object.

RCs are usually divided into restrictive as in (4) and non-restrictive, as in (5) and (6):

(5)   Hillary Clinton, who just returned from a trip to Cuba, intends to write a book.
(6)   Queen Elizabeth the first, who was born in 1533, was the last sovereign of the house of Tudor.

The reason we discuss the difference between restrictive and non-restrictive clauses is that the use of one over the other has grammatical (and possibly other) consequences.

Three differences between restrictive and non-restrictive relative clauses are listed in Table 10.1. First, restrictive RCs can have a *that,* as in (7), or a *who/which,* as in (4).

In the non-restrictive RC (5) and (6), on the other hand, only a *wh*-pronoun occurs and *that* is not possible, as (8) shows:

(7) The stories that he told us often are boring. (restrictive)
(8) *Hillary Clinton, that just returned from a trip to (non-restrictive)
       Cuba, intends to write a book.

The second difference is that restrictive RCs provide essential information, unlike non-restrictive ones. For instance, in (4), *the stories* is so general that the RC restricts and specifies the stories that are meant. In the case of (5), everyone living in the US at the beginning of the 21st century is expected to know who Hillary Clinton is and therefore the NP *Hillary Clinton* does not need to be restricted. The RC just provides background information that is not essential in knowing which noun is meant. That's why it is called non-restrictive.

Third, since the information in non-restrictive RCs is background information, the non-restrictive RC in (5) can be surrounded by commas or parentheses, and is therefore sometimes referred to as a parenthetical, whereas the restrictive RC in (7) cannot be.

Table 10.1. Restrictive and Non-Restrictive RC

Restrictive	Non-Restrictive
wh-pronoun or *that*	only *wh*-pronouns
highly relevant information	additional information
commas cannot surround it	commas may surround it

As an illustration of the difference, (9) and (10) are given. The restrictive RC in (9) contrasts interestingly with a non-restrictive in (10). In (9), only a small set of climbers reached the top, but in (10), all the climbers did:

(9)   The hikers who reached the top were very tired. (restrictive)
(10) The hikers, who reached the top, were very tired. (non-restrictive)
        (Thanks to Johanna Wood for the examples)

Another set that I sometimes use is (11) and (12). If you were a journalist, you'd be ok using the restrictive (11) but might get into trouble using the non-restrictive (12):

(11) Bankers that are crooks should be fired. (restrictive)
(12) Bankers, who are crooks, work overtime nowadays. (non-restrictive)

Of course, you could substitute *bankers* with *politicians, investors, house keepers, professors,* or *doctors* as well.

2.2 Complement clauses

There is a type of clause that looks deceptively like the RC, namely the complement clauses in (13) and (14):

(13) Reports [that he reached Mars] are exaggerated.

(14)   The fact [that he reached Mars] went unnoticed.

The finite clause following the noun in (13) and (14) is a complement (and not a RC) for several reasons. The first is that noun (*reports* and *the fact*) can be left out, as in (15) and (16):

(15)   [That he reached Mars] is exaggerated.
(16)   [That he reached Mars] went unnoticed.

The nouns can be deleted because the complement spells out what *reports* and *the fact* are.

The second reason this clause is not a relative clause is that the head N *reports* plays no role inside the clause. If we changed (13) to (17a), we would force the complement to be a relative clause. Now, *reports* (through *that*) is the object of *reached* but the result is very strange (indicated by the question mark) since report is not an object you would expect with *reached*. If we change the verb to *read*, as in (17b), we do get a RC because one can read reports:

(17)   a.   ?Reports [that he reached] are exaggerated.
       b.   Reports [that he reads] are (always) exaggerated.

The third reason that the clause in (13) and (14) is a complement and not a RC is that the complementizer has to be *that*. This *that* is not a relative pronoun. When we change *that* in (13) and (14) to *which*, the result is very strange, indicated by an ungrammatical mark in (18) and (19):

(18)   *Reports which he reached Mars are exaggerated.
(19)   *The fact which he reached Mars went unnoticed.

Table 10.2 summarizes the differences between relative and complement clauses. I have added a fourth one, namely that the type of noun complemented by a clause is quite restricted, e.g. *story, fact, dream, idea* and *concept*.

Table 10.2. Relative Clauses and Complement Clauses

Relative Clause (RC)	Complement Clause
relative pronoun has a function in the RC	*that* has no role in the clause, as in (17)
relative marker: *which, who, that*, etc	only *that* as marker, as in (18) and (19)
noun preceding RC cannot be deleted	noun can be deleted (see (15) and (16))
any noun can have a RC follow	noun is *fact, story, idea, ...*

2.3   Reduced relative clauses

Non-finite clauses, as in (20) to (22), just like their finite counterparts above, can be modifiers to N:

(20)   The stories [to tell him] are the following.
(21)   That story [written by him] is awful.
(22)   The author [writing those marvellous books] lives in Antarctica.

These non-finite clauses are called reduced relative clauses since one can paraphrase them with full relative clauses. For instance, (20) to (22) are similar to the relative clause structures in (23) to (25):

(23)   The stories [which you need to tell him] are the following.
(24)   That story [which was written by him] is awful.
(25)   The author [who is writing those marvellous books] lives in Antarctica.

In cases where there is a PP present, as in (24), we can often further reduce it, as in (26), in which case the modifier is a PP, not a (reduced) RC:

(26)   That story [by him] is awful.

We don't generally distinguish between restrictive and non-restrictive clauses in (20) to (22). Unlike finite clauses, non-finite clauses cannot be complements to nouns. Don't memorize this kind of information; just be able to analyze the structure of phrases.

Thus, the functions of finite clauses inside the NP are complement and modifier. Modifiers are referred to as relative clauses (RCs) and can be restrictive or non-restrictive. Non-finite clauses only function as modifiers and are referred to as reduced relatives. Some examples of reduced RCs appear in Table 10.3.

Table 10.3. Examples of Reduced RC

Infinitival	The plumber [to find the leak in the White House]
Present Participle	The ship [exploring Antarctica]
Past Participle	The book [written in an Edinburgh café]
	A dictionary [plagiarized in 1803]

In this section, we have looked at clauses that go with a noun. The next section will look at categories other than a noun that can be modified or complemented.

3.   NPs as compared to AdjPs, AdvPs, and PPs

As we've seen, inside an NP, clauses can function as relatives (i.e. modifiers) or complements, as (27) shows:

(27)   [The man [who crossed Antarctica]] was happy.

Let's look at the AdjP, AdvP, and PP.

Finite and non-finite clauses, as in (28) to (31), can be complements to AdjPs:

(28)   They were [happy [that he enjoyed his sugar-coated zucchini]].
(29)   Are you [confident [that your full Social Security benefits will be paid to you]]?

(30)   He was [unsure [what to do with the elephant in the room]].
(31)   She was [proud [to have grown the largest blue eggplant]].

Since adjectives can be compared, we also have comparative clauses, as in (32) and (33). These clauses function as modifiers since they indicate the degree of happiness and niceness. With adjectives, don't worry too much about the difference between complements and modifiers:

(32)   Most people are as [happy [as they want to be]].
(33)   She was [nicer [than I had thought]].

As shown in the previous chapter, AdvPs do not have complement or modifier PPs. They have no clausal complements or modifiers either. They only can have degree modification by another adverb.

Prepositions have complement clauses such as in (34) but do not generally admit object clauses with a *that* complementizer, as (35) shows. Instead, a non-finite clause, as in (36) or (37), appears:

(34)   I relied [on [what he wrote about clauses]].
(35)   *I insisted [on [that he/Stan should pay the bill]].
(36)   I insisted [on [him/Stan paying the bill]].
(37)   I insisted [on [his/Stan's paying (of) the bill]].

Some prepositions, such as *before* or *after* in (38), do introduce a clause but, as I mentioned in Chapter 7, they are then complementizers rather than prepositions:

(38)   He left [after she arrived].

4.   More on RCs

In this section, we'll briefly discuss a few other facts about English RCs. First, we'll look at relativized adverbials. Then, we'll look at prepositional and possessive relatives.

In Sections 1 and 2, most examples have the relative occupying a subject position or an object position. There is another frequently relativized function, namely that of adverbial, such as in (39) to (41):

(39)   The time [when you decide to discuss that] is important.
(40)   The place [where you plan to live] is important.
(41)   The reason [why/that I avoided that party] is clear.

The difference between subject, object, and adverbial relative is in the relative pronoun used. For subjects, *who* is used for humans, as in (2), (5), (6), (9), and (10) above; *which* for non-humans, as in (4) above; and *that* for both if it is restrictive, as in (7). For (direct, indirect, and prepositional) objects, *whom* is used for humans in very formal English, *who* in less formal English; *which* for non-humans, and *that* in restrictive relatives for both subject and object. Relativized adverbials, as in (39) to (41), use the relative pronoun most appropriate to the adverbial, *when* for a time adverbial, *where* for place, etc, but can sometimes also use *that*.

RCs that relativize PPs occur and English has many options. They can 'strand' the preposition, as in (42), or 'pied pipe' it (as in the Rat Catcher of Hamelin), as in (43):

(42)   The translation [which I insisted on] was unavailable.
(43)   The translation [on which I insisted] was unavailable.

The relative pronoun can be left out, as in (44); and *that* can be used, but only when the preposition stays in place, as in (45):

(44)   The translation [I insisted on] went missing.
(45)   The translation [that I insisted on] went missing.

When *who* is used, there are some other possibilities, depending on whether the objective marked *whom* is used; *that* is still a possibility too:

(46)   The man [about whom she heard that rumor] is in prison.
(47)   The woman [who(m) I heard this rumor about] is pleasant.
(48)   The woman [that I heard this rumor about] is pleasant.

Possessives can be relativized too, as in (49). They have an alternative as in (50), but the use of *whose* is not restricted to human antecedents, as (51) shows. And there's an alternative in (52):

(49)   You start with S, [whose daughters are always NP and VP].
(50)   You start with S, [the daughters of which are always NP and VP].
(51)   The book, [whose author is well-known], was on NPR this morning.
(52)   The book, [the author of which is well-known], was on NPR this morning.

5.   The structure of modifiers and complements (optional)

Relative clauses and complement clauses have a structure very similar to those clauses discussed in Chapters 7 and 8, with a CP, a C, and an S. The CP will be the same for all; the crucial difference between the different kinds of RCs and complement clauses is how close the CP is to the noun, i.e. what they are sister to. In this section, I provide the trees for some of these, namely for restrictive and non-restrictive RCs, complement clauses, reduced relative clauses, and complements to adjectives.

Structures of NPs with restrictive and non-restrictive RCs are given in (53) and (54) respectively. Structurally, the restrictive RC is closer to the head noun than the non-restrictive. In (53) and (54), this is indicated by being sister to the N′ and to the NP respectively:

(53)

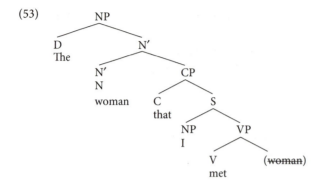

(54)

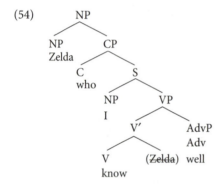

To indicate the function of the modified noun inside the RC, a copy in parentheses is introduced. It has a line through it to show that it is not pronounced there. In (53), for instance, *the woman* is met, i.e. *the woman* functions as the direct object in the RC. Similarly, in (54), *Zelda* is the object in the RC and a copy indicates that. I am focussing on trees in which the copy is an object since they are the least complex. In the (advanced) exercises, there will be other trees to draw.

Structurally, the restrictive RC is said to be closer to the N head but not as close as the complement clause shown below. The non-restrictive RC is often said to be sister to the NP, i.e. outside the NP. In Chapter 3 (Section 3), a number of structures were discussed that have a similar structure (with one NP branching to another), namely, coordinated NPs and appositive NPs. Many grammarians have noticed the similarities between non-restrictive RCs and appositive NPs, hence the alternative name of appositive RC. Thus, as mentioned, the appositive NP *We, the people of the United States, ...* could be rewritten as *We, who are the people of the United States, ...*

Now, let's turn to the clause with the closest connection to the noun, the complement clause as in (55). Note that the CP is sister to the N *reports*:

(55)

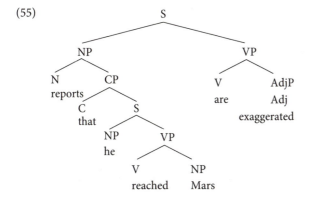

The reduced RC in (56) is similar to (53) but with more empty positions:

(56)

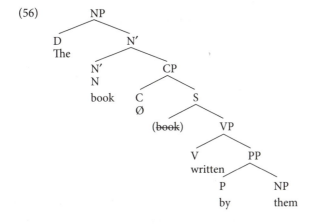

Finally, some trees for complements to adjectives are provided in (57) and (58), one
finite and the other non-finite:

(57)

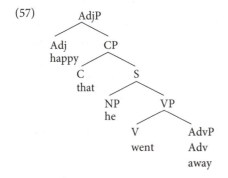

(58)

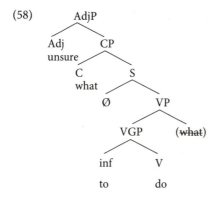

To summarize the differences in the positions of the clauses in relation to their heads, I provide Table 10.4.

Table 10.4. The sisters of CP

Complement Clause	CP is sister to N	Adjective Clause	CP is sister to Adj
Restrictive RC	CP is sister to N′		
Reduced RC	CP is sister to N′		
Non-restrictive RC	CP is sister to NP		

6. Conclusion

In Chapters 7 and 8, functions of finite and non-finite clauses were discussed at sentence level, namely subject, direct object, adverbial, and subject predicate. In the current chapter, we have discussed finite and non-finite clauses at phrase-level, namely functioning inside an NP or AdjP. These phrase-internal clauses have two functions: modifier and complement.

Sections 1 and 2 are the most important of the chapter. It is first explained that finite clauses that function as modifiers are called relative clauses and can be divided into restrictive and non-restrictive relatives. Clauses that function as complements to a limited set of nouns are also discussed as are non-finite clauses functioning as modifiers, namely those called reduced relative clauses. Section 3 examines clausal modifiers and complements to the P and Adj heads. Section 4 adds complexity to the RC by providing three additional varieties and Section 5 provides tree structures for the clauses discussed in Sections 1, 2, and 3.

The key terms are **relative and complement clauses; restrictive and non-restrictive relative clauses;** and **reduced relatives.**

Exercises

A.   Label the clauses in (59) to (64) as complements or relatives and as finite or non-finite:

(59)   The javelina [that I saw next door] was unafraid of coyotes.
(60)   The report [that javelinas are dangerous] is exaggerated.
(61)   Gerald, [who lives next door], will be leaving soon.
(62)   The yellow fog [that rubs its back upon the window-panes]
       (from T.S.Eliot's *Love Song* for J.A.P)
(63)   The president [that founded this organization] was arrested twice before he was
       replaced.
(64)   I am the man [to fix this].
(65)   The story [that Kissinger went to Moscow for Obama] seems true.

B.   In the text below, from Harry Potter, there are three RCs. Find them and label them as
       restrictive, non-restrictive, or reduced. If there are relative pronouns, what is their function
       inside the RC?

       Harry's feet touched road. He saw the achingly familiar Hogsmeade High Street: dark
       shop fronts, and the outline of black mountains beyond the village, and the curve in
       the road ahead that led off towards Hogwarts, and light spilling from the windows
       of the Three Broomsticks, and with a lurch of the heart he remembered, with pierc-
       ing accuracy, how he had landed here nearly a year before, supporting a desperately
       weak Dumbledore; all this in a second, upon landing – and then, even as he relaxed
       his grip upon Ron's and Hermione's arms, it happened. The air was rent by a scream
       that sounded like Voldemort's when he had realized the cup had been stolen: It tore
       at every nerve in Harry's body, and he knew immediately that their appearance had
       caused it. (J.K Rowling, *Harry Potter*, volume 7: 554)

C.   Change one of the finite clauses in (63) into a non-finite one.

D.   In the (challenging) text below, identify the relative clauses by putting brackets around
       them:

       To educate as the practice of freedom is a way of teaching that anyone can learn. That
       learning process comes easiest to those of us who teach who also believe that there
       is an aspect of our vocation that is sacred; who believe that our work is not merely to
       share information but to share in the intellectual and spiritual growth of our students.
       To teach in a manner that respects and cares for the souls of our students is essential
       if we are to provide the necessary conditions where learning can most deeply and
       intimately begin. (from bell hooks *Teaching to Transgress*, 1994: 13)

Optional (Section 5)

E.   Draw trees for (59) to (65).

Class discussion

F.   What is the basic structure of (65)? (Don't draw a tree!) Which are the relative clauses?

(66)   Shakespeare, *Loves Labour's Lost*, I, 2, 157

Armado: I doe affect the very ground (which is base) where her shooe (which is baser) guided by her foote (which is basest) doth tread.

G.   Can clauses (relative or complement clauses) ever precede the head? If yes, give examples. If no, give ungrammatical examples.

Keys to the exercises

A.   In (59), *that I saw next door* is a (restrictive) RC which is finite; in (60), *that javelinas are dangerous* is a finite noun complement; in (61), *who lives next door* is a (non-restrictive) RC which is finite; in (62), *that rubs its back upon the window-panes* is a (restrictive) RC, also finite; in (63), *that founded this organization* is a (restrictive) RC which is finite, and in (64), there is a reduced (non-finite) RC. Sentence (65) contains a finite complement to the noun *story*.

B.   The first RC is restrictive (and finite), the second reduced (and non-finite), and the third restrictive (and finite). The two relative markers function as subjects.
    Harry's feet touched road. He saw the achingly familiar Hogsmeade High Street: dark shop fronts, and the outline of black mountains beyond the village, and the curve in the road ahead [that led off towards Hogwarts], and light [spilling from the windows of the Three Broomsticks], and with a lurch of the heart he remembered, with piercing accuracy, how he had landed here nearly a year before, supporting a desperately weak Dumbledore; all this in a second, upon landing – and then, even as he relaxed his grip upon Ron's and Hermione's arms, it happened. The air was rent by a scream [that sounded like Voldemort's when he had realized the cup had been stolen]: It tore at every nerve in Harry's body, and he knew immediately that their appearance had caused it.

C.   The president that founded this organization was arrested twice before **being replaced**.

D.   To educate as the practice of freedom is a way of teaching [that anyone can learn]. That learning process comes easiest to those of us [who teach [who also believe that there is an aspect of our vocation [that is sacred]]]; who believe that our work is not merely to share information but to share in the intellectual and spiritual growth of our students. To teach in a manner [that respects and cares for the souls of our students] is essential if we are to provide the necessary conditions [where learning can most deeply and intimately begin]. It is not clear how the clause starting with *who believe* … is connected to the rest of the sentence and that's why I haven't marked it.

E.   (59)

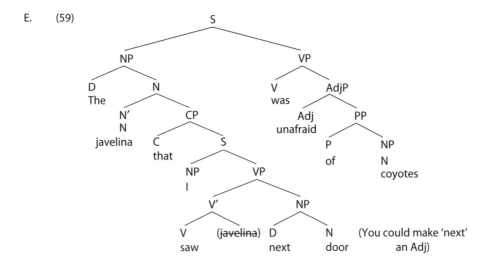

In (60), you could also argue that *exaggerated* is the past participle form of the verb and part of the VGP. Then, *is* will be an auxiliary, not a copula as in the tree below:

(60)

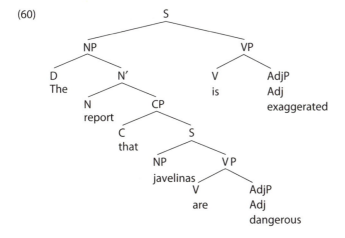

In (61), I have indicated that *soon* and *next door* are adverbials by making them sisters to V':

(61)

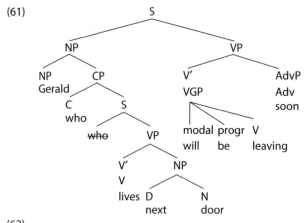

(62)

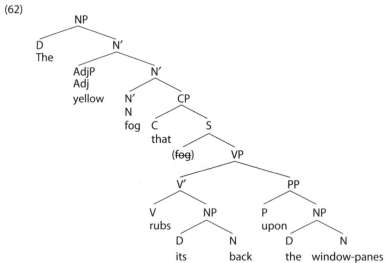

(63)

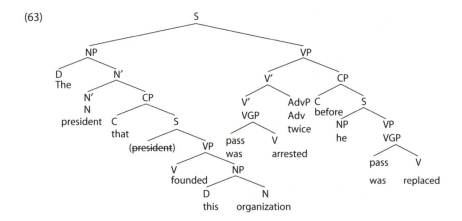

In (63), I have expressed that *twice* and *before he was replaced* are adverbials by making them sisters to V's. (Note that VGP is used when auxiliaries are present, but that V suffices when there is just the lexical verb).

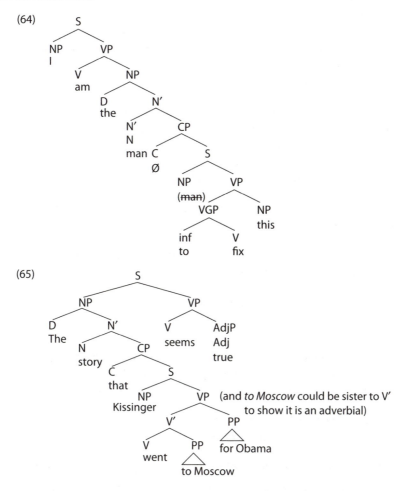

(64)

(65)

Special topic: Relative choice and preposition stranding

In spoken language, our most favorite relative marker is *that*. In writing, we predominantly use a *wh*-pronoun. This shows that there are some strong prescriptive rules at work where relatives are concerned. Fowler has definite ideas on all of these issues. In the older edition, he says: "Relative pronouns are as troublesome to the inexpert but conscientious writer as they are useful to everyone, which is saying much" (1926 [1950]: 709). Other style books have similar ideas. Three of these rules can be phrased as follows:

(67)   **The case of the relative:** "The case of the pronouns *who* and *whom* depends on their function within their own clause. When a pronoun serves as the subject, use *who* or *whoever*; when it functions as an object, use *whom* or *whomever*" (Kirszner & Mandell 1992: 376–7).

(68)   **The antecedent:** "*who* refers to people or to animals that have names. *Which* and *that* usually refer to objects, events, or animals and sometimes to groups of people" (Kirszner & Mandell 1992: 381).

(69)   **Do not strand prepositions.**

The choice between nominative or accusative case has been talked about in the special topic to Chapter 4, as well as briefly in the chapter above. The only position where speakers still use *whom* is directly following a preposition, as in (70):

(70)   This is a man about **whom** I know very little.

The debate about the use of *who, which*, or *that* is a very lively one. Many argue that *that* can only be used in restrictive relatives when the antecedent is non-human. Sentence (71) violates both:

(71)   'was her Brother, **that** in pure kindnesse to his Horse, buttered his Hay.
        (Shakespeare, *King Lear* II, 4, 128)

Fowler is careful about criticizing the use of *that* and thinks it will change (1926[1950]: 716) "at present there is much more reluctance to apply *that* to a person than to a thing. Politeness plays a great part".

The dislike of stranding prepositions allegedly started with John Dryden. Many 'good' writers employ constructions with stranded prepositions, and would rewrite (70) as (72) with a stranded *about*. Sir Winston Churchill is said to have ridiculed the construction by uttering (73):

(72)   This is a man (who) I know little **about.**

(73)   This is something **up with which** I will not put.

Stranding prepositions does not just occur with relatives, but in questions as well, as in (74):

(74)   who did I want to talk **to**?

Chapter 11

Special sentences

1. Questions/interrogatives: The CP
2. Exclamations
3. Topicalization, passive, cleft, and pseudo-cleft
4. Conclusion

In this chapter, I discuss sentences in which elements have moved around for a particular reason, e.g. to enable the speaker to ask a question, to make an exclamation, or to emphasize something. The latter occurs through topicalization, passive, cleft, and pseudo-cleft. Question sentences are referred to as interrogatives, whereas most of the sentences we have seen up to now assert something and are called indicatives or declaratives.

In Section 1, we look at questions, both *yes/no* and *wh*-questions and suggest a tree for them using a CP. In Section 2, we briefly cover exclamatives and how they differ from questions. Section 3 goes into topicalization, passives, and clefting. Some of the material in this chapter has been covered, e.g. questions and passives, but in slightly different contexts.

1. Questions/interrogatives: The CP

Questions can be main clauses (*Will she leave?*) or embedded clauses (*I wonder if she'll leave*). They can also be classified according to whether the entire sentence is questioned, in which case a *Yes* or *No* answer is expected, or whether another element is questioned using a *wh*-word (also called an interrogative pronoun) such as *who, what, why*, etc., in which case a full answer is expected.

In *yes/no* questions, the only appropriate answer is *Yes* or *No* (or *Perhaps/maybe*). To make a question, e.g. of (1), the auxiliary *has* is fronted, as in (2):

(1)   She has gone.
(2)   **Has** she gone?

If there is no auxiliary present, a dummy *do* is used, as in (3), as discussed in Chapter 6:

(3)   **Did** you see Santa?

A structure for *yes/no* questions is given in (4), where the auxiliary moves to C (indicated by its copy left in the VGP that is not pronounced): [9]

(4)

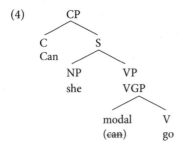

A main clause *wh*-question starts with a *wh*-word (*who, what, why, when, where,* and *how*) or wh-phrase (*which book,* etc). The auxiliary follows. There are empty positions in the sentence, indicated by copies (crossed out because we do not say them out loud). Examples are given in (5) to (7):

(5)   Who will you (will) see (who) in the Highlands?
(6)   How heavy is that box of chocolates (is) (how heavy)?
(7)   How much wood would a wood chuck (would) chuck (how much wood), if a wood chuck could chuck wood?

Evidence that the question word was at some point in the position of the copy is that, with special intonation, movement is not necessary. Thus, (8) is possible with emphasis on *what*. In this case the auxiliary stays in place too, as (8b) shows:

(8)   a.   You saw WHAT?
      b.   You would do WHAT?

Questions such as (8) are called 'echo-questions'

As to the structure, I will suggest (9) for *wh*-questions. The *wh*-word moves to the position immediately underneath the CP and the auxiliary moves to the C position. The original position of the *wh*-word and the auxiliary is indicated by means of a copy:

---

9.   Some people indicate that the sentence is a question by having a Q in C in (4) and in (9).

(9)

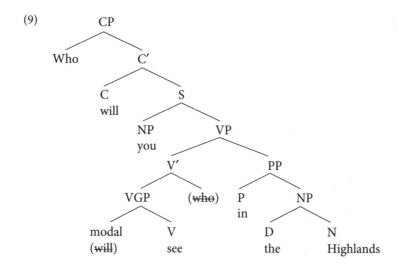

Using C, C′, and CP makes sense for these sentences and also makes the CP similar to the VP, the NP, and the other categories that have a phrase, a head, and an intermediate category.

2.   Exclamations

Sentences such as (10) can be analyzed using a CP as well, namely as structures where the phrase *what a nasty person* is in the same position as the *wh*-word in (9). Notice that in sentences, such as (10) and (11), the auxiliary does not move, unlike in the questions in (5) to (7):

(10)   What a nasty person he is (~~what a nasty person~~)!
(11)   "What an excellent father you have, girls," said she, when the door was shut.
       (Jane Austen, *Pride & Prejudice*, Chapter 2)

This was not always the case in English, as (12) shows. In (12), *have* has moved to before the subject *I*, unlike *is* in (10) and *have* in (11):

(12)   O what a Scene of fool'ry **haue** I seene. Of sighes, of grones, of sorrow, and of teene:
       (Shakespeare, *Love's Labor's Lost*, IV, iii, 163)

Modern English exclamatives differ from questions in not fronting the auxiliary, but they do involve movement of a *wh*-phrase to a position in the CP.

3. Topicalization, passive, cleft, and pseudo-cleft

Even though the structures of topicalizations, clefts, and passives look very different, they have in common that the order of words is rearranged to emphasize a part of the sentence. Examples such as (13) are similar to exclamations but occur without the question word. I have marked where *tomatoes* comes from by means of an arrow. In (14), the topic is preceded by *as for*, and repeated by a pronoun:

(13) **Tomatoes**, I really don't like __ in my cereal.

(14) and **as for herself, she** was too much provoked . . .
      (Jane Austen, *Emma*, Vol 1, Chap 15)

Some topicalizations serve to front old information, which is convenient to listeners.

In the same way, passives and clefts can shift phrases to put old information at the beginning of a sentence and new information towards the end. In a passive, as seen in earlier chapters, the subject *she* in (15) is the object *her* of the corresponding active in (16). This shifts the attention:

(15) **She** was persuaded to go by Columbo.   (passive)

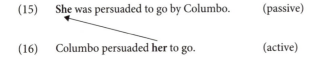

(16) Columbo persuaded **her** to go.   (active)

Examples of a cleft and pseudo-cleft are given in (17a) and (18a). I have provided a declarative version of each in (17b) and (18b). A cleft starts with *it is* or *it was* and a pseudo-cleft starts with a *wh*-word:

(17) a. **It was** on the wedding-day of this beloved friend that Emma first sat in mournful thought of any continuance. (Jane Austen, *Emma*, vol 1, Chap 1)

      b. Emma first sat in mournful thought of any continuance on the wedding-day of this beloved friend.

(18) a. **What** he threw away was the winning lottery ticket.
      b. He threw away the winning lottery ticket.

The cleft picks out one phrase from the sentence to focus on, e.g. *on the wedding-day of this beloved friend* in (17a). By doing so, it separates the phrase from the rest of the sentence which becomes subordinate to the first part. The pseudo-cleft focuses on a phrase by doubling it through a *wh*-word and then having the focussed phrase come after the copula.

The structure of clefts is that of a restrictive relative clause, as in (19). The structure of pseudo-clefts is controversial and will not be given:

(19)

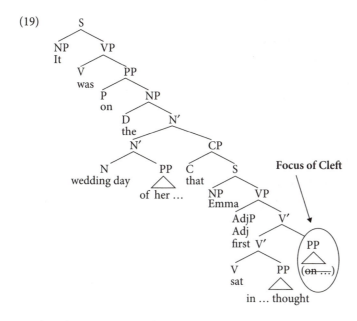

Note that I have represented an NP and PP by means of a 'coathanger' since the internal structure is not relevant here; and I haven't filled in the words to some of the phrases. This is for reasons of space.

4. Conclusion

In this chapter, I briefly describe a number of special constructions, where movement seems to be taking place to achieve a special effect, namely questions, exclamations, topicalization, passive, and clefting. Tree structures using a CP are provided for the *yes/no* and *wh*-questions and the cleft.

Key terms are **questions (*wh* and *yes/no*); exclamations; topicalization, cleft, pseudo-cleft, and passive.**

Exercises

A.   Identify the special constructions in:

    (20)   It is his character that I despise.

    (21)   She was recognized going into the store.

    (22)   Higgins I hate.

    (23)   Who did Anne say that she saw?

B.   Draw trees for:

    (24)   Will she go then?

    (25)   What will they think?

C.   Explain the ambiguity in the following headline:

    (26)   Stolen Painting Found by Tree.

Keys to the exercises

A.   Sentence (20) is a cleft; (21) a passive; (22) a topicalization, and (23) a *wh*-question.

B.   (24)

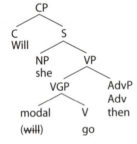

(25)

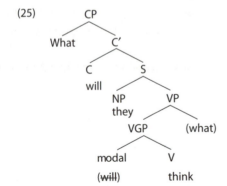

C.   The sentence can be a passive in which case the meaning is strange/funny since typically trees are inanimate objects and don't find things. The intended meaning is not a passive, but one where *by tree* is a place adverbial, i.e. the painting was found by someone at the site of a tree; the finder has been left out or is unknown.

Special topic: Comma punctuation

Commas are used in writing to indicate a slight pause in speech. Pauses help disambiguate structural ambiguities, i.e. are syntactic in nature. The discussion below is not meant to be exhaustive but merely discusses commas in connection to some of the constructions dealt with in this book. The main use of commas is to indicate that some information is not crucial. Since objects and complements are more important than modifiers and adverbials, we don't use commas for the former but we may do so for modifiers and adverbials (some people argue that one must use them there).

Some specific rules are (26), (27), and (28):

(26)   Commas are not used inside the core sentence to separate the subject, verb, and object.

(27)   Commas may be used for non-restrictive relative clauses and for adverbial clauses but not for restrictive clauses. Sentence adverbials are always surrounded by commas.

(28)   Commas are not used between independent clauses. If they are, the construction is called the comma splice.

As to (26), subjects, as in (29), cannot be separated from their verbs, even if the subject is a clause, as in (30), and neither can commas appear before objects, as in (31), or before subject and object predicates:

(29)   *He, left.
(30)   *That he didn't want to meet the Dalai Lama, is true.
(31)   *I noticed, that she …

I have marked these as ungrammatical but that is perhaps too radical since technically they aren't.

Commas are used for non-restrictive relative clauses, as in (32), sentence initial adverbials, as in (33), but are not used for restrictive relative and complement clauses, as in (34):

(32)   Pure Empiricism, which he was disposed not to accept, leads to scepticism.
(33)   Fortunately, she was on an urban safari tour.
(34)   *The story, that he met the Dalai Lama, is true.

The comma splice is well-known from composition classes. An example appears in (35):

(35)   Scientists think they have detected life on the Moon, visions of people living in lunar colonies that stop off to refuel on the way to Mars can be envisaged.

Where would you put a period in (35) to fix this?

I'll now give some examples where pauses in speech and commas in writing do make a difference. The well-known (36) is ambiguous; it is sexist either way but illustrative. When (36) is pronounced without pauses or written without commas, it is unclear:

(36)   Woman without her man is a savage.

The two possible interpretations are either (37) or (38):

(37)   Woman, without her, man is a savage.
(38)   Woman, without her man, is a savage.

The tree structure of (38) is given in (39), with *woman* the subject and *is a savage* as the predicate. The structure of (37) is more complex since *woman* is topicalized and, as shown in (40), *man* is the subject and *is a savage* is the predicate:

(39)

(40)

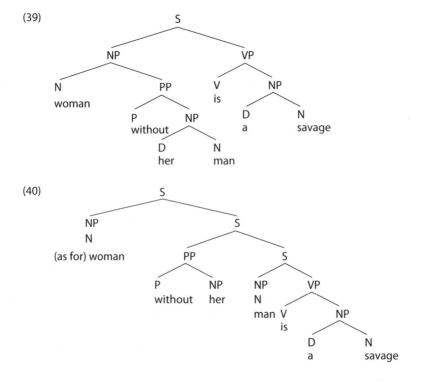

A construction where there is no agreement about when to use commas in coordinating three or more elements. Some argue that all commas should be present in (41), e.g. Fowler and Oxford University Press; others argue the last can be left out. Allegedly, it once became the matter of a law suit, when something like (42) appeared in a will:

(41)   The books, magazines, and records in this store are on sale.
(42)   Equal parts of the estate will go to Mary, Jane, Edward and Michael.

Apparently, Mary and Jane assumed they would each get a third and Edward and Michael each a sixth, whereas Edward and Michael assumed each would get a quarter. I now put all commas in!

Review of Chapters 9 to 11

In Chapters 9 and 10, the inner structure of the phrase is examined. PPs and AdvP are the simplest: PPs have a head and a complement and AdvPs have a modifier and a head. AdjPs and NPs are more complex. The AdjP can have an Adj head, an Adv(P) modifier, and a complement; an NP can have a determiner, a head, several modifiers (both preceding and following the head) and one complement (either preceding or following the head). DON'T memorize this; just be able to analyze a given sentence. A relatively complex NP is given in (1):

(1)

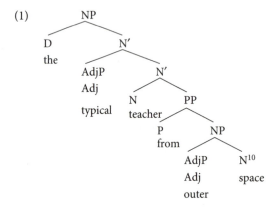

In Chapter 10, we give names to the different kinds of clauses. These include restrictive and non-restrictive relative clauses, complement clauses, reduced relatives, and complements to adjectives. Trees for these are provided in the last section of that chapter. Chapter 11 gives examples of some special effect sentences such as topicalizations, passives, questions, and clefts. Just be prepared to recognize these. A tree for some of these is also given in that chapter, using a CP, with a C and a C′.

Rather than providing separate exercises, I include three homework assignments, a short one that covers the special topics, a second one that I use regularly and that students find very helpful, and a third, very comprehensive and difficult one, that covers Chapters 7 to 11 and that I often use as a special credit assignment. No keys are given because they are meant to be real homework or take home assignments. There are also three samples of final exams covering the entire book. A key is provided on the website. (I have tried to balance convenience and too much convenience by doing this).

---

10. If you want to show that the PP in (1) is a modifier, make it sister to an N′.

Homework 1, on Chapter 1 and special topics

The book has discussed prescriptive grammar in Chapter 1 and has covered 11 special topics. Some of these topics include well-known prescriptive rules, e.g. the one on the split infinitive (Chapter 1), the multiple negative (Chapter 3), the dangling participle (Chapter 8), and preposition stranding (Chapter 10). Some topics help explain a grammatical category, for instance, the adjective and adverb (Chapter 2) or the complementizer (Chapter 7) and how these categories change over time. Case and agreement phenomena (Chapter 4) are very relevant to the grammar of English and the changes it is undergoing while other phenomena are stylistic choices, such as the use of the passive (Chapter 5). Thus, in an academic paper, one must use the correct agreement on the verb but, depending on the field, the use of the passive is fine.

Choose one of the special topics and show by means of examples from your own writing whether or not you follow the prescriptive rule. Then, choose an audience (perhaps first year students taking a composition class) and write a short (200 words) explanation on how, and possibly how not, to use this construction.

Homework 2, covering Chapters 2–11

Take a page of your own writing (an academic paper might be the easiest) and analyze it in terms of the grammatical structures it uses. For instance, we have seen that Hemingway ((76) in Chapter 5) uses relatively short sentences with copulas and that Tolstoy ((43) to (45) in Chapter 9) uses lots of PP modifiers. Use similar observations about your own writing.

To analyze your own writing, consider the ten points below. You could mark the page of your writing in a different color or use multiple copies of your text. Then write a paragraph summarizing what you see. If you think it is easier to compare your writing to someone else's, do that, still using these points.

A.   Modification of nouns. Do you use a lot of adjectives and PPs as modifiers?
B.   Types of verbs used? Do you use a mixture of intransitives, transitives, copulas, and other types?
C.   Do you use coordination? If so, which coordinators do you use and is your coordination of phrases or of clauses?
D.   Adverbials. Are there many adverbials and, if so, which kinds (clausal or PP)?
E.   Auxiliaries.
F.   Passive.
G.   Embedded clauses. What functions do they have?
H.   Finite as opposed to non-finite clauses.
I.   Dummy elements.
J.   Split infinitives, dangling modifiers, or anything else banned by prescriptive rules?

(For fun, you could use http://textalyser.net. This site will give you the frequency of words in a text you want).

Homework 3, or take-home exam, covering Chapters 7–11

In the text below, taken from Thomas Kuhn:

A.   Locate the relative clauses and indicate whether they are restrictive or non-restrictive.
B.   Find all the finite verbs and indicate whether or not they are lexical.
C.   Analyze the last sentence of the first paragraph in terms of basic sentence structure. Try to draw a tree.
D.   Draw a tree for the NP *its practitioners' insistence . . . being considered* (second paragraph)
E.   How might one analyse a sentence with *if* as in (last but one sentence in the second paragraph).

Anyone who studies the history of scientific development repeatedly encounters a question, one version of which would be, "Are the sciences one or many?" Ordinarily that question is evoked by concrete problems of narrative organization, and these become especially acute when the historian of science is asked to survey his subject in lectures or in a book of significant scope. Should he take up the sciences one by one, beginning, for example, with mathematics, proceeding to astronomy, then to physics, to chemistry, to anatomy, physiology, botany, and so on? Or should he reject the notion that his object is a composite account of individual fields and take it instead to be knowledge of nature *tout court*? In that case, he is bound, insofar as possible, to consider all scientific subject matters together, to examine what men knew about nature at each period of time, and to trace the manner in which changes in method, in philosophical climate, or in society at large have affected the body of scientific knowledge conceived as one.

Given a more nuanced description, both approaches can be recognized as long-traditional and generally noncommunicating historiographic modes. [note deleted] The first, which treats science as at most a loose-linked congeries of separate sciences, is also characterized by its practitioners' insistence on examining closely the technical content, both experimental and theoretical, of past versions of the particular specialty being considered. That is a considerable merit, for the sciences are technical, and a history which neglects their content often deals with another enterprise entirely, sometimes fabricating it for the purpose. On the other hand, historians who have aimed to write the history of a technical specialty have ordinarily taken the bounds of their topic to be those prescribed by recent textbooks in the corresponding field. If, for example, their subject is electricity, then their definition of an electrical effect often closely resembles the one provided by modern physics. With it in hand, they may search ancient, medieval, and early modern sources for appropriate references, and an impressive record of gradually accumulating knowledge of nature sometimes results. (from Kuhn "Mathematical versus Experimental Traditions in the Development of Physical Science")

Examples of final exams

Example 1

This exam is based on a text adapted from *The Games Helmet* (the *London Sunday Times*, 25 Nov 2007).

A.   Label the categories (N, V, D, etc.) in the sentence below:

   (1)   The fact that an advanced system has been developed
          for computer games should come as no surprise.

B.   Label the six lexical verbs (Intransitive, etc) that are underlined:

   Think carefully before you answer: is a device that <u>is</u> capable of <u>reading</u> people's minds
   fact or fantasy? We knew you'd say that. But scientists at an American laboratory have
   been brainstorming the same question for more than five years and have <u>thought</u> up
   a mind-blowingly different answer. They <u>call</u> it Epoc, but when it is launched early next
   year in Britain and the US we will probably <u>give</u> it the name of "mind-reading helmet",
   capable, supposedly, of <u>knowing</u> what users are thinking.

   is: reading:
   thought: call:
   give: knowing:

C.   Identify the functions of the eight underlined and numbered phrases (Su, Dir Object, etc. or Modifier):

   The device is being hailed as a revolutionary breakthrough in the way that humans
   will be able to interact (1) <u>with computers</u>. Its implications are (2) <u>massive</u>, opening
   the possibility that one day (3) <u>people</u> will be able to control everything from light
   switches to the cursor on their computer screen simply by thinking about it. (4)
   <u>However</u>, for now, the technology will be used as the ultimate gimmick: to play
   computer games simply by thinking your screen character (5) <u>into action</u>. Emotiv
   Systems, the San Francisco company that has developed the technology, says Project
   Epoc could mean the end of joysticks and keyboard bashing. Instead games players
   will be able to visualise a move in their head and that move will be replicated (6)
   <u>on the screen in front of them</u>. So, for example, Harry Potter could be ordered to
   cast exotic spells, or a jedi might exert "the force" to fling (7) <u>his enemies</u> around – all
   through the willpower (8) <u>of the gamer,</u> with no buttons pressed.

D.   AND name these phrases (e.g. NP, PP):

Function (e.g. Adverbial)	Name (e.g. NP, PP)
1	....
2	....
3	....
4	....
5	....
6	....
7	....
8	....

E.   Draw a tree for:

(2)   Scientists at an American laboratory brainstormed the question for five years

F.   Circle the lexical verbs and underline the auxiliaries in the text. Which are finite?

So how does the helmet work? In simple terms it relies on the fact that every time a human thinks about something, electrical impulses are triggered in the brain. This has been known for years in the medical world and is the basis of an electroencephalogram (EEG) – the technique that measures the electrical activity of the brain by recording from electrodes placed on the scalp. Emotiv claims to have refined the technique to isolate and identify the electrical patterns that are given off when humans think about a given course of action, such as moving their arm to the left or right or depressing their right thumb or index finger. The Epoc helmet recognizes these electrical patterns and translates them into "real" movements on the screen.

G.   Identify the function and type of the clauses in brackets, e.g. modifier/reduced RC, Subject/non-finite, etc. in:

[To look at], the helmet resembles nothing so much as a novelty head massage gadget with several spidery arms [curving around the head and meeting at the top]. The arms are fitted with a total of 16 sensors [that are positioned so that they are in contact with the relevant part of the head and pick up electric signals in the brain]. The system's software analyzes these signals and then wirelessly relays what it detects to a receiver plugged into the USB port of the game console or PC. Emotiv says that it has mapped 12 specific actions [that the helmet will recognize].

H.   Draw a tree for:

(3)   Emotiv says that it has mapped specific actions to use in its program.

I.   Circle the phrasal verbs, if any, and underline the passives, if any, in:

If true, the implications are huge. Gaming is believed to merely be the way to popularize the technology rather than being an end in itself: the tip of the virtual iceberg. In the long run the headset could be used widely, from the use of brain scanners as lie detectors to see whether suspects can make out a crime scene, to enabling consumers to turn machines on or off or change television channels without a remote control.

Example 2

Please read the following text. Most questions are based on it. It is adapted from *The New York Times*, 4 December 1996, but even as late as 2009, the debate on ice/water on the moon continued.

The Moon May have Water

Scientists think they have detected water on the Moon. Suddenly, visions of people living in lunar colonies that stop off to refuel on the way to Mars are less far-fetched. After two years of careful analysis, scientists said yesterday that radar signals from an American spacecraft indicated the moon was not bone-dry. The spacecraft's radar signatures suggested the presence of water ice in the permanently cold shadows of a deep basin near the lunar south pole.

The survey revealed a vast landscape in which ice crystals are mixed with dirt. It seems a kind of permafrost that is presumably the residue of moisture from comets striking the Moon over the last three billion years.

Even though scientists are not positive, they see signals consistent with ice. Dr. Paul Spudis, one of the scientists reporting on the discovery, acknowledged that the discovery needed to be confirmed by an independent investigation. That might come a year from now because then another spacecraft will orbit the Moon with instruments of even greater precision for determining the presence of lunar water.

This discovery gives astronauts hope for longer stays in space. Told of the new discovery, Dr. Story Musgrave was very enthusiastic. He said that this implied there might be water and water is extraordinarily important to establishing a permanent base on the Moon. Other scientists reacted to the report with a mixture of caution and enthusiasm. They noted that the radar results were particularly difficult to interpret.

A.   Identify all the categories in (1), e.g. D, N, etc.:

(1)   a kind of permafrost that is presumably the residue of moisture from comets striking the Moon over the last three billion years.

B.   List all PPs used as adverbials in the first paragraph (or underline them clearly in the text).

C.   Indicate function and name (or realization) of the phrases at sentence/clause level in the sentences/clauses below, e.g. *the world is round*: SU: NP/Pred: VP/SubjPr: AdjP. DO NOT ANALYSE THESE UNITS ANY FURTHER.

(2)   Suddenly, visions of people living in lunar colonies that stop off to refuel on the way to Mars are less far-fetched.

(3)   The survey revealed a vast landscape in which ice crystals are mixed with dirt.

(4)   …   another spacecraft will orbit the Moon with instruments of even greater precision for determining the presence of lunar water.

(5)   This discovery gives astronauts hope for longer stays in space.

D.   Locate all non-finite clauses in the third paragraph. List them here or underline them clearly in the text.

E.   What is the function and name of the following phrases in the structures in which they occur (e.g. Su/NP):

(6)   positive (l. 10)
(7)   consistent with ice (l. 10)
(8)   Told of the new discovery (l. 15)
(9)   that the radar results were particularly difficult to interpret (ll 18–9)

F.   List the modifiers in the fourth paragraph. Also indicate what their name is (e.g. PP, CP, etc.)
G.   List all auxiliaries. Indicate what kind they are (perfect . . .)
H.   Draw trees for (10) and (12):

(10)   After two years of careful analysis, scientists said yesterday that radar signals from an American spacecraft indicated the moon was not bone-dry.

(11)   Paul Spudis acknowledged that the discovery needed to be confirmed by an independent investigation.

Example 3

Please read the following text, A Life of Fiction, adapted from Jane Smiley (*New York Times Magazine*, 3/12/00)

When Charles Dickens was traveling home from France in June 1865, the train he was riding in went off the tracks while crossing a bridge over a river. Seven first-class carriages dropped into the river. The eighth, which was the one Dickens was travelling in, dangled off the bridge. Dickens calmed his companions and clambered out. He was indefatigable and helped to free his friends in the carriage and many others.

When all that could be done for the victims had been done, Dickens, who was 53 years old and not in very good health, climbed into the carriage again and retrieved from the pocket of his coat the installment of 'Our Mutual friend' he had just finished.

The author, who hadn't shrunk from describing the lurid and the terrible before, made no effort to describe what he had seen. "I don't know what to call the accident" he wrote to a friend. He also refused to give testimony to the subsequent inquest. Why did Dickens hide his heroism? It so happens that Dickens' traveling companions were his mistress Ellen Ternan and her mother. What is really interesting is that a man whose volume of writings approach logorrhea could dissemble his most intimate concerns and feelings so consistently and for so long.

A. List all adverbials in the second paragraph.

B. Indicate function and name of the phrases/clauses at sentence level, e.g. Su/NP; Adverbial/PP in the sentences below. Do not go further than the first layer:

    (1) I don't know what to call the accident

    (2) When all that could be done for the victims had been done, Dickens, who was 53 years old and not in very good health, climbed into the carriage again

    (3) … helped to free his friends in the carriage and many others

C. What is the function and name of the following:

    (4) his mistress … mother (ll. 12–3)

    (5) testimony (l. 11)

    (6) off the bridge (l. 3–4)

    (7) a man … logorrhea (l. 13)

D. List all auxiliaries in the second paragraph. Indicate what kind they are.

E. List all finite verbs in the third paragraph.

F. Indicate the relative clauses in the first and second paragraphs. Are they restrictive, non-restrictive, or reduced?

G. Draw trees for:

    (8) When Charles Dickens was traveling home from France in June 1865, the train he was riding in went off the tracks while crossing a bridge over a river.

    (9) Why did Dickens hide his heroism?

Glossary

At the end of each chapter, there is a list of key terms. These are the most relevant and should be understood. The glossary tries to be somewhat comprehensive, and lists key terms, abbreviations, non-key terms, and some common terminology not used in this book, e.g. attributive adjective, but perhaps used elsewhere. Don't attempt to memorize the glossary! There is also an index to the book so, if the definitions in the glossary do not suffice, check the index and read the relevant pages.

accusative case   The case of the object or prepositional object, only visible on pronouns in English, e.g. *me*, in *He saw me*, also called the objective case.

active   A sentence in which the doer of the action is the subject, as in *She guided the elephant*.

Adj   = adjective.

Adj′   Adjective-bar, intermediate category, see Chapter 9, Section 1.

adjective   A word which often describes qualities, e.g. *proud, intelligent,* or physical characteristics, e.g. *short, strong*.

adjective complement   Complement to an adjective, e.g. *of him* in *proud [of him]*; see Chapter 9, Section 1.

AdjP   = Adjective Phrase: group of words centered around an adjective, e.g. *very nice*.

adjunct   Term not used in this book; alternative for 'adverbial'.

Adv   = adverb, i.e. the category

Adv-ial   = adverbial, i.e. the function

adverb   E.g. *proudly*; it is similar to an adjective but it modifies a verb, adjective, or other adverb, whereas an adjective modifies a noun.

adverbial   A function at sentence level providing the background on where, when, how, and why the event described in the VP takes place.

AdvP   = Adverb Phrase: group of words centered around an adverb, e.g. *very nicely*.

affix   Cannot stand on its own, e.g. an ending such as *-ing*; see Table 6.2.

affix-hop   Process where an affix belonging to an auxiliary 'hops' and attaches to the verb immediately to the right of the auxiliary; see Chapter 6 and Table 6.2.

agreement   E.g. *-s* in *she walks*, ending on the verb that 'agrees' with the subject.

ambiguity/ambiguous   Word (lexical ambiguity) or sentence (structural ambiguity) with more than one meaning; see Chapters 1 and 3.

antecedent   What a pronoun refers to, e.g. the noun that a relative pronoun such as *who* refers to in *the man who(m) I saw*; see Chapters 9 and 10. Antecedent is used more generally though for any pronoun that refers to a noun.

antonym   A word with the opposite meaning, e.g. *hot/cold, good/bad*; Chapter 2.

appositive NP   The second NP in *Tegucigalpa, the capital of Honduras*; see Chapter 3. It rephrases the first and provides extra information; similar to a non-restrictive relative clause.

appositive relative clause   Another word for non-restrictive relative clause; see Chapter 10 and below.

article   *A, an, the* in English; see Chapter 2, Section 2.1.

aspect   When the type or duration of the action is emphasized, as in *he is reading*, rather than when the action took place, Chapter 6.

attributive adjective   Term not used in this book; an adjective that modifies a Noun inside an NP.

AUX   = auxiliary, see below.

auxiliary   A 'verb' that cannot stand on its own, but that 'helps' (combines with) another verb, e.g. *have* in *They have seen a riot*; see Chapters 2 and 6 and Table 6.1.

bare infinitive   Infinitive without a *to*; e.g. *leave* in *I saw her leave*, see Chapter 8.

branch   A line that marks the relationship between two nodes in tree; it shows how a phrase is divided up; see Chapter 3.

C = complementizer, see below.

C' = C-bar, intermediate category, only used in Chapter 11.

case   In English, case is only visible on pronouns. Thus, *she* in *She saw me* has nominative case, i.e. is used in subject position, and *me* has accusative or objective case, i.e. is used in object position.

clause   Unit containing a lexical verb, see also main clause, subordinate clause.

cleft   A construction of the form *It is Catweazle who caused the problems*; see Chapter 11.

coathanger   Not dividing a phrase into separate branches (to save space); used rarely in this book.

comma splice   A comma between two independent clauses; see extra topic Chapter 11.

comparative   Forms such as *greater* that compare one situation or entity with another.

complement   There are complements to V, N, Adj, and P. Complements to VPs are divided into direct and indirect object, subject predicate, object predicate, prepositional and phrasal object. Nouns, adjectives, and prepositions can also have complements.

complementizer   E.g. *that, if,* and *whether*; connects two clauses, one subordinate to the other; see Chapters 2 and 7.

complex transitive   A verb with a direct object and an object predicate; see Chapter 4.

compound   When two words are put together to form one word, e.g. *blackboard* and *sleepwalk*.

conjunction   Not generally used in this book, except in quotes and to indicate an alternative phrasing. It is a general term to describe a word that joins two or more words or phrases or sentences together. There are subordinating (*that*) and coordinating (*and*) conjunctions; see Chapter 2.

consonant   Sound such as *b, p, f, v, t, k*, made by somehow modifying the airstream; see Chapter 1, 1.1. for use in a rule.

constituent   Not used in this book; a group of words that form a unit, typically a phrase.

contraction   A word that is shortened, e.g. *he's* for *he has*; see special topic Chapter 6.

coordination   Connecting two phrases or clauses that are equal to each other by means of e.g. *and*; see Chapter 3.

coordinating conjunction   Not used in this book; same as coordinator, see there.

coordinator   Connects two phrases or clauses that are equal to each other, e.g. *and/ or*, also called coordinating conjunction; see Chapter 2.

copula   A verb with a subject predicate, typically *to be* or *to become*, see Chapter 4.

corpus   A set of texts collected to provide a representative view of the language of a particular time, social group, or genre.

CP   Complementizer Phrase, see Chapter 7 and 8.

D = determiner.

(D)Adv   Degree adverb, see below.

dangling modifier   An adverbial clause whose subject is not the same as the subject of the main sentence, see special topic Chapter 8.

daughter   For example, P is a daughter of a PP, i.e. lower in the tree but connected to the 'mother' by a branch; see Chapter 3.

declarative   A neutral sentence that is a statement, not a question or command.

definite article   The article *the*.

degree adverb   Adverbs that indicate degree, e.g. *very, too, so, more, most, quite, rather*; see Chapter 2.

descriptivism   Describing what language users really say, as opposed to what they 'should' say; see Chapter 1.

determiner   Word that points or specifies, e.g. *the*; see Chapter 2, Section 2.1.

direct object   Object of a verb such as *eat*, *see*, and *enjoy*. For instance, *him* in *They saw him*.

ditransitive   Verb that has both a direct and indirect object, e.g. *tell, give*; see Chapter 4.

dummy   A word used to fulfill a grammatical requirement, see dummy *do* and dummy subject below.

dummy *do*   If no auxiliary is present in a sentence, *do* is used with questions and negatives; see Chapter 6.

dummy subject   If a subject is not present, *it* or *there* are used, also see pleonastic subject; see special topic to Chapter 5.

E   = Event time, used in Chapter 6.

echo question   Question formed by special intonation, as in *You saw WHAT?* See Chapter 11.

ed-participle   See past participle.

elided/elision   Word or phrase left out to avoid repetition after a coordinator, e.g. in *He wrote a poem and painted a pictures*, the subject of *painted* has been left out.

ellipsis   Word or phrase left out to avoid repetition.

embedded sentence/clause   A clause or sentence inside another phrase or sentence/clause; see Chapter 7.

emphasizer   Words such as *even* and *just* that are used to emphasize a phrase, also called focusser; see Chapter 9.

exclamation or exclamative   Sentences such as *What a fool he is!!* See Chapter 11.

extraposed/extraposition   When an embedded clause (usually in subject position) is placed at the end of the sentence, e.g. *It was nice [that he left]*. A dummy subject *it* is put in the original position.

finite clause   A clause with a finite verb (see below) and a nominative subject; see Chapter 7.

finite verb   A verb expressing agreement and tense (past or present), e.g. *has* in *He has left*; see Chapters 6 and 7.

flat structure   A tree that does not express hierarchies because many braches descend from one node; see Chapter 3, Section 1.

focusser   Words such as *even* and *just* that are used to emphasize a phrase, also called emphasizer; see Chapter 9.

formal language   Language used in formal situations such as ceremonies, formal lectures, or meeting a government official; see Chapter 1.

fragment   An incomplete sentence, i.e. one missing a finite verb.

functional category   Not used in this book, alternative to grammatical category.

functions   Phrases (and clauses) have functions, such as subject and direct object, at the level of the sentence. There are also functions inside the phrase, namely as determiner, modifier, and complement. See Chapters 4 and 5 for functions at sentence level and Chapters 9 and 10 for functions at phrase level.

future (tense)   E.g. *will see* in *They will see the new bridge on their trip*.

future perfect   E.g. *will have done* in *They will have done that by 5*; see Chapter 6, Figure 6.1.

genitive case   The case that a possessive has, e.g. *Catweazle's* in *Catweazle's book*; see special topic Chapter 4.

gerund   A verbal noun that ends in *-ing*, briefly discussed in Chapter 8 and special topics Chapter 8.

gradable   Not used in this book. Adjective that can be modified in terms of degree, e.g. *very happy, happier*.

grammar   The rules to form and understand language. In this book, we focus on how to analyze sentences, rather than full texts, words, or sounds. We also focus on descriptive, rather than prescriptive rules.

grammatical   A sentence (or word) that native speakers consider acceptable.

grammatical category   Word with little lexical meaning, e.g. Determiner, Quantifier, Auxiliary, Coordinator and Complementizer; see Chapter 2.

head The most important part of a unit/ phrase, e.g. the N *seadog* is the head of the NP *the blue seadog*.

hypercorrection When speakers are so conscious that a prescriptive rule exists that they make a mistake. The use of *between you and I* is a good example.

inf = infinitival marker *to*; see Chapter 8.

ing-participle See present participle.

imperative A command such as *Go away, shut up!* See Chapter 6, Section 3.

indefinite article The articles *a* and *an*.

indicative A 'normal' sentence, i.e. not asking a question, indicating a wish or command. Declarative is also used.

indirect object Object that can be preceded by *to* or *for*, e.g. *Doris* in *Clovis gave Doris a flower*; see Chapter 4.

infinitive Form such as *to go, to be, to analyze*; it is one of the non-finite constructions. See Chapter 8.

informal language Language used in informal situations such as casual conversation. In/ formality depends on the situation, the participants, the topic. See Chapter 1.

innate faculty Enables us to acquire language; see Chapter 1.

interrogative pronoun Pronouns that start a *wh*-question such as *who left*; see Chapter 11. In form, they are similar to relative pronouns.

interrogative sentence A question such as *who will go there*; see Chapter 11.

intransitive A verb without an object, e.g. *laugh, swim*; see Chapter 4.

irregular verbs The past tense and past participle of these verbs are not formed by adding -*ed* to the present, as in the case of regular verbs. Some examples of irregular verbs are: *go, went, gone; see, saw, seen; write, wrote, written*. See Chapter 6.

lexical category Word with lexical meaning, such as a Noun, Verb, Adjective, Adverb, and Preposition; see Chapter 2. It has a synonym and antonym.

lexical verb Verb that can stand on its own, e.g. *see, walk*; see Chapters 2 and 6.

light verb Verbs such as *make, do, take* with a very general meaning that combine with nouns, such as *take a walk*. They can be replaced by verbs, e.g. *walk*; see Chapter 4.

linguistic knowledge Knowledge about linguistic notions and rules that we have in our heads, e.g. consonants and vowels, structure, question formation; see Chapter 1.

linguistics The study of language.

main clause Independent clause, i.e. a sentence that can stand on its own, minimally containing a subject and a predicate and not embedded within another clause.

modal Auxiliary such as *must, will, would, can, could* that expresses necessity, uncertainty, possibility; see Chapter 6.

modifier An element whose function is to provide more information on another element, e.g. *purple* in *purple sage*; see Chapter 9.

modify Describe the quality of something.

monotransitive See transitive.

morphology Rules for how to build words, e.g. *formal* + *ize*; see Chapter 1.

mother In a tree, the node above another node, e.g. PP is the mother of P.

multiple negation When two or more negative words (*not, nobody*) occur in the same clause, e.g. *I didn't eat nothing*; see special topic Chapter 3.

N = noun.

N′ = N-bar, intermediate category; see Chapters 3 and 9.

negation/negative E.g. *not* or *n't*, or a negative word such as *nothing*.

node a point in the tree, e.g. NP is a node, see Chapter 3.

nominative case The case of the subject, only visible on pronouns, e.g. *she* in *She left early*; see special topic Chapter 4.

non-finite clause A clause lacking a finite verb; see Chapter 8.

non-finite verb A verb that lacks tense and a nominative subject, e.g. *to be* in *to be or not to be is the question*; see Chapters 6 and 8.

non-linguistic (or social) knowledge   Knowledge of social rules; see Chapter 1, Section 3.

non-restrictive RC   A clause that provides background information to the noun it modifies; is often set apart from the rest of the sentence through commas or comma intonation; see Chapter 10.

noun   A word such as *table, freedom, book, love*; see Chapter 2.

noun complement   *Of chemistry* in *teacher of chemistry*; see Chapter 9.

NP   = Noun Phrase, group of words centered around a noun, e.g. *the red balloon*; see Chapter 3.

numeral   A word such as *one* or *two*. They can be seen as Adj or D; see Chapter 2 and Table 2.4.

objective or accusative case   In English, case is only visible on pronouns, e.g *him*, in *Hermione saw him*. Objects typically get this case, hence the name objective. See special topic, Chapter 4.

object predicate   Realized as an AdjP, NP, or PP, making a claim about the object, e.g. *nice* in *I consider her nice*. It occurs together with a complex transitive verb such as *consider, elect*; see Chapter 4.

OED   Oxford English Dictionary, see references.

P   = preposition.

participle   Either accompanied by an auxiliary, see Chapter 6, or on its own heading a non-finite clause, see Chapter 8.

particle   Similar in form to prepositions and adverbs, but a particle is only used together with a verb; see Chapter 5.

passive auxiliary   A form of *to be* used together with a past participle. For instance, *was* in *She was arrested*; see Chapter 6.

passive construction   A construction where an undergoer of the action is functioning as a subject, e.g. *she* in *She was met at the airport*.

past (tense)   An event took place in the past, i.e. the speech time and event time do not overlap.

past participle   Typically follows auxiliary *to have* to form a perfect, or *to be* to form a passive. It can function on it own in a non-finite clause. The participle ends in *-ed/-en (walked, written, chosen)* or may be irregular, such as *gone, swum, begun, learnt*.

past perfect   E.g. *had done* in *She had done that by five*; see Chapter 6, Figure 6.1.

perfect auxiliary   *To have* when used together with a past participle. For instance, *have* in *I have done that already*.

phonology   The structure of the sound system; see Chapter 1.

phrasal verb   A verb that is always combined with a preposition-like element but which has a special meaning. For instance, *look up* does not mean 'see upwards', but 'go to the library and check on something', see Chapter 5.

phrase   A group of related words, centered around a head; see Chapter 3.

pied piping   Taking the preposition along in a relative clause or a question, as in *the man [to whom] I talked*; see Chapter 10.

pleonastic subject   See dummy subject, see also Chapter 4 and special topic to Chapter 5.

possessive   E.g. *his* or *Catweazle's* in *his book* or *Catweazle's book*; see Chapter 2. It is of the D category.

postmodifier   Modifier that follows the head, e.g. *from Venice* in *a stone from Venice*.

PP   = Prepositional Phrase: group of words belonging to the preposition, e.g. *in the garden*.

pre-D   = Pre-determiner, quantifiers such as *all, both, half* can occur before the determiner, e.g. in *all that trouble*; see Chapter 2.

predicate   Says something about the subject, realized as a VP, e.g. *saw him* in *Hermione saw him*.

predicative adjective   Term not used in this book; an adjective that heads an AP with the function of subject predicate or object predicate.

premodifier   Modifier that precedes the head, e.g. *blue* in *a blue hat*.

preposing   Moving a word or phrase to a position towards the beginning of a sentence.

preposition   A word indicating location (in place and time), such as *at, in,* and *on,* direction, such as *to, into,* and *towards,* relationship, such as *with, between, among,* and *of;* see Chapter 2.

preposition stranding   Leaving the preposition behind in a relative clause or a question, as in *the man who I talked to;* see Chapter 10.

prepositional verb   A verb that has a PP as a complement, e.g. *rely on, refer to;* see Chapter 5.

prescriptive rules   A rule typically learned in school, see Chapter 1, e.g. don't split an infinitive or don't use multiple negation.

present (tense)   The event occurs at the time of speech.

present participle   Forms that end in *-ing,* e.g. *walking,* used after a progressive auxiliary, as in *he is walking,* or on its own in a non-finite clause, as in *walking along the street, I saw a fire.*

present perfect   A Verb Group like *have lived* in *I have lived here for ever.* See Chapter 6 and Figure 6.1.

progressive (aspect)   Indicating that the action is or was going on; see Chapter 6.

pronominalization   Referring to an NP, PP, VP, AdjP, or AdvP, i.e. a phrase, by means of a pronoun.

pro-form   Word that pronominalizes a PP, VP, AdjP, or AdvP. Used as a broader term than pronoun.

pronoun   Words such as *he, she, it, me* that refer to an NP; pronouns replacing PPs (*there*), AdjPs (*so*), AdvPs (*thus*), or VPs (*do so*) are called either pronoun or pro-form.

pronoun resolution   Determining the proper antecedent for a pronoun. See special topic to Chapter 9.

proper noun   Not used in this book. A noun that used for names, e.g. *Bertha, Arizona.*

pseudo-cleft   A construction such as *What he did was stupid,* used to emphasize/focus a part; see Chapter 11, Section 3.

pun   The use of a word to suggest two meanings; see Chapter 1.

quantifier   Words such as *all, some, many, each;* they are either like determiners or adjectives, or occur before determiners.

question   See *yes/no* question and *wh-*question.

RC   = relative clause, see below and Chapter 10.

reflexive pronoun   The pronouns *myself, yourself, himself, herself, ourselves* and *themselves.*

regular verbs   Verbs formed by adding *-ed* to the present to form the past tense and the past participle, as in the case of regular verbs such as *walk, walked, walked.* See Chapter 6.

relative clause   A clause/sentence that typically modifies a noun, e.g. *the tree which I see from the window;* see Chapter 10.

relative pronoun   pronoun such as *who, whose* that introduces relative clauses; see Chapter 10. The same set is used in questions and then they are called interrogative pronouns.

restrictive RC   A relative clause with highly relevant information; see Table 10.1.

S   = sentence: a group of words that includes at least a verb/VP

    = Speech on a timeline; see Chapter 6.

S'   = S-bar, used in the first edition of this book, replaced by CP.

S-adverbial   An adverbial that modifies the entire sentence or expresses the feelings of the speaker, e.g. *unfortunately,* as opposed to a VP-adverbial. See Chapter 5.

SC   = Small Clause, see below.

sentence/clause   A unit that contains at least a verb. The subject may or may not be expressed; see Chapters 7, 8, and 10.

semantics   The linguistic aspects to meaning.

semi-modal   Auxiliary such as *dare (to), need (to), used to, ought to, have to.* They have properties of both main verbs and modal verbs; see Chapter 6.

simple sentence/clause   Sentence or clause with only one lexical verb; see Chapter 7.

sister   For example, a P and NP are sisters of each other; each has a branch going up to the 'mother'; see Chapter 3.

specify   Point to something, i.e. a determiner's function in a phrase.

split infinitive   Separating the *to* from the verb, e.g. as in *to boldly go ...*; see special topic Chapter 1.

small clause   A sentence in which the verb has been left out; see Chapter 4.

stacking   When more than one adjective precedes the noun; see Chapter 9.

strong verbs   A term for a verb that has a different vowel for the present, the past, and the past participle, e.g. *swim, swam, swum*.

subject   In English, the subject agrees with the verb in person and number, see Chapter 4.

subject predicate   Often realized as an AdjP, making a claim about the subject, e.g. *nice* in *She is nice*. It occurs after a copula verb such as *be, become*; see Chapter 4.

subject verb agreement   Finite verbs agree with subjects in English. Evidence for it is fairly limited, e.g. the *–s* on *she walks*.

subjunctive   Expressing a wish or intention or necessity, e.g. *go* is a subjunctive verb in *it is important that he go there*. In Modern English, most of these are replaced by modal verbs; see Chapter 6, Section 2.1.

subordinate clause   Dependent clause, or clause embedded in another by means of a complementizer such as *that, because, if*; see Chapters 7 and 8.

subordinating conjunction   Not used in this book, same as complementizer, see there.

superlative   An adjective such as *greatest*, see Chapter 2.

synonym   A word with an almost identical meaning, e.g. *often* and *frequently*; see Chapter 2.

syntax   Rules for how words are combined into phrases and sentences, the topic of this book; see Chapter 1.

tag-question   A repetition of the subject and the auxiliary, as in *She has been there before, hasn't she?* See Chapter 4.

tense   Indicating past or present time.

trace   Not used in this book. When used, it indicates that a word or phrase has been moved. In Chapters 10 and 11, I have used copies in brackets instead. These copies have a line through them to show they are not pronounced.

transitive   Verb with one object, e.g. *see*; see Chapter 4.

tree   A representation of the units/phrases of a sentence by means of branches and nodes; see Chapter 3.

two-part coordinator   Coordinator with two parts, e.g. *both Mary and John, neither Mary nor John*; see Chapter 2.

Universal Grammar   Grammatical properties shared by all languages; see Chapter 1.

V   = verb

V′   = V-bar, an intermediate category; see Chapter 5.

verb   A lexical category often expressing a state, act, event or emotion; see Chapter 2.

VGP   = Verb Group; see Chapter 6.

vowel   Sounds such as *i, e, a, o*, and *u*, made by not blocking the airstream; see Chapter 1, for use in a rule.

VP-adverbial   An adverbial that modifies the action of the verb, e.g. *quickly, slowly*, as opposed to an S-adverbial; see Chapter 5.

weak verbs   A term for a verb that has a *-ed* past and past participle, e.g. *walk*.

wh-question   A question that starts with *who, what, how, why, when* or *where*; see Chapter 11.

word order   Linear sequencing of words and phrases.

yes/no question   A question for which the appropriate answer would be 'yes', 'no', or 'maybe/perhaps'; see Chapter 11.

References

British National Corpus, http://www.natcorp.ox.ac.uk.

Chomsky, Noam 1975. *Reflections on Language*. Fontana.

Corpus of Contemporary American English, http://www.americancorpus.org.

Fowler, H.W. 1926 [1950]. *A Dictionary of Modern English Usage*. Oxford: Clarendon.

Kirszner, Laurie & Stephen Mandell 1992. *The Holt Handbook* [third edition]. HBJ.

O'Dwyer, Bernard 2000. *Modern English Structures*. Broadview Press.

O'Grady, William & Michael Dobrovolsky 1987. *Contemporary Linguistic Analysis*. Longmans [1st edition]

Oxford English Dictionary (OED). online edition. Oxford: Oxford University Press.

Quirk, Randolph & Sidney Greenbaum 1973. *A University Grammar of English*. London: Longman.

Strunk, William with E.B. White 1959[2000]. *The Elements of Style*. Boston: Allyn and Bacon.

Swan, Michael 1980. *Practical English Usage*. Oxford: Oxford University Press.

Index